CU00592125

A Family Occupation

to Gregory

A Family Occupation

Children of the War
and
the Memory of World War II
in
Dutch Literature of the 1980s

JOLANDA VANDERWAL TAYLOR

AMSTERDAM UNIVERSITY PRESS

Author and publisher gratefully acknowledge generous grants given this book by the Prins Bernhard Fonds and University of Winconsin.

Cover design: Erik Cox, 's-Gravenhage
Typesetting: te *Giffel* Publishing Services, Amersfoort

ISBN 90 5356 221 4 (hardbound)
ISBN 90 5356 236 2 (paperback)

© Amsterdam University Press, Amsterdam, 1997

All rights reserved. Without limiting the rights under copyright reserved above, no part of this book may be reproduced, stored in or introduced into a retrieval system, or transmitted, in any form or by any means (electronic, mechanical, photocopying, recording, or otherwise), without the written permission of both the copyright owner and the author of this book.

Table of Contents

Acknowledgments

This book was written with the help of many friends, and I received financial support from several sources. I would like to thank them here.

The early research for this book was made possible by a Fulbright grant to the University of Utrecht during the fall semester of 1989, and by repeated support from the University of Wisconsin Graduate School. I am grateful to both, as without their help this book would not exist.

Although it is impossible to thank adequately every person who has contributed to this project, I wish at least to acknowledge some of those to whom I am indebted.

I am grateful to my parents, from whom I first learned the value of learning, to Willem Dwarshuis of the Baudartius College in Zutphen, who demonstrated what literature can mean, and to Sander Gilman, who showed me what writing can do.

I am grateful for the hospitality of the Department of Dutch at the University of Utrecht, particularly during the time of my Fulbright grant, and especially to W.J. van den Akker for his advice and support over the years.

I wish to thank Berteke Waaldijk and Peter Romijn, whose friendship and ongoing conversation have contributed to the development of this project and whose hospitality has in very real ways supported the research.

I am grateful to the writer known as Hanna Visser for her generously long conversation with me, in which she helped to clarify my thinking on a difficult subject.

The archive at the RIOD (Dutch Institute for War Documentation) in Amsterdam provided some of the photographs which illustrate this book, and the Letterkundig Museum in The Hague provided both photographic and textual sources. The staffs at both were unfailingly kind and helpful.

At Amsterdam University Press, I am grateful to Saskia de Vries, Wardy Poelstra and Peter van Roosmalen, and others whose names I may not know for their careful work and helpful suggestions.

Many people listened to presentations of pieces of this work at conferences and offered thoughtful questions, suggestions, resistance, and enthusiasm. I cannot mention them by name here, but wish to acknowledge in general the contributions of members of the American Association for Netherlandic Studies and the Internationale Vereniging voor Neerlandistiek. Their spirited engagement and intellectual generosity provide a superb context for thinking and writing.

I would like to thank many colleagues who read parts of this book at various stages of completion and offered me the benefit of their knowledge and experience. Much of what is good about this book is the result of their suggestions; any mistakes and infelicities that remain are my own. For generous collegiality I particularly thank Hans Adler, Klaus Berghahn, Sabine Gross, Nancy Kaiser, G.P.M. Mourits, Cora Lee Nollendorfs, Valters Nollendorfs, and James Steakley.

I thank Robert B. Howell for being an unfailingly supportive colleague. In starting and nurturing a lively Dutch Program at the University of Wisconsin-Madison, he has helped to make it a place where scholarly work on Dutch literature can be done. Joseph-"that's not going to happen"-Salmons deserves my gratitude for his enthusiastic support of the Dutch program and for providing a much-needed sense of perspective.

I thank Gregory A. Taylor, without whose help and encouragement I would not have written this book or any other. He has in many ways made my involvement in academic pursuits possible. Many of the ideas presented here were formulated in conversation with him, and he is still my best and favorite editor.

1. *Introduction*

In the summer of 1992, when the nomination by the Bush administration of an American named Donald Alexander for the post of Ambassador to the Netherlands was retracted, possible reasons that the candidacy had run into trouble in Washington and elsewhere were mentioned in Dutch newspapers. First of all, it is clear that there were objections on the basis of the fact that Alexander had made sizable political contributions, and secondly that Alexander was also Honorary Consul of the Netherlands in Kansas, a fact which was thought to create a possible conflict of interest. A third possible reason was mentioned in *NRC Handelsblad*[1]: Alexander, whose last name at birth had been Buitenhuis, was the son of a man who had been indicted in the Netherlands after World War II as one who had collaborated with the Germans. However, a brief mention of the retracted nomination in the *Volkskrant* the next day[2] mentions the issue of his political contributions and the potential conflict of interest due to his history as Honorary Consul, and then ends the report with the curious statement that knowledge of his father's war history had had no bearing on the decision.

The apparent contradiction among these reports is interesting. It suggests that the events of World War II still played an important role in Dutch, even Dutch-American relations, nearly 50 years after the fact. As for collaboration, Donald Alexander had committed no crime, except to be his father's son. And although one might readily understand why an infamous name might be a burden – Germany, for instance, might not nominate a person named Himmler as ambassador – in this case the family name had been changed to one which nobody would associate with war crimes. Nevertheless, the issue had been raised, and it may have hurt Alexander's chances. This story points to two facts about the history of World War II as it is remembered in the Netherlands: first, what happened fifty-odd years ago is still quite relevant to many people. But second, individuals often have mixed feelings, and many Dutch citizens disagree with each other about whether the history of half a century ago still matters and what its meaning should be.

The effects and aftereffects of World War II are not limited to those actively engaged in combat, but touched civilians to an unprecedented degree as well. In the European arena, this involvement was intensified by the implementation of Hitler's "final solution". Since the regimes in various countries occupied by Nazi Germany were instructed to round up and deport not only all Jews, but all members of several other religious and ethnic groups, the Nazis' goals included not just gaining military or political control over the conquered countries, but a direct involvement in their day-to-day governance as well. Such close association among the occupiers and the occupied was particularly strong in the Netherlands, where the Nazi occupation installed a civilian, rather than a military, government and waged a hearts-and-minds campaign, in hopes of converting Dutch citizens to Nazi ideals and thus gaining their wholehearted cooperation. Because of this effort, ordinary Dutch citizens – even those who had never before been interested in politics – were forced to devise a practical response to Nazi policies, sometimes without prior time for reflection. In the heat of the moment, and in the belief that one's life, the lives of family members, or one's livelihood might be in jeopardy if one chose not to cooperate with the regime, some made quick decisions which they would later come to question or even regret.

Regret for one's behavior under Nazi occupation took several forms. Some of those who collaborated out of principle later found that they had been deceived about the Nazis' plans; others, who collaborated – perhaps just in insignificant ways – out of fear of reprisal, later wished that they had been more valiant. Some members of both groups suffered after the war had ended; either they were punished by agents of the new regime for their political crimes, or they – often with their families – faced various degrees and kinds of social isolation because their compatriots demanded retribution for their – real or imagined – offenses against ideals of loyalty to the nation or to ethical standards. This atmosphere of retribution and punishment put great pressure on families, as uninvolved spouses and children suffered because of the choices which perhaps only one member of the family – often the father – had made, and because the suffering was not distributed fairly among offenders. Since minor infractions could lead to social isolation, it is easy to imagine that fear of exposure was widespread. Such pressured atmospheres after the end of the war even affected the families of bystanders and victims, not just those of collaborators. This book offers evidence that many civilians and in some cases their offspring were deeply affected by the occupation, whether by its direct effects or its collateral varieties.

COMPLEX ISSUES

The Dutch populace was affected by World War II on several levels. Two major factors which had a deep impact include, first, the relatively far-reaching physical destruction of the country, which meant a desperate need to rebuild at the end of the war. Secondly, the loss of life, particularly the lives of Jewish-Dutch citizens, sometimes with the active cooperation of Dutch compatriots, had profound implications, not least of which are various issues of guilt which presented themselves after the end of the occupation. Responding to these two results of the war set up contradictory impulses. The struggle for physical survival, the need to reconstruct the physical infrastructure of the country, and to re-establish some semblance of a social fabric was pre-eminently important. Punishing, in some cases making an example of the offenders, appeared to be an important way to reconstruct the social fabric, a step toward making life return to normal.

In addition to these legitimate goals and concerns came an undercurrent of sometimes undefined guilt, felt either on a personal or collective level. Some people definitely had reason to feel guilty: opportunists who had taken advantage of the conditions presented by the occupation to further their own political and financial ends at the expense of their compatriots. For others, those who had operated within the many gray areas which modern wars and occupations create, guilt may have presented itself as a confused sense of unease: Should they have done more – or less? Had it been right for parents to protect their children, or should they have given up normal family patterns in order to save those the Nazi regime was out to destroy? Even if one had assisted the Resistance, it was still possible to ask whether one could or should have done more. In addition, some must have wondered whether offenders were being punished appropriately, or rather whether big fish were getting away while lesser fry were treated more harshly than they deserved. My intent here is not to answer such questions definitively, but rather to point to their complexity and to the difficulty of deciding on their validity.

Common knowledge holds that in the years following the war, most individuals and families were too busy with both rebuilding the nation and its infrastructure and seeing to their families' physical survival amidst chaos to spend much time mourning the past. Indulging one's regrets for a tragic past was viewed as a "luxury" which required more investment of time and energy than was affordable in light of the pressing need to restore the nation to normalcy. But clear patterns cannot be identified in the literature of the Netherlands at this time. This fact seems puzzling on the surface. After all, one would expect to find the confusion of the time reflected in the literature being published and/or also in a silence surrounding the most difficult issues. But only later did the entire picture become clearer.

It is not until later – approximately the 1980s – that a common "pattern" or interpretive convention emerges which allows readers to compare works and notice certain commonalities in these various texts. As this study will show, the issue of memory is a central theme around which the many other clusters of variables are arranged: the notions of heroism, victimhood and culpability, of family dynamics and coming of age, and issues of sexuality and national identity.

Nevertheless, however scattered the attempts, Dutch writers did begin the work of thematizing, analyzing, reworking, re-evaluating and reconsidering World War II in various kinds of texts almost as soon as the war ended – in some cases, even before it had run its course. As is the case with the work of writing which takes as its raw material the stuff of history, it is easier to locate the events of history itself – the succession of dates and events and the networks of correspondence which accompany them – than it is to locate and define the work done by these writers and their texts. Therefore, it is the intention of this study to sketch the outlines of the way that this work and reworking continues into the present time. One index of the relative importance of the experience of World War II for a Dutch reading public can be found in the comforting "historical" realities of numbers. Dick Schram estimates that some six to seven hundred literary narratives exist in Dutch which thematize the war; if plays and those texts which tend more toward documentary are included, that count approaches a thousand.[3] As suggested by the sheer force of numbers, the effects of the war upon the lives of the Dutch as individuals and as a society and culture as a whole have persisted until the present and continue to be an important cultural factor into the decade of the 1990s.

Schram's count of thematic texts seems an inversion of our expectations for a study of writing as a cultural practice; we would expect to begin with "documentary" texts and then proceed to include literary approaches. However, the image of a collection of events such as war, its function as a set of collected and distilled stories, the perception of memory, and the meaning of the ways in which the passage of time has altered our views of those events in the course of the intervening decades may also be understood as the quintessential domain of fiction. Thus, in some sense, the Dutch interest in the experience of the war could be said to grow gradually beyond its "literary" treatment to include more "documentary" materials and, by implication, a broader range of remembering than can be fully described by looking at explicitly fictional works. However, as is also to be expected, the image of the war, the function of this collection of events in fiction, the perception of its memory, and the meaning of the passing of time have altered in the course of the intervening decades. Although such changes are by no means uniform or programmatic, various attempts have been made to identify several broad developments.

VARIOUS LITERARY HISTORIES

The interest of the Dutch public in the history of the war has seen an ebb and flow in the last five decades. This variance is perhaps the result of the factors mentioned above: an interaction between the pressing need on one level – for physical and psychological reasons – to forget and on another level the intermittent and inconsistent need to remember. There is no one canonical history of "war literature" in the immediate postwar decades. Several (literary) historians have proposed different models which are at variance with each other. I will not attempt to harmonize their views, as their different proposals reflect the reality of how complex and diffuse literary treatments of the war/occupation were in the postwar era.

One analysis, in the so-called "Menten report" from 1979, asserts that the Dutch interest in remembering the war years follows a "wavelike motion".[4] The general pattern is presented as one of overwhelming interest in patriotic texts about recent history during the first two years after the war, followed by an attitude of satiety by the end of the 1940s.

The immediate postwar years did indeed see the publication of a number of novels which take the war or occupation as its theme. Unfortunately, almost none of this literature is available in English translation and I will therefore mention a few well-known examples. *Die van ons* by Willy Corsari, published in November 1945 and reprinted twice within a year, contrasts the story of a cynical Gentile with that of a Jewish man who dies an idealist in Bergen-Belsen; its point is that the horrible experiences of the war can be somewhat redeemed if survivors are chastened and purified by the experience. Bert Voeten's war diary *Doortocht* (1946) optimistically proclaims the triumph of art over life: despite the fact that the spirit is put upon by physical hardship, one may find comfort in the knowledge that a perfect poem will not perish. In 1946, Simon (later Gerard) van het Reve published *De ondergang van de familie Boslowits* in the journal *Criterium*, a work which very effectively presents events from the perspective of a young boy who is initially excited at the prospect of war and only slowly comes to realize what the Nazi occupation has in mind for his Jewish friends.

The publication of Simon Vestdijk's *Pastorale 43*, in 1947 and 1948, offers a different perspective. It represents the resistance as constituted of poorly organized, inefficient people whose motivations are often less than altruistic. Anbeek van der Meijden[5] offers three reasons for the fact that its reception was nevertheless mostly favorable. He cites the presence of a patriotic twist at the end of the novel and the fact that, since Vestdijk was always fond of irony, the reading public did not expect him to present unambiguous heroes. Furthermore, he reads the appearance and acceptance of *Pastorale 43* as a sign that the appetite for heroic war memories had been satiated.

This work brings us to the juncture which Anbeek van der Meijden describes as the "coma" thesis: according to the Menten report, the moment in which a lively interest in the history of the war turns to collective forgetting or repression occurs in 1947. On the face of it, this thesis pertains. However, the silence after 1947 is by no means complete. *The Diary of Anne Frank*, which was written during the war years and derives a part of its interest for readers from the way it foreshadows the author's death in the Holocaust, was first published in Dutch in 1947 and immediately reprinted that year, then twice in 1948 and again in 1949 and 1950. A period of silence does occur with reference to this book: after 1950, it was not reprinted until 1955, when repeated reprints became necessary – as many as seven in 1957. This second wave of interest was probably stimulated by the success of the American edition and its adaptation for Broadway.

The supposed disinterest in war topics within Dutch letters which started in 1947 then ended in 1953 with the publication of J.B. Charles' *Volg het spoor terug* ("Follow the Track Back"); the work was well-reviewed and merited two reprints that year and one in each of the two years thereafter, followed by a lacuna. This line subsequently leads to Marga Minco, the publication of whose *Het bittere kruid (Bitter Herbs)* in 1957, a brief and poignant novel about a Jewish woman who loses her family but herself survives the Holocaust in hiding, was followed by regular reprintings which suggest the existence of an enthusiastic readership.

The end of this period of activity is punctuated by the publication of two important texts which, as Anbeek van der Meijden stresses, are not best described as "war novels", but are rather fictional texts which use the war as a setting in which they investigate philosophical or ethical issues: W. F. Hermans' *De donkere kamer van Damocles* (1958) and Harry Mulisch's *Het stenen bruidsbed* (1959). Anbeek van der Meijden points to the fact that these novelists develop an original, personal point of view toward the war and takes this to indicate that the war has to a certain extent receded into the past. Neither work glorifies the war, and, according to Anbeek van der Meijden, neither is specific to World War II: they could also have been set in another war. Both express a decided disenchantment with Enlightenment values and the optimistic views of human nature which are their legacy. They illustrate the negative expectations associated with a demoralized generation which survived the occupation.

6   The fact that not all literature from this period which is thematically related to the war has a negative view of human nature is illustrated by *De nacht der girondijnen* (*The Night of the Girondists*) by Jacob Presser (1957), which tells the story of a protagonist who, with the support of a rabbi, persists in making moral and humane choices, even at the cost of his own life. Anbeek van der Meijden further remarks upon the fact that the most positive books about the war were written by three Jewish authors: Etty Hillesum, herself a Holocaust victim, Willy Corsari, and Presser.

Although, as Anbeek van der Meijden states, Dutch interest in the war years is ascendant in the 1960s and 1970s, literature is not the arena in which issues related to this period in the past are primarily dealt with. The "backlog", as he calls it, is taken on in the literature of the 1980s, the subject matter of *A Family Occupation*.

HISTORY ITSELF

In addition to the fiction being produced and read, however, the war was also being replayed in the Dutch national consciousness in a different forum. Even at times when fiction which dealt thematically with the occupation was not plentiful, an interest in the history was kept alive. One extra-literary author deserves particular mention, as his influence is nearly unmeasurable. For decades, L. de Jong was a central figure as a scholar and historian of the war in the Netherlands.

During the war, De Jong[6] edited and read broadcasts by Radio Orange from London, the voice of the Dutch government-in-exile, which were beamed across the Channel to the occupied Netherlands. Shortly after the liberation, De Jong became the first director of the Dutch Institute for War Documentation,[7] and – at least until his retirement in 1979 – was responsible to a large degree for its reputation in academic circles as well as among the general public. His greatest impact on the Dutch memory of World War II, however, may be attributed to two important and high-profile projects. First, he wrote and narrated a series of television programs on the Dutch history of the war, broadcast on TV between May of 1960 and May of 1965; a version in print form was also published.[8] It would be difficult to overestimate the impact of such innovative use of technology. The programs did not rely on flashy graphics, but consisted mostly of De Jong telling the story of the war using minimal props; they nevertheless made a deep impression on the viewing public. De Jong's style was personal and engaged, a fact which contributed to its impact on viewers.

De Jong's second high-profile project was his popular multivolume history of the war: *Het Koninkrijk der Nederlanden in de Tweede Wereldoorlog,* [9] ("The Kingdom of the Netherlands during World War II"). De Jong received criticism from some of his scholarly colleagues for the idiosyncratic style he employed in these studies, but it is clear that his style was one factor which attracted an audience outside academic circles. In addition, in order to make the work accessible to a broad audience, the series was published not only in a scholarly edition, but in a more "popular" one as well. As De Keizer shows,[10] the strategy was justified: on average, each volume was published in an edition of 75,000. The first volume, *Voorspel,* was reprinted nine times for a total of 200,000 copies, and it is estimated that 74,000 Dutch individuals own the entire series. The very large editions indicate that, while it is true that the 1960s and 1970s are not the heyday of Dutch "war" literature, and thus of the themes of personal memory-work, the Dutch were collectively occupied with (their past during) the war. This occupation apparently contributed to the backlog to which Anbeek van der Meijden refers, an incremental build-up of a store of unresolved issues which was still to be worked out in literature and in public debate surrounding literary and non-literary texts, as will occur in the 1980s.

NEW DEVELOPMENTS IN THE 1980s

During the 1980s, narratives which deal with experiences of World War II not only continued to appear in Dutch literature but even increased in number. Although it may be tempting to ascribe the renewal of interest in World War II novels during the decade of the 1980s as a mere function of some important anniversary (i.e., the 40th anniversary of the occupation or the liberation of the country), a look at the scope of these novels might suggest that some broader set of social constructs were being engaged – for these narratives were not only about World War II as a kind of moral "stage" on which the novelists of the decade moved their characters about. A list of the works which were published and read by the Dutch public includes novels about citizens who suffered during the occupation, such as Harry Mulisch's *The Assault*. Several works by Marga Minco published in the 1980s such as *The Fall* and *The Glass Bridge*,[11] Rudi van Dantzig's *For a Lost Soldier*, texts by Jona Oberski such as *Kinderjaren* ("Childhood Years"),[12] Frans Pointl's *De kip die over de soep vloog* ("The Chicken which Flew Over the Soup"), Sera Anstadt's *Een eigen plek* ("A Place of One's Own"),[13] and Kati David's *Een klein leven* ("A Small Life"),[14] while set during the time period of World War II, are further notable as texts which place children centrally among the war's victims. Various texts by Armando (a pseudonym for Herman Dirk van Dodeweerd) such as *De straat en het struikgewas* ("Street and Foliage") engage the question of enmity and aggression among people(s), the central role prejudice plays, and the ways in which language contributes to our memory of past offenses.[15]

The decade of the 1980s also saw the publication of a number of narratives from a new group of persons – the children of collaborators. These include such texts as Hanna Visser's *Het verleden voorbij* ("Beyond the Past"),[16] Rinnes Rijke's two memoirs[17] *Niet de schuld, wel de straf. Herinneringen van een NSB-kind* ("Punished, Though Innocent: Memories of the Child of a Member of the N.S.B.")[18] and *Op zoek naar erkenning* ("In Search of Recognition"),[19] and *Niemandsland* ("No Man's Land") by Duke Blaauwendraad-Doorduyn, as well as texts about collaboration clearly marked as novels such as Louis Ferron's *Hoor mijn lied, Violetta* ("Hear My Song, Violetta"), D.A. Kooiman's *Montyn* ("Montyn"), and Ten Hooven's (pseud.) *De lemmingen* ("The Lemmings").

A final sub-genre within this group is comprised of narratives dealing with the experience of World War II in Indonesia, then the Dutch East Indies, the occupation by the Japanese, and the consequences of the fact that the colonials were forced to repatriate when Indonesia gained independence after the war. Works about this period and the memory of it include Jeroen Brouwers' novel *Sunken Red*, numerous memoirs such as Beb Vuyk's *Kampdagboeken*,[20] ("Camp Diaries") the voluminous writings of Rudi Kousbroek, and novels about the desire to return to one's parents' homeland, such as Ernst Jansz's *De overkant* ("The Other Side").[21] The publication of these works was supplemented by a flood of books, booklets, articles and studies in various fields which signaled the fact that the Dutch were still very much interested in the history of the war and its aftermath.

What is of particular interest in the Dutch literature of the 1980s which deals with the memory of the occupation is not just the fact (which may surprise some) that such narratives are still being published and that the memory of the war is still a matter for public discussion, but also that there has been a clear shift in the locus and meaning of such arguments. Those traditionally assumed to have been affected by the war include victims such as survivors of the Holocaust, their children (for whom "survivor's guilt" is a central concept), and members of the Resistance (whose position as Dutch heroes has long been firmly established). In the 1980s the exclusivity of these two groups was challenged to include a much broader spectrum of the population. Members of more and more constituencies, all of whom we may identify as "children of the war", begin to identify themselves as having been affected by the events of World War II, as having their lives and identities changed by the memories – the history – of what happened in the first half of the fifth decade of this century, even events which happened to their families when they were very young or not even born yet. What emerges is a "continuum of survivors" which begins with the groups acknowledged as victims from the start, such as survivors of the Holocaust and members of the Resistance, and now includes other groups as well.

Another striking feature of these texts concerned with the memory of World War II and its aftermath is not merely their number, but also the fact that so many of these fictional and nonfictional works which portray the experience and memory of the occupation of the Netherlands during World War II consist of representations of children, of their experience of childhood, and of the ways in which the rest of their lives are influenced by their early experiences. The World War II period is represented as having a profound effect, whether protagonists experienced it as young people, as children, or only indirectly, mediated by their parents; all these categories of not-yet-adult persons affected by World War II are included in the term "children of the war".[22]

These texts presenting childhood memories of World War II confront the critical reader with problems of the relationship between childhood memory and historical accuracy. Are such texts an objective statement concerning the period of World War II, or are they portrayals of troubled childhood years? On a more specific level, they also raise questions concerning the development of the self-image of the Dutch.

It is instructive to note a central feature of common speech in Dutch when thinking of the course of Dutch history in the 20th century. In common parlance, World War II is known to speakers of Dutch as "de oorlog" (the war). What is curious about this widespread usage is not merely the inclusion of the definite article – "the" war – but the choice of noun itself: "war" rather than the more historically accurate "occupation" (*de bezetting*). Admittedly, the famous televised history of the years 1940-1945 featuring Dr. L. de Jong mentioned above bears the title *De bezetting*.[23] However, the more commonly used term reflects the historically less accurate expression of the experience of the Dutch populace. The Netherlands was forced to surrender a mere four days after the surprise attack by the Germans in May of 1940. Although Dutch individuals joined in the war effort, for instance as members of the SS, their behavior was considered treasonous by the bulk of the population, in a move that per definition made such a person "un-Dutch".[24] The northern part of the Netherlands, the last to be liberated, was under German occupation from May of 1940 until May of 1945, but the population nevertheless often refers to this period as "the war". In the course of this study, I investigate the implications of this definitional relocation as it is practiced in contemporary literary culture.

THE OCCUPATIONS OF FAMILIES

The community's practice of writing/producing and reading/consuming narratives about this occupation renamed "war" invites interesting questions about the functions these cultural practices fulfill. For example, the shift in terminology creates and sustains the image of an occupied populace as combatants rather than citizens, and of communal behavior during the occupation as a protracted (either overt or inner) conflict. In addition, these narratives, in presenting history and memory on the same stage, contribute to a discourse on the nature and function of memory. The experience of the war fades into history, and its literary treatment also changes; the minds of those who lived through the war display a shift in focus from the experience of that period to memory, on the one hand, and to its implications for the survivor, on the other. Alongside this shift, one also finds an interesting and useful dynamic posed by representing "remembered" time, which coincides with the childhood of the texts' central characters. Their memory of "the war", seen through the lens of a depicted childhood and its traditional thematic connections within the circle of family and peers, becomes a story of a kind of "family occupation" in three senses. In the first place, there is an occupation (one could call it a pre-occupation) of the dynamics within the family by (and with) issues in the forgotten or repressed past. Secondly, the much-maligned occupying forces were paradoxically viewed, by some at least, as ethnic "brothers", and were sometimes aided by local collaborators. This fact of family resemblance between the Dutch and German peoples and between loyal Dutch citizens and Dutch Nazis fundamentally complicates attempts to equate foreignness with the enemy and to view one's own nation as purely the victim. This phenomenon begins and ends within the realm of the childhood subject and the larger circle of family as I consider various seminal Dutch-language novels and investigate the interactive construction of notions of childhood and occupation by exploring broader concerns about the maintenance of binary oppositions such as victimization/collaboration and fiction/nonfiction in these contexts.

The third meaning suggested by "A Family Occupation", has to do with the long-standing discord among Dutch victims of the occupation. They are permanently related to each other, but they nevertheless insist on comparing their differences, much as sibling rivals do.[25] Some non-Dutch readers will be surprised at the notion that survivors of the occupation would sort themselves into individual constituencies – the groups along the "continuum" I name in my study – rather than immediately recognize their essential solidarity. It is easier to understand when one keeps in mind the 20th-century tradition in the Netherlands of "pillarization", the principle of dividing society into groups of people who share similar epistemic commitments ("pillars") rather than just along class lines ("strata"). Although pillarization has withered in the course of the century, the predisposition toward joining groups of like-minded people has persisted in the Dutch character.[26]

In the following pages, I will briefly describe the most important points along this continuum, i.e. the various "kinds" of survivors. I present a number of works of fiction and non-fiction from the 1980s which have the memory of World War II as their central theme. The titles which I have chosen from the many available in order to attend to them in this study are representative of certain approaches and themes which were prominent in the 1980s.

I do not claim to be offering complete or final interpretations of the texts I discuss, or the final word on any of the texts I mention, nor do I claim that these texts are the only ones which qualify for inclusion in a study of the discussion of the memory of World War II. This study is intended as a necessarily limited, unabashedly engaged, but certainly good-faith contribution to a centrally important discussion.

I expect that some readers will disagree with some of my interpretations. Perhaps others will offer examples from texts or writers other than those I discuss. Both the facts worthy of remembrance and the meanings accorded to such facts are negotiable. I am persuaded that memory is a community project as well as a personal reality, and that it is in the interplay – be it push-and-pull or give-and-take – between those poles that we human beings can work out our "family arguments".

VARIOUS VICTIMS : THE CIRCLE WIDENS

Harry Mulisch's *The Assault,* Marga Minco's *The Glass Bridge,* and Rudi van Dantzig's *For a Lost Soldier* look at children as victims of the occupation, and introduce some paradigms of what it means to be a victim. This problem, I argue, became important in the 1980s. From several texts of Armando's published in the 1980s, I have chosen *De straat en het struikgewas.* All his literary works up until that point, to be sure, would be thematically relevant; I chose this text because it can in some sense be said to be a novel (most of his literary work is much more fragmentary) and because its protagonist is a child. For my discussion of narratives by the children of collaborators, I pay closest attention to Rinnes Rijke's *Niet de schuld, wel de straf. Herinnerin-*

gen van een NSB-kind ("Punished, Though Innocent; Memories of the Child of a Member of the N.S.B.")[27] and Hanna Visser's *Het verleden voorbij* ("Beyond the Past"). Rijke's book more clearly illustrates some of the ways in which the Dutch have fashioned their memories of the darker sides of their history in the middle of the Twentieth Century in such a way that collaboration becomes a useful foil for other social problems. Visser's work is illustrative of an honest search for reconciliation and is particularly interesting because of the author's close connection with "Herkenning", the Dutch "self-help" group for children of collaborators.

The main characters of all these works are too young to have experienced the war as adults, too young to have participated in the wrenching political and moral choices which adults were forced to make during the occupation. Nevertheless, their lives were fundamentally influenced by the legacy of the war, and particularly by the effect the war had on them and their families. This "trans-generational traumatization" bears some resemblance to an effect which has been well known for a long time and has been treated as a syndrome among the families of Holocaust survivors.

Individuals who survived the Holocaust are commonly said not only to be deeply traumatized by their experiences, which frequently cause flashbacks and nightmares and a general habit of distrust toward other human beings, but also often to suffer "survivor's guilt", a deeply troubling response to the arbitrary factors which determined who died in the camps, and who survived. Their children are traumatized because they sense their parents' pain, and because they are aware that their parents have had experiences too terrible and painful to discuss. They suffer from communication difficulties within the family, difficulties attributable to their own reluctance to ask questions or discuss painful issues.

In the 1980s, a surprising number of Dutch novels and nonfiction works, such as memoirs and diaries, presented the children of different groups, that is, children whose parents had experienced a wide variety of war histories, as suffering from similar symptoms. The syndromes presented in these novels can be traced back to the wartime experiences of the character's family. A pattern develops; I will show that these "children of the war", be they the children of victims, of bystanders, of collaborators, or of survivors of the Japanese concentration camps in Indonesia, are all shown to have suffered in similar ways.

"Children of the war" ("Kinderen van de oorlog") was the topic of a convention of lay people and therapists interested in these war-related problems, which was held in Amsterdam in 1989. G. Bögels states that there were two reasons for choosing that title: first, because then-standard references to "second generation" had been under fire in the political arena, and secondly, based on an argument I find fully convincing, because "counting" generations appears to involve making distinctions which are more rigid than is necessary or useful. It is in all probability less relevant to a person's development whether he or she was born after, during or even just before the war. More important is the fact that such a person grew up as offspring of parents seriously affected by the war, and in the midst of a culture still seriously focused on the war, its aftermath, and its meaning for the present and the future.

12 Besides allowing one to skirt any distinctions based on the exact years of birth, the term "children of the war" also makes it possible to consider together children with a variety of family war histories. As I will show in the chapters to come, Dutch literary and non-literary texts often present the children of collaborators as being more similar than dissimilar to the children of camp survivors. This premise may surprise some, but its accuracy has begun to emerge not only in literary texts but also in texts from the field of psychology and counseling. The point is not to suggest that there is an ethical equivalence between the purposeful attempts at destruction of the Jews (and other groups) during the Holocaust and the experience of the occupation. The point is rather that current theories of psychological damage assume that trauma is the result of perceived threat, of a subject's response to events, rather than an objective index of historical realities.

The stage for the phenomena I study in these texts is set by defining the expulsion of the child from the family and his/her relocation as subject/narrator within the wider context of the adult "histories" and human conduct during wartime occupation. Three recent Dutch novels, prime exemplars of the representation of childhood and the role of one's childhood memory in textual treatments of the "war", provide the starting point, as each of the three protagonists is only one step removed from individuals who would be widely and readily recognized as victims. The first of these is Harry Mulisch's well-known novel *The Assault*, which I analyze in detail. Doing so allows me initially to present issues which I will again raise in reference to the other texts. Since my discussion of *The Assault* serves as a benchmark, I treat its themes, the language in which these are represented, and the assumptions which lie behind them, in some detail. *The Assault* functions as a paradigmatic text for my investigation; my discussion of it serves as a case study to which I refer back in subsequently presenting the problems at issue in other works.

To some it may seem unnecessary to offer a close reading of a well-known novel at the beginning of my text. Many readers are familiar with *The Assault* and with analyses of it, and they might indeed proceed to later chapters without losing the thread of my argument. Nevertheless, I include this chapter at the beginning of my book for several reasons. First, those who are not familiar with Mulisch's work would be missing an important piece of the picture. Secondly, my analysis of *The Assault* functions as a "case history" – a summation of many of the themes which are central to all the texts I study here – and by providing a thorough discussion of this one text I set the stage, describe the territory within which the rest of my analysis is embedded, and define a number of issues to which I refer back in the course of the discussion of the other texts in later chapters. Thirdly, in this first chapter I suggest connections which will interest even a reader already familiar with *The Assault*.

The Assault makes a case for viewing bystanders – Dutch citizens who attempted to avoid any contact with potentially dangerous events related to the war – and their descendants as victims of the occupation. As such, it is the first step away from the previously "recognized victims" on the imaginary continuum of survivors identified above. This novel questions the strong distinctions traditionally made between perpetrators and victims in its suggestive comparison of the children of a collaborator and of victims of the occupation; a thought which would have been so outrageous as to be unthinkable in the decades immediately after the war. Further, starting with a child protagonist, it paints a compelling picture of delayed expressions of emotional and social damage which may have been caused by traumatic experiences earlier in life: it places the amnesia and recovered memories associated with traumatic stress disorder, such as is sometimes associated with wartime experiences, in the foreground. These three features I identify as fundamentally important in Dutch texts of the 1980s which deal with "the" memory of World War II.

Next, but not far from *The Assault* along the continuum, I place two other texts which permit a discussion of similar issues, and of dissimilar issues raised in a similar context. Looking at these texts together offers a palette of views of childhood as they relate to remembering and forgetting. Rudi van Dantzig's *For A Lost Soldier* and Marga Minco's *The Glass Bridge* engage some of the same issues, but from significantly and unexpectedly different perspectives. Minco's main character is a "traditional" victim, a Jewish child who at the end of the war is the sole survivor in her family. She spends the next four decades under the spell of buried memories. I include this work because it extends the consequences of her traumatic experiences into a character's middle age and thus represents a phenomenon typical of these 1980s' texts. Van Dantzig tells the emotionally complex story of Jeroen, a child from Amsterdam who is not affected in any direct way by the war itself. Like the parents of Anton, the protagonist of *The Assault*, Jeroen's parents are "innocent bystanders". But unlike Anton's parents, they are not harmed. Jeroen is only indirectly a child of the war: he is changed forever when an Allied soldier transgresses the boundaries of his role as "liberator" and takes this child as his lover. Despite significant differences between the characters of *The Assault* and *For A Lost Soldier* as "types", they participate in similar representations of the damage done by or during the occupation. The emphasis is on the role assigned to childhood, which is delineated in terms of issues of coming of age, with sexuality as a marker for the end of childhood. At the same time, these texts investigate narrative as memory. These three works viewed together function as a dialogue within the context of this community practice; they constitute three approaches, three different varieties of experiences, three sets of presuppositions, all within the range of "normal" community approaches to the history and memory of the occupation and the post-war period, and the narratives which rehearse them.

NON-TRADITIONAL VICTIMS: BLACK SHEEP OF THE FAMILY

From these novels whose subjects may be construed as "victims", I move along the imaginary continuum of survivors which I have posited toward narratives of children who are the offspring of perpetrators, and from treatments of obviously "fictional" subjects to texts which appear on the surface to be more explicitly nonfictional – and perhaps, more "historical". The movement along this line fittingly pauses in the center of the continuum to invite the intervention of the writer and artist Armando. His early, nonfictional text, *De SS'ers* ("SS-ers", 1967), problematizes the easy distinctions between victims and perpetrators; his more abstractly fictionalized study of language and place *De straat en het struikgewas* ("Street and Foliage", 1988) undermines whatever simplistic notions one might entertain of individual subjects who are simply good or entirely evil. Armando offers a multi-faceted exposé of the role of language and culture in determinations of right and wrong and of memory as a determining factor in the present. In Armando's work, I interrogate language as the vehicle and place as the setting of a culture of enmity. In Armando's work, the problems of war and occupation are reduced to their constitutive parts and are layered over the issues I have come to associate with memory in the earlier parts of this book. Armando has a finely-tuned ear for language and the implications of the way we talk for what we do, and for how – and why – we remember.

Moving on from these more abstract issues – but abstract issues which are directly applicable – of language and representation, the next point on the continuum of children of the war is populated by children of collaborators. Several narratives representing this group include the working-class narrative of Rinnes Rijke's *Niet de schuld, wel de straf* ("Punished, Though Innocent"), Duke Blaauwendraad-Doorduijn's more educated and "literate" tale *Niemandsland* ("No Man's Land"), and an impassioned memoir written under the pseudonym of "Hanna Visser" on the beginning stages of her memory-work. The decade of the 1980s marks the historical moment when it first became possible within Dutch culture at large to recognize that in the postwar period the children of collaborators suffered for their parents' earlier political offenses.[28] Visser's memoir, *Het verleden voorbij* ("Beyond the Past"), involves a large measure of grief at the (relatively) small part her father and his political allies played in cooperating with the Nazi occupation and thus furthering the Holocaust, and offers a genuine attempt to reject the values which led to her father's collaboration and to somehow disassociate herself from the hated past. Rijke's text on the other hand is remarkable for the way he constructs his tale of suffering: presumably an indictment of the "good" Dutch citizens who visited their post-war anger on the "innocent" child of a petty collaborator, the narrative reveals a much more complex tale of a wicked stepmother and seemingly run-of-the-mill domestic child abuse.

Since notions of victimization and child abuse are of central importance in the discussion of these texts, and since memory is arguably the basic problem which is at issue in the debates surrounding collaboration and child abuse, I consider evidence from the realm of psychotherapy to shed light on the problematic issues concerning memory of abuse. I illustrate that what these two separate debates have in common is a central and very pointed question about the reliability of memory and its critical importance for and within culture. There are several intriguing reasons or explanations for why these different aspects of social interaction have become the locus for the debate about memory.

Historically, World War II took place on two fronts for citizens of the Netherlands – the occupation of the Low Countries by Germany, and the occupation of Indonesia by Japan. It is interesting to note that a similar set of thematic concerns recurs in recent Dutch fiction whose setting is the Japanese occupation – to the point that some of the linguistic and visual vocabulary associated with the German occupier is appropriated for use in a Southeast Asian setting. To illustrate the last outpost along my continuum of those groups recently recognized as survivors, I consider these now-familiar themes in Jeroen Brouwers' fictional narratives which provide an adult perspective in *Sunken Red,* of the narrator's internment in a Japanese concentration camp in Indonesia during his childhood, and the consequences of these experiences in later decades of his life. It is instructive to examine the explicitly different cultural settings of Brouwers' work in terms of both the construction of the idea of the perpetrator in the context of shared cultural memory and the place it occupies in the Dutch discussions of war victims of the occupation(s) and the function of memory within fiction and life. I therefore offer a brief description of several strains of the pitched debates which followed the publication of this novel, including criticisms presented in Rudy Kousbroek's *Het Oostindisch Kamp Syndroom,* and investigate what these arguments mean in a cultural sense, that is, what these arguments imply for the notion of what it means to be "Dutch" in the 1980s. I do not attempt to offer an exhaustive analysis of each of the many memoirs, diaries, commentaries, and even novels which have been published since the 1980s about the experience of the war in Indonesia, but rather focus on the debate about the accuracy or reliability of Brouwers' (former-)child protagonist's memory, the relationship between fact and fiction, and about both appropriate doubt and the reasons why in certain contexts it is important to people to insist on truth-telling.

This debate in effect asks for definitions of appropriate roles for both fiction and memory. Kousbroek and others point to what they view as historical inaccuracies in Brouwers' text. Three responses are conceivable: first, that the text is in fact not inaccurate, second, that it is a work of fiction, to which different standards of verisimilitude apply than to a non-fictional text, and third, that the need to remember is itself more important than the literal accuracy of individual facts.

Responses of these three types have in fact been offered. In the first place, a debate ensued about certain facts mentioned in *Sunken Red.* The picture which emerges after the dust has settled is that some elements which had been alleged to be historical mistakes in Brouwers' text were not necessarily errors, but facts which pertained to some localities and specific points in history, but not to others. Thus when Indonesian camp survivors weigh in with testimonials concerning their individual experiences ("I was in a camp, and we never experienced x"), such statements do not necessarily count as counter-arguments to Brouwers' presentation of the facts. However, beyond recognizing that facts are often contingent, this approach is of little interest.

A second species of response in the debate concerning *Sunken Red* is to recognize that the text is fictional and not primarily meant to be a literally accurate representation of specific individual facts about the past. In my discussion, I show that Brouwers deliberately raised the issue of the truth status of fiction in his text, that he plays with the reader's tendency to expect accuracy under certain circumstances. What is of even more interest, however, is to consider the possibility that if inaccuracies exist in the text, they may not be merely random errors, but may represent a tendentious retelling of the events. Brouwers' choices of imagery are significant in themselves, and relate to the third point in this series of responses.

Lastly, what interests me about the debate concerning the historical accuracy of Brouwers' work is an emphasis on the inherent importance of remembering itself. Brouwers claims that the history of the camps in Indonesia is in danger of being forgotten. I accept and discuss this point with some sympathy, and return to Blom's argument about what it means to be Dutch to ponder the social and historical reasons why it may indeed be the case that those repatriated from Indonesia were treated less sympathetically than they perhaps should have been. It is significant that Kousbroek *names* that which he has identified as a phenomenon, the "tendency" to lie deliberately about the past. He calls it the "East Indies Camp Syndrome", and by naming it thus he fills it with a greater claim to reality than it would otherwise have had; it has thus been identified as a significant fact, an event with an identifiable meaning within Dutch postwar culture.

CHILDHOOD AND SUFFERING

Childhood is commonly assumed, in the context of the cultures of the "West" (in the First World, and in the twentieth century), to be a separate stage of life which sets the child apart from the rest of society. In addition, childhood is viewed in a utopian light. I posit that the complaints implicit in the texts I consider about the lack of perfect happiness expose an assumed consensus of expectations for childhood, such as happiness and mental and physical well-being. Further, childhood is viewed as a period of preparation for adult life, and thus a stage which one outgrows. Given these parameters, it is to be expected that a "former child" would look back on his or her childhood with either nostalgia or regret, and probably with an admixture of both simultaneously, and that the memory of that childhood would have great constitutive and explanatory power for the individual's adult life.

Contemporary western views of the world posit an idealized conception of childhood as a time which is assumed to be kept devoid of burdensome responsibility or any preventable suffering. Although such hopes are laudable and understandable, it is clear that they are essentially utopian. On one hand, there are forces at work in the world which cannot be controlled by parents and other well-meaning adults, or even by governments at their best, and the limits of the adult world's finite ability to control living conditions during wartime are nothing more or less than an extreme example of an everyday truth, which marks boundaries which normally remain invisible. Under the conditions which middle-class members of the dominant cultures in the West consider "normal", parents are able to control to a certain degree the conditions under which their children are raised: they can provide sustenance, shelter, education, perhaps a loving family. The fact that there are factors in life (such as catastrophic illness or serious accidents) which cannot be controlled even in the best of circumstances is usually studiously ignored and denied as long as circumstances permit. The result is that we are caught short whenever events do not allow us to continue to repress our knowledge of the less pleasant realities of life. We respond by considering suffering by children particularly tragic or unfair. Some of the recent literature which considers the fallout of the memory – and memories – of the occupation of the Netherlands during World War II provides an opportunity to face such concerns. It deals through memory with a time when the barriers which adults set up to protect their children were ineffective because the adults themselves were essentially powerless to control their environment.

The occupation is a time when children suffer, as do adults. One of my purposes in this book is to examine narratives about war and memory with an eye to exploring their social and cultural meanings. To what uses are the memories of the occupation put? What do these writers and readers "do" when they consider the effect the memories of the occupation have on the lives of individual characters, and on Dutch society as a whole? How does and how should the community respond to the events of fifty years ago, and to their continued presence (through memory and/or repression) among us?

Why then are there so many recent Dutch novels which concern themselves with the plight of children during and following the occupation? A simple answer would be that it is because of the natural progression of generations: many of the authors writing today are at an age when they are coming to terms with the earlier experiences of their generation – they, after all, *were* children during or just following the war. In addition to the historical factors, which are surely relevant, I posit and explore several other conditions of the community's investment in discussions about "former children" and the occupation.

The historical accident that a certain generation of Dutch readers and writers experienced childhood during wartime (that is, during the occupation), and that this generation is now reflecting on that childhood, young adulthood and even middle age – forever influenced by the events of the occupation – which followed it, is arguably a necessary condition of the production of this body of literature. I posit, however, that this circumstance does not completely account for its prevalence and does not entirely explain the community's enthusiasm (though a passion often also reflected in distaste) for negotiating and renegotiating the questions which this literature raises and the views which it represents.

More important than simply our time in history, I would argue, is the fact that looking at texts about children set in an unusual, notoriously "dangerous" time allows us to bracket the experience, to set it apart in order to gain a different perspective or assume a different stance toward momentous issues which are true always and everywhere. Setting the narratives in the past allows the community to temporarily avoid some of the sentimental or idealistic notions which might otherwise distract from the work at hand. The process of writing, reading, and arguing about these texts at least provides writers and readers with an opportunity to set aside certain utopian presuppositions in order to test some received notions of childhood, and to consider what we mean by coming of age, or the end of childhood. Asking why such topics are so prevalent in recent literature, though interesting, may prove a less productive way of approaching the issue than to ask to what end the discussion is taking place: it is important to explore which views of the occupation and of childhood are proposed, whether they are widely accepted or contested, and which consensus-building values are represented.

The works I have selected allow a look at childhood from a fresh point of view, an opportunity to consider why the memory of the war provides a unique perspective on childhood and what this view of childhood is. Also, these novels explicitly investigate the role of one's memory of childhood, and – unavoidably – the perspective of the same character from the vantage point of adulthood while looking back; this perspective of "pastness" offers different textual opportunities than would pertain in a work written about a child-hero set in the present, or a tale about the experiences of an adult in the past.

The texts I present construct the lives of characters who because of the occupation, were denied what twentieth-century Western culture would consider a "normal childhood". When we investigate these texts, the reason for the persistence of expressions such as "Dat heeft-ie van de oorlog overgehouden", (to refer to a nervous tic; loosely translated: "That's his souvenir from the war", or "That's what he has brought back from the war", or "That's what's left over from the war (for him)",) or "Die heeft de oorlog niet meegemaakt", (said of a person who does not eat all of the food on his or her plate; "He/she didn't live through (experience) the war"), that is to say, the reasons for the centrality of the image of the war's privations and wounds to Dutch thinking, will become clear.

The frequency with which recent fiction is still set in the war years indicates that the occupation continues to fulfill a crucial function in Dutch consciousness. As a fictional setting, of course, the war can serve various functions. In addition to providing a stage on which acute moral dilemmas may be played out, and creating an atmosphere of grave danger which heightens the reader's sense of adventure, it offers an opportunity to investigate the culture through the eyes of children. The presentation of main characters who are children introduces an interesting dynamic, as the children become interesting and unusual heroes or protagonists. Since our culture views children as relatively helpless, the text's representation of children-as-(anti-)heroes questions the reader's casually held and possibly unexamined notions of agency: children may be helpless, but in the end, if we are honest with ourselves, we must admit that adults are too, particularly while under a brutal occupation.

Bystander parents who were unable to feed their children felt powerless. Collaborators in many cases were better able to provide for the physical needs of their families, but they were often ashamed of what they did in order to feed their offspring. Resistance fighters, the heroes of the war, were often frustrated in their desire to prevent all the evil they could see, and were often unable even to avoid indirect complicity. Examples of the moral dilemmas the resistance faced are presented in *The*

Assault, such as when members of the resistance decided to act while aware that the
Nazis were likely to retaliate by executing hostages.

Thinking about the helplessness of children is a practice which allows the reading public to entertain indirectly the notion of the helplessness of adults without being forced to squarely face an uncomfortable reality. If we do not enjoy considering the powerlessness of an individual grownup, it may be easier to confront the more acceptable truth of the helplessness of a child. (This remains true, although, as has already been noted, we are less comfortable about entertaining the notion that children may suffer, and there is a clear connection between this helplessness and this suffering). In addition, given our culture's tendency to associate helplessness with innocence, there is by implication an opportunity to appropriate the innocence of children as well. Since children are viewed as not being strong agents, they are also more likely to be innocent; that is, they will be viewed as less likely to be guilty of any moral or political offense. Because of their innocence, any ill or evil which befalls them will be viewed as all the more "unjust" or "unfair", and thus as particularly salient. It is true that adults – resistance fighters, collaborators and bystanders – suffered traumatic wounds during the occupation and that these traumas need to be treated. It is easier, however, to make the same point if the victim was a child – that is, "innocent" – at the time when the traumatic event occurred. Then, as a next step, once the issue of trauma as a condition which is to be taken seriously has become socially acceptable, it becomes much easier to include those hurt in adulthood in this therapeutic circle, the company of victims.

A SENSE OF MEANING

I proceed to show that this "culture of victimhood" is thought to apply not only to the individual groups of survivors, but also to the Dutch people collectively. Following arguments by Dutch historian J.C.H. Blom,[29] I argue that the attitudes about victimhood which I identify in these novels about the memory of the occupation are entirely consistent with traditional definitions of "Dutchness". As Blom states, suffering and innocence are central to Dutch definitions of national identity. Thus, the child protagonists of the novels I present may serve as representations of a helpless victim nation, which in its innocence was unable to prevent the evils of occupation by a powerful enemy.

A final implication of the fact that Western culture of our age views children as innocent (at least of the political sins of their parents) is that such an assumption implies a possible leveling effect between "victims" and perpetrators: it suddenly and perhaps surprisingly[30] becomes thinkable that a continuum, however tenuous, be constructed from Jews, and particularly Jewish children, and other victims of the Holocaust,[31] to "uninvolved" Dutch citizens, bystanders, and their children, to the children of casual or petty collaborators, and finally to the children of wholeheartedly committed collaborators (traditionally the most manifest "bad guys" on the Dutch literary horizon). This scheme implicitly suggests the possibility of leveling the perceived ethical differences between victims and perpetrators, a move experienced as subversive by some of those traditionally considered war heroes, and welcomed by members of those groups who consider themselves (unjustly) vilified and excluded from the mainstream culture. In this context, I find the work of the Israeli psychologist Daniel Bar-On instructive. His research indicates that the children of perpetrators suffer(ed) in ways remarkably similar to the wounds of the offspring of victims, such as Jewish camp survivors, that the syndrome described as "survivor's guilt" and its effects on the survivors' offspring are paralleled by similar effects which occur in the families of perpetrators. Bar-On's research shows that both effects impede the "processing" of the events of the war, and tend to perpetuate social and psychological dysfunction in children of the war.

Thus the choice of children as heroes carries distinct advantages for the potential impact of the text: it allows the author to highlight specific, otherwise inaccessible, inexpressible or invisible aspects of the situation, to introduce a new point of view, and to study the age-old problems of utopia and culpability from a fresh angle. It is worth noting that this emphasis on children as victims – not of their mothers' child-rearing practices, as in the popular stereotype of the view of Freudian psychology – but of forces outside the family which in turn affect various behaviors within the family, reflecting a trans-generational (diachronic)[32] chain of culpability, is also a common phenomenon in contemporary subcultures of the legal and therapeutic professions, and thus also in popular culture[33] of the United States of America in the 1980s and first half of the 1990s. In both the Dutch and American settings, the question of the reliability and function of memory, in particular as it relates to events which cannot be readily verified because of the secretive circumstances under which they occurred, is a centrally important issue. A second common factor is that the acts being remembered are so far beyond the pale for the culture in which the discussion is taking place that they are said to be "unthinkable".

In the US, these concerns about the function or usefulness of memory center around issues of child abuse, and specifically, child sexual abuse. In the Netherlands, in the works on which I elaborate here, the concern is with traumatic experiences which occurred during the occupation, or later as a result of events associated with the war. Such events were often not directly experienced by an adult protagonist, so that the emotional responses are not caused by any guilt belonging to the individual, but rather they are cases of a "secondary traumatization" passed from parents to children. This pattern also echoes the conviction in many American circles that abusers were themselves abused as children, and that those who are abused will themselves likely become abusers unless a successful therapeutic intervention is accomplished.

Thus, in insisting that what is at stake in investigations of child abuse in the US or the war past in the Netherlands is memory itself, I mean not just the memory of the individual, but this trans-generational transference of the "sins of the fathers". I particularly attend to these similarities in approach and in the meaning attributed to these events in the second half of *A Family Occupation*. In order to tease out the meaning of the narratives about the occupation, I ask various questions: What are the narrative strategies used to tell the stories, and why are they told as they are? How is language employed to obtain a certain effect, does the writer do so effectively and what is the outcome of these techniques for community practice? How does the community of readers and writers thus express its various views about the function of memory – and specific memories of the occupation – and simultaneously move to alter those views in a variety of ways, and for a variety of purposes?

In summary, I present not just texts concerning the experiences of victims of the German occupation, but also others, such as a novel by Armando which challenges many common and facile assumptions about the sources of evil during the occupation by looking at language, as well as texts which consider the suffering of the children of collaborators (a topic which really raises the question of how we re/present the issues of collaboration and/or child abuse which we wish to discuss) and lastly, a novel which presents the suffering of "colonials" both in Indonesia during the war in Japanese concentration camps, and after their subsequent return to the Netherlands. I argue that both their pain and the importance of correct memory (the proof which these texts provide that memory is an important issue) are evident from the discussion about *Sunken Red* in the press. This evidence bolsters my claim that these arguments are not *only* about the occupation, but about the relationship between memory and truth as well. In effect, the debates about these texts from the 1980s which engage the memory of World War II invite the reader to participate in a debate about what is important, including questions concerning morality and character, on a national and on an individual level.

When examining these different texts together – texts from various points along the "imaginary continuum" of parental culpability – it is possible to delineate explicitly not only their representations of childhood, but also the role of "innocence" as it relates to Dutch thought about the occurrences and experiences of the occupation. I take into account a collection of texts which represent all of the groups which fall within the range from "Jews and Jewish children" to "uninvolved" Dutch citizens and their children, to the children of casual or petty collaborators, and finally to the children of wholeheartedly committed collaborators. Thus I can sum up and attempt to understand the dynamics involved in negotiating the assignment of relative levels of innocence or culpability as allowed by the culture.

Sem Dresden, writing about those whose extermination was the explicit goal of the Nazis, considers the consequences for narrative, history and truth of the fact that the murderers failed to kill all their intended victims:

> Suppose, however, that all European Jews had been massacred. Numerous and important accounts and reports from eyewitnesses would then have disappeared. Now that the intention did not quite succeed, however, we find therein the opportunity for written or oral transmission. The *almost,* that is to say, the void that exists between (a series of) actions and their intended but unreached result, leaves room for the irreplaceable expressions of the victims, which within the perspective of the perpetrators would not have had any right to exist.[34]

This book is not in the first place about those who died, but about those who had to go on living with the knowledge – the memory – of what had happened. They had survived while others were massacred. In some cases, the survivors end up wondering whether their survival came at the expense of someone else's death, as does the main character in Marga Minco's *The Glass Bridge*. Theirs is the burden known as "survivor's guilt". The fact that I study the consequences of that fact not just for survivors of the Jewish Holocaust, but for survivors from other groups as well, should by no means be taken as a lack of recognition of the victims of the Shoah. I believe that the outcome of any genuine and thoughtful attempt to come to terms with the memory and history of the war will have as a major consequence the creation of a space in which all survivors can remember how and why Jewish suffering occurred, and I hope in some small way to contribute toward enabling such acts of memory. It is a truism in psychology that individuals and groups suffering from the effects of unprocessed traumatic experiences cannot empathize – even with survivors of disasters much worse than those they have experienced. It is also true that part of the dialogue between victims and survivors – from every group – must have as its point of departure an honest attempt for each to understand the other. For, as I show in the course of my study,[35] people from various walks of life have come to believe that the wounds sustained by children of the war collectively described by the word "trauma" and the unresolved memories – even private memories passed down only within families – can affect subsequent generations. Further social problems are more likely to occur as long as we have not faced the past, grieved for the victims, and faced our failure to protect them. In this book, I trace this view of an entire generation – the children of the war – in which individuals belonging to various groups were affected and who express in fiction and non-fictional texts the need to resolve the past.

In the final analysis, these narratives must be studied in order to ask to what end – "what for?" – these stories with their readings of the consequences of memory are written and read. The most interesting question remains this: how these narratives "interactively" both reflect and participate in shaping the culturally received notions of what the war period – and its aftermath – was like, and what, if anything, a given understanding of what the time was like means for the generation of people who were children during those times, as well as for their children and even their grandchildren. Thus my primary interest lies not in determining whether the narratives reflect a "historically accurate" view of the times – though if I were to "catch" an author or narrator in an apparently intentional distortion of history, or a tendentious telling thereof, it would certainly be interesting to discover the reason for that particular sleight of hand. I assume it is true that the role I play when I read a text in the context of literary practice differs from the one of a historian when she reads a text in light of her discipline. If, however, as Lynn Hunt put it, the discipline of history is "an ongoing tension between stories that have been told and stories that might be told",[36] then in that sense history has a thing or two in common with my approach.

2. Anton's Story

Before I proceed to discuss the variety of texts published in the Netherlands in the 1980s which engage the memories and histories of the children of the war, I begin with a detailed and deliberate discussion of the novel *The Assault*,[1] a text which offers opportunities to identify and illustrate many of the issues central to the other texts which contribute to the debate about memory and the history of the children of the war. The detailed analysis of this one representative text will function as a benchmark for more abbreviated treatments of other novels in subsequent chapters, and will permit a careful delineation of the function which language inhabits in mediating the memory of World War II, the Holocaust, and the occupation of the Netherlands in Dutch literature.

This novel has been exceptionally successful.[2] One reason for its popularity is identifiable and particularly instructive as a starting point for this study. *The Assault* resonated with much of the Dutch reading public because it may be the quintessential story of the Dutch child who survived the occupation. Mulisch's "achievement" (if one wishes to call it that) is two-fold: He has told a story which incorporates many or most of the elements which belong to the cultural store of collected memories of

1. Harry Mulisch standing in front of a poster-size photograph of his mother and himself. (1975) (Letterkundig Museum)

the "war" as experienced, or rather, remembered, by the "average" Dutch person, and – more significantly – he has succeeded in convincingly portraying the child (the novel's protagonist Anton Steenwijk) of a family of bystanders as a war victim. It is worthy of note that *The Assault* does not mention the (Dutch) Jewish experience of the occupation or the Holocaust; although the secret at the very heart of the novel is certainly connected to that experience, it accounts for a very small fraction of the entire novel. Rather, this text is dedicated to the experience of the ethnically Dutch gentile population who had no direct active involvement in the war or the occupation on either a military, governmental or resistance level. Because of this fact, *The Assault* paints the image of the suffering of this child without having to deal with comparative issues such as the calculus of suffering often encountered in post-war life and discussions of the past. The main character in this text is a victim in his own right, and one is not explicitly invited to discount his suffering because others have suffered more. Nevertheless, while the text does mention the suffering of a collaborator's child, the narration does not dwell on his experience; and the protagonist, Anton, is too involved in his own suffering to extend much sympathy to the other. However, some readers will do so, and are thus sensitized to the damage done to children of collaborators, although this issue is not given a central place or exhaustive treatment in this text.[3]

Mulisch's narrator tells the story of Anton Steenwijk, a young boy whose life is completely changed by a single, apparently random, event. The narrative takes pains to present not only him, but his entire family, as innocent and even ignorant of the events which lead to the catastrophe. Thus Anton's parents and brother function as the paradigm of the "innocent" Dutch family – the perfect example of people who view themselves as "average" Dutch citizens and who attempted to survive the occupation by staying out of the public eye by neither collaborating with the occupying forces, nor by resisting. As the Steenwijk family is quietly playing a board game (the well-known traditional game called "Mens erger je niet" in Dutch)[4] inside their house, Fake Ploeg, the Chief Inspector of Police, a collaborator and reputedly exceptionally brutal torturer, is liquidated near their home by members of the Dutch Resistance. The Steenwijks watch in horror as their neighbors move the body and deposit it in front of the Steenwijks' house. The Nazis avenge the assassination by burning down the Steenwijks' house, and killing its inhabitants – except for Anton, who is saved, either because of his youth or perhaps as the result of an oversight, but in any case, under circumstances which seem to him to be random. The average Dutch reader will recognize an appeal to several well-known features of the memory of World War II which have become stock elements in the cultural history of the occupation: the theme of the winter of starvation and the trope of the nasty collaborator. The winter of 1944-45 was particularly bitter. It featured a combination of cold weather and an acute shortage of food, particularly in the cities of the (Northern) part of the country which the Allied forces had failed to liberate after their failure to take Arnhem.

The narrator immediately alerts the reader to the symbol of the stone which serves a central interpretive function in the story. Just before the assault, Mr. *Steen*wijk[5] is tutoring his elder son, Peter, in the classics, which precipitates the following exchange:

> "...Remember the word 'symbol', which comes from symballo, 'to bring together', 'to meet'. Do you know what a symbolon was?"

> "No," said Peter in a tone implying that he couldn't care less.

> "What was it, Papa?" asked Anton.

> "It was a stone that they broke in two. Say I am a guest in another city..."

> "That's great," said Anton, "I'm going to try that someday."

> Groaning, Peter turned away. "Why in God's name should I learn all that?"

> "Not in God's name," said Steenwijk, peering at him over his glasses. "In the name of humanitas. You'll see how much pleasure it will give you for the rest of your life." (14-15)

Peter, the intended audience of the lecture, is not interested in his father's enthusiasm for classical culture, but Anton, the younger child, takes the lesson to heart: "I'm going to try that someday." This childish prediction sets up the dynamic by which Anton will later remember a past he has attempted to forget. The father identifies himself as an educated man who has achieved social status and found meaning in his education. As the family plays the game, the narrative makes clear which symbol the reader is expected to trace in Anton's life, and alerts the reader to the fact that Anton is not insensitive to the influence of symbols: Anton wants to have the green game pieces; the fact that his brother makes fun of Anton's superstitious belief that "having green" will help him win, serves to focus the reader's attention on the scene, which contains a crucial hint to the path of memory in this novel.

This conversation between the two brothers also serves to foreground Anton's youth: his brother Peter's disgust with him highlights Anton's childlike faith in magic, his credulous attitude toward the game pieces' instrumentality, and their power to influence the future; this moment will prove to be the end of Anton's childhood. Whereas Peter, the older brother, rebels against his father's enthusiasm for humanistic values, Anton is not yet developmentally ready to grasp them.

> Steenwijk laid down his book. A moment later the only sounds were those of the dice being shaken and the pawns being moved across the board. It was

almost 8 o'clock: curfew. Outside all was as still as it must be on the moon. (15-16)

The phrase "the dice being shaken and the pawns being moved across the board" suggests a symbolic narrative device – the dice and pawns used in the game of "mens erger je niet" obviously foreshadow the fateful event which is about to occur in the lives of the Steenwijks. The Dutch word for "die" is "dobbelsteen",[6] and throughout the book any stone or rock will signify fate to Anton;[7] although he will do all he can to forget the events of that night, stones and rocks will continue to appear in the narrative as stumbling blocks placed in his path. As long as he succeeds in repressing from his consciousness memories of the events of that evening, he will have migraine headaches brought on by the presence of rocks, which in fact are prominently displayed throughout the narrative.

Dice constitute a carefully chosen symbol for Anton's experience: he views his parents' and brother's deaths as an example of essentially arbitrary fortune – a fate so inexplicable and meaningless that he blocks it out or isolates it in his memory. The text repeatedly indicates that he attempts to view the events of that night as irrelevant to his later life, beginning in the sentence quoted above:

> ... the only sounds were those of the dice being shaken and the pawns being moved across the board. It was almost 8 o'clock: curfew. Outside all was as still as it must be on the moon. (15-16)

When he hears the sound of shots ringing out in the night in front of his house, on impulse Anton puts one of the dice in his pocket. The Steenwijks look out the window to see that Fake Ploeg, the Chief of Police, has been assassinated in the street near their house.

After the assassination of Ploeg, chaos breaks out in the Steenwijk household. Ploeg has been killed in front of the neighbors' house. The neighbors – a father and daughter named Korteweg – quickly run outside and move the body away from their house, laying it in front of the Steenwijk residence. Ignoring his mother's protests, Anton's older brother Peter goes outside to attempt to move Ploeg's body back to where it had initially fallen, so that the corpse would not be found in front of the Steenwijks' house – everyone was aware of the German regime's penchant for reprisal. This element of the plot constitutes an appeal to a presumed shared history: Dutch readers will recognize the theme of retribution by the occupation authorities. Acts of sabotage or violence against German soldiers or officials of the government were routinely followed by retribution toward the civilian population. At the end of the novel, in Anton's discussion of this event with Karin Korteweg, it becomes clear that the Kortewegs expected some retributive act such as the burning down of a house, but that they were aware that the pattern up to that point did not include taking the lives of the inhabitants of the house. This assumption of limited consequences was cited as a partial explanation for the Kortewegs' willingness to pass the anticipated punishment on down the street to their neighbors. The mention of this detail calls to mind

the careful analysis by the Dutch population of the formal and informal rules in occupation culture – rules set and adhered to by the occupation forces – and well known
to the occupied, even to such families as the Steenwijks and the Kortewegs, who were
attempting to avoid all involvement.

The boys' mother is portrayed as (appropriately) concerned for Peter, and the
father – the exemplar of the classical humanist – is unable to act. He has frozen in
place, helpless to prevent the catastrophe which he must see coming. The issue of the
father's lack of involvement in politics, his status as essentially a "bystander", engages
questions concerning the behavior(s) of an important segment of the Dutch population during World War II. I should note in passing that Mulisch saw his father as a
politically ignorant "bystander", actually a hapless collaborator in the end, someone
who did not understand where his involvement would lead, and never made a conscious choice to be involved as he was. During the war, the elder Mulisch separated
from his wife, whose Jewish mother and grandmother were deported. Meanwhile,
according to Harry Mulisch in *Mijn getijdenboek*, Harry's father was a director of personnel for Lippmann-Rosenthal & CO. As J. Presser describes it in *De ondergang*[8],
the Nazis forced all Dutch Jews to deposit their financial resources into this bank, so
that when the time came to deport the people, the funds were easily collected and
confiscated. It is on the basis of this personal history that Harry Mulisch states with
an undeniable sense of drama: "I *am* World War II".[9]

Mulisch has given voice to a warning that attempting to remain uninvolved does
not necessarily allow one to escape danger, as he stated in the autobiographical *Mijn
getijdenboek:* [10]

2. A Dutch policeman named Fake Krist, shot by the Resistance on October 25, 1944.
(RIOD)

But for my father, a new stage of his life began that afternoon – which is a text-book case of the inner defenselessness of someone who does not involve him-self in politics. He becomes guilty and is subsequently crushed by politics. Therefore it is better to go ahead and become involved with politics, for that way, one would at least know why one is being crushed when one is crushed. (23)

COMMITMENT, A GOOD CAUSE, AND FATE

As Anton learned later, both his parents and Peter were killed that night of the assault, while he was taken away. For reasons which remain unclear – the decision is chal-lenged later on – little Anton is temporarily put into a jail cell, which he shares with someone he does not know. The details of the scene in the cell are of central impor-tance for the narrator's construction of the memory of the occupation as a constitu-tive element of Dutch postwar experience, and especially for survivors such as Anton. After Anton is put into the darkened cell, the following conversation takes place:

"Come and sit next to me."

He stood up and felt his way step by step in her direction.

"Yes, here I am," she said. "Put out your hand." He touched her fingers; she took hold of his hand and pulled him close. On the cot she embraced him with one arm and with her other hand pressed his head against her breast. She smelled of sweat but also of something else, something sweetish that he couldn't identify. Perhaps it was perfume. Within the darkness there was a sec-ond darkness in which he heard her heart pound, really much too hard for someone who was just comforting someone else. (32-33)

The image is touching: a frightened child being comforted by a kind, maternal woman. But the narrative raises significant ambiguities, which will be further devel-oped as the night wears on: Anton notices that he is touching her breast, his sense of smell is acute, and his interpretation of the scents he perceives is sensual: the sweet smell he notices is blood, as the reader will discover later, but he thinks of it as per-fume. The description of the loud beating of the woman's heart is equally ambigu-ous: although the reader realizes that it is due to a surfeit of adrenaline (she has just killed a dangerous and much-hated collaborator, has been wounded and apprehend-ed, and expects to be tortured and executed in retribution for her act), the narrative clearly raises the possibility that the situation may be confusing to Anton, presenting to the reader a young boy who is forced to grow up rapidly in more than one respect during this awful night.

The woman and the young boy comfort each other and converse. She attempts to prepare Anton for a hurtful view she fears he will later confront, namely, that the

Resistance is to blame for the ills that befall him and his family as a result of the assault on Ploeg. Thus the narrative recalls to the reader a stock theme in discussions of situational ethics during and after the occupation.

> "…but will you never forget one thing for the rest of your life?"…
>
> "Listen. They'll try and make you believe all kinds of things, but you must never forget that it was the Krauts[11] who burned down your house. Whoever did it, did it, and not anyone else."
>
> "Of course I know that," said Anton, a little offended. "I saw it with my own eyes, after all."
>
> "Yes, but they did it because that pig had been liquidated, and they'll blame the Underground and say they were forced to do it. They'll tell you that the Underground knew what would happen and therefore the Underground is responsible."
>
> "Oh," said Anton drawing himself up a little and trying to formulate what he thought about it. "But if that's the case, then…then no one's ever at fault. Then everyone can just do as they please." (33)

The child may be smarter than she had anticipated, but she has offered him a way of thinking about history which she hopes will help him to live with the consequences of her act, and she has attempted to assuage her feelings of guilt or regret at being the proximal cause for the suffering to which she has alluded. The reader will later learn that the position she takes on the ethics of retribution is the result of long discussions of the topic with her colleagues in the Resistance. She does not respond to the philosophical parry the boy offers her; she needs to be reassured that his and her suffering will not turn out to have been in vain, and she is not disappointed. As the reader already knows, the boy will indeed be able to reassure her on this account.

Consider, meanwhile, the language in which this scene of comforting and information-gathering is presented. Although the woman's intentions are decidedly not sexual, the language used to describe the encounter craftily suggests gestures and physical positioning that would echo the language of a first, timid sexual experience from the little boy's point of view:

> He felt her fingers caressing his hair. "Do you happen to know, by the way…" she began hesitantly, "what that fellow's name was?" (33)

To the woman's great relief, Anton confirms that he made a positive identification of Ploeg and that Ploeg is indeed dead and thus – the reader understands – that she had succeeded in her mission. Anton declares Ploeg dead "as a doornail": the jocularity reminds the reader as well as the female character of the fact that little Anton has not yet grasped the negative implications of this fact for his future.

Anton blithely mentions that he knows Ploeg by sight because he is a classmate of Ploeg's son, also named Fake, and so upsets the woman even more. His subsequent attempt at comforting her will prove to have been determined by fate, and determining of his future, in the careful structure with which Mulisch shapes the narrative:

> She pulled her arm away and began to sob. It frightened Anton; he wanted to comfort her but didn't know how. He sat up and carefully reached out till he felt her hair: thick, springy hair. (34)

When he asks her why she is crying, she comforts him:

> She took his hand and pressed it against her heart...

> Under the palm of his hand he felt her soft breast, a strange softness such as he had never felt before, but he didn't dare remove his hand. (34)

Almost as palpable to the reader as the intimacy between the two, is the sense of dread when the woman declares that "it" is almost over: everyone except Anton knows that they will soon be separated, and that she will be tortured and put to death in retribution for the assassination of Ploeg. The narrative describes the light as faint but sufficient for Anton to see his companion's silhouette: "he could just see the outline of her head and body, her loose, somewhat wild mass of hair, the place where she sat, an arm approaching him." (35) This image will be burned into his memory; or rather, into his heart, and prove to be an ineluctable influence for the rest of his life. The woman asks permission to touch his face in order to discern his features. Again, Anton finds her touch, her maternal tenderness exciting:

> Softly her cold fingertips caressed his forehead, his eyebrows, cheeks, nose, and lips. He sat motionless, his head slightly tilted back. He felt that this was something very solemn, a kind of initiation, something they might do in Africa. All of a sudden she pulled her hand back and moaned. (35)

An initiation indeed, though not one "they might do (only) in Africa"; it will turn out that Anton habitually thinks of events, customs or behaviors with which he is not familiar in terms of geographical distance. This description of a solemn, only barely understood act is strongly reminiscent of a passage in the Prologue[12] to *The Assault*, where the theme of coming-of-age, of the promise of a delicious and still inaccessible adult world, including the experience of the ineffable, is also heralded:

> Occasionally in the late twilight when his mother forgot to call him in, a fragrant stillness would rise and fill him with expectations – of what, he didn't

know. Something to do with later, when he'd be grown up – things that would
happen then. Something to do with the motionless earth, the leaves, two sparrows that suddenly twittered and scratched about. Life someday would be like
those evenings when he had been forgotten, mysterious and endless. (4)

Thus when one reads the narration of Anton's experience of having his face touched
by the as-yet-anonymous woman in the jail cell in the context of the earlier narrative
of his expectations of the ecstasies of adulthood, one notes a resonance of a language
traditionally associated with sexuality and coming of age in Western culture. I will
show that the notion of coming of age is an important index of the sudden "adulthood" which the experience of the war foists upon young protagonists in Dutch fictional texts set during the occupation.

Anton and the mysterious woman spend a good deal of time talking that night.
The content of this conversation is important because it will form the link to other
characters later, who will help Anton begin to deal with his memories and to start
putting together the pieces of the puzzle which – when completed – will explain what
happened to him the night of the assault. Without identifying herself, the woman
describes to Anton her relationship with a fellow worker in the Resistance, to whom
she has denied her love for him because he is married, and she does not wish to cause
any harm to his family. She also relates a story of how she got lost in the dark one
night[13] while trying to walk home after curfew – how she lost her way, became frightened, and waited on the street, and how, at daybreak, she realized she was just several steps from her home. Her description of her fear echoes the way Anton thinks of
his experience of the occupation and the assault:

> But I was scared, believe me! Perhaps even more by the silence than by the
> darkness. I knew that there were lots of people all about, but everything had
> disappeared. The world stopped at my skin. My fear had nothing to do with
> the War anymore. Besides, I was terribly cold. (36)

The story provides a point of connection between the two characters: Anton sympa-
thizes, recalling a visit to his uncle and aunt's house, during which he awoke in the
middle of the night to find the wall on the "wrong" side of the bed. She reminds him
that the fear evaporated when an adult came and turned on the light, obviously wish-
ing that an adult would come and shed light on his future for him before soon. The
little narrative about being lost in the dark will later become important within the
overall narrative. Anton will remember this story when the plot uses it to link this
woman to her lover, whom Anton will meet later on.

The story of being lost in the middle of one's neighborhood, literally right next to
one's own house, closely mirrors the way Anton will construct his life. Anton will
come to associate his literal displacement (the burning down of his family's house by
vengeful German soldiers) with his social displacement: as the rest of his family will
turn out to have been executed during the night of the assault, he will not return to
Haarlem, but go to live with his uncle and aunt in Amsterdam. Thus, it is no coin-

cidence that later on he will be intrigued by the sextant which he displays in his apartment, and which he explains repeatedly to the young women with whom he half-heartedly and diffidently establishes relationships. The night of the assault ends for Anton with a sign, although he does not consciously interpret it at the time:

3. Harry Mulisch at Schiphol Airport (ca. 1939). (Letterkundig Museum)

... he walked out into the winter day. He was sobbing but hardly knew why, as if his tears had washed away his memories. His other hand felt cold. He stuck it into his pocket, where he touched something he could not place. He looked: it was one of the dice. (52)

The dice will recur throughout the rest of Anton's recovery as a reminder of the arbitrariness of his family's fate.

EPISODE TWO: KEEPING THE ENEMY AT A DISTANCE

The Second Episode of *The Assault* is set in 1952, in the context of the Korean War, but declares the centrality of the events of 1945 in its opening sentence: "All the rest is a postscript – the cloud of ash that rises into the stratosphere from the volcano, circles around the earth, and continues to rain down on all its continents for years." (55) The events of the past may have receded as far away as the stratosphere, but their fallout continues to affect life in the present. The notion of the arbitrariness of Anton's victimization represented by the image of the dice is reinforced by the motto of the book ("By then day had broken everywhere, but here it was still night – no more than night." – Pliny the Younger, *Letters*, IV, 16//"Overal was het al dag, maar hier was het nacht, neen, meer dan nacht." – C. Plinius Caecilius Secundus; *Epistulae*, VI, 16), which is recalled by the "cloud of ash" here: the motto is taken from Pliny the younger, who was reporting on the volcanic eruption which buried Pompeii. The quotation also simultaneously describes the situation in Europe: the Dutch winter of starvation was experienced as particularly difficult because most of Western Europe had already been liberated, and the still-occupied part of the Netherlands had anticipated its liberation as well. Thus by a process of association, the narrative here reflects and reinforces Anton's view that the evil which befell his parents could not be blamed on any individuals, just as a volcanic eruption cannot, nor could it have been prevented. The notion of burying (by ash) also resonates with how Anton deals with his memories of the assault. One might certainly argue that Anton is wrong in this regard, that (as the woman in the cell said) individuals are responsible for their choices; the fact is that Anton found this fact too painful, or the puzzle too complicated, and therefore simply resorted to viewing the whole event as a catastrophe and leaving it at that.

The Assault provides an occasion to question the popular notion that the end of the occupation caused universal happiness among the population of the Netherlands. The narrative jumps to the period of time just after the Liberation in May 1945, when Anton discovers that his parents have been killed, and later, that his brother Peter has too. The Dutch nation celebrates the liberation, but Anton does not, because, as the text explains succinctly:

...none of this was really a part of him or ever would be. His entire universe had become that other one which now fortunately had come to an end, and about which he never wanted to think again. Nevertheless it was a part of him, so that all in all, he didn't have much left. (55-56)

Anton constructs his entire being in terms of the events which occurred during the occupation, and yet he simultaneously chooses to repress them from his conscious memory, thus leaving himself with a severely limited repertoire of modes of existence. Unfortunately this statement describes in fact the conflicts experienced by many survivors of the occupation – the knowledge that many of the events which had taken place were among the most important that can occur in a human life, combined with a natural unwillingness to go on existing in that mode of heightened anxiety, a wish to return to a more "normal life", and linked with a lack of understanding of the fact that this set of attitudes placed very high demands on postwar existence, raising the expectations for happiness beyond the reach of the possible. The wrenching differences between life under the occupation and life following the end of the war is expressed in Anton's sense of the discontinuous passage of time:

> For Anton that distance of five months between January and June, 1945, was incomparably longer than the distance between June of 1945 and the present day. It was on this distortion of time that he later blamed his inability to explain to his children what the War had been like. His family had escaped from his memory... (57)

The sense that the "meaning" of an important experience or historical event can not be communicated in language is a well-known problem in both philosophy and literature, and a frequent complaint in Dutch post-war society. Hence the familiar complaints and expressions such as "Die heeft de oorlog niet meegemaakt",[14] said in exasperation of a person who does not eat all of the food on his or her plate. In this expression, attitudes toward food serve as an index of the effect of one's experience on post-war existence. The sentiment – though understandable – constitutes an overgeneralization: anyone who has survived the war knows from experience what it is like to be hungry, and will therefore eat any food offered. Although many Dutch citizens experienced hunger, and some starved to death, while others were rescued just in time, it does not follow that every survivor will respond by valuing and consuming every scrap available: some, clearly, respond to deprivation by going to the other extreme, that of enjoying the luxury of being able to be choosy about their food, and having the option of wasting it at whim. In this case, the experiences may have been similar, but the responses differed. The common expression inscribes only one response into the culture, but clearly articulates the difficulty of communicating the memory and meaning of certain events to those who have not experienced them first hand.

In *The Assault*, Anton's refusal to remember is presented as a strategy by which he shields himself from a terrible experience – an experience which the narrator describes as "hermetically sealed somewhere deep inside him". (57) (Hermetic means impervious to air, and – Anton hopes – also to thoughts). Anton's sense of intentional isolation from the experience by repression or dissociation mirrors his sense of its arbitrary character – since he cannot connect his experience to some rational construct, he cannot connect it to himself and thus he rejects it. However, as the narrative makes clear, there are times when memories intrude, and these events are tied to cues he cannot avoid. Although Anton is able to rebuff such attempts most of the time, the aspect of this whole experience which makes him vulnerable to memory is "the fingertips of the girl caressing his face". This does not mean that he is condemned to remember every detail: he succeeds very well in refusing to remember any details for a long time, as the text states: "he remembered a dream, but not so much what the dream had been about", and yet that was bad enough from his perspective. It is not an accident on the narrator's part that dice become for Anton one of the symbols of the events of that night; the perceived unpredictability and thus "irrationality" of what happened makes him want to forget. Also, the impulse to remember is presented as "non-rational": the caress of a woman – whether one interprets his experience of her caress as love, or as a more straightforward sensual experience, it is clear that he cannot deny the event, and invests it with meaning, when he thinks of it as his "rite of passage". I have already considered the passage where the text states that "He felt that this was something very solemn, a kind of initiation, something they might do in Africa." (35)

> At such moments it was as if he remembered a dream, but not so much what the dream had been about, as simply the fact that it had been a nightmare. Yet at the core of that hermetic darkness now and then flashed a single source of blinding light: the fingertips of the girl caressing his face. Whether she had had anything to do with the assault, and what had happened to her, he did not know. He had no desire to know. (57)

This appears on the surface to be a case of willful ignorance, of a determination to not know – after all, by virtue of raising the question whether the woman "had had anything to with the assault", the narrator points out that in spite of himself Anton had an awareness of the assault (thus relegating to paradox the statement that all that had been hermetically sealed away), and secondly, that Anton could and must have known (or at least "suspected") that the woman was somehow involved in the assault. "Knowing without being aware of this knowledge" is a situation common in families with "awful secrets": it is possible for the child to be aware of the fact that there is a topic which cannot, must not, be discussed with the parents, or with anyone else, even though – paradoxically – this injunction has supposedly never been discussed among the members of the family. On the surface, the child's knowledge of the forbidden status of the concealed fact is paradoxical – if the thing is a secret, and has never been discussed, then how does one become aware of the fact that one should not ask questions about the topic? However odd, this "knowing that one is not supposed to know" is a well-documented phenomenon among survivors.[15]

The text shows the progression of memory from almost complete repression to its slow resurfacing. In the second period (as subdivided by the narrator of *The Assault*), of Anton's life, successfully and consistently denying the past is not as easy as the narrator made it seem above. In Section 2 of the Second Episode, he reports: "But things don't vanish all that easily." (58) Anton, who has not returned to the city of his childhood since the assault, is invited to a birthday party in Haarlem. He goes, but cannot avoid thinking thoughts such as: "The burned-out truck had been removed...", at which the reader asks: did Anton expect a truck which was bombed during a night in 1945 to still be there seven years after the end of the war? It is clear that Anton's internal landscape of Haarlem has no relationship to a Haarlem in the normal space-time continuum of 1952. Having "hermetically sealed" his memories, having sent them far away, Anton becomes oblivious to the fact that life has gone on in the meantime.

Anton is a typical survivor in this respect. That is exactly the point of forgetting; the notion that life might go on "as usual" without Anton's parents and his brother Peter – and Anton himself, now that he has moved to Amsterdam to live with his uncle and aunt – is too horrible to contemplate, and therefore he ignores the possibility. In repressing the past, it is as if Anton has attempted to flash-freeze it, to hold it in place until (if ever) he is ready to return to that point. He has not thought about Haarlem for seven years, and has not wondered about what happened to the burned-out truck.

During his visit to the street where his house used to be, one of the neighbors has noticed Anton, to his deep dismay:

> Looking closely, he recognized Mrs. Beumer. She had already noticed him and waved.

> He was upset. Not once had it occurred to him that she or any of the others might still be living here. That was inconceivable. He cared only about the place, not the people. Whenever he had thought about it [the neighbors] had not been present. That the people too had remained the same ... he wanted to run away, but she was already standing in the doorway. (64)

Anton's distress has several sources. He views the history of his experiences as discontinuous, and thus expects the same to be true for the other neighbors as well. He had hoped to be able to visit the site as a detached observer. He had, after all, "hermetically sealed" his memories of the place. Secondly, thoughts of the neighbors present special dangers to the young man's equanimity; one set of those neighbors, after all, almost directly brought the catastrophe upon Anton's family, and the others, by their sheer existence and survival after the war, pose the difficult question why Anton's family should have been chosen to suffer as they did, rather than the others?

Like a child who closes his eyes in order to be invisible, Anton has assumed that history froze while he was refusing to pay attention. It will require considerable memory-work on his part before he can absorb and accept not only what happened during the night of the assault, but during the "normal" years after the war as well.

On the other hand, things not remembered might also continue to exist, as when the narrator reports the thought: "Even though he had not thought about them, these ruins had been here all these years, without interruption." (63) It is telling that Anton thinks of the place where his family's house had stood as "these ruins". It is true that the house had been burned down and never rebuilt, but the text also makes it clear to the reader that the neighbors' houses are still there, and still occupied. To the newer neighbors, the lot where Anton's house used to stand is just that: an empty lot in the middle of their neighborhood. The ruins – ashes, really – may remind Mrs. Beumer of Anton and his family, and thus of the events of the occupation, but the neighbors have continued to build their lives, despite and around the empty lot, which is a monument to the events which took place during the occupation. Anton, however, has attempted to live by leaving the ruins of his former life untouched and forgotten. While the neighborhood has remodeled itself around his ruins, he has let the ground upon which his former life had been built lie fallow. The disruption engendered by forgetting is of wide-ranging consequences. Forgetting is portrayed as a force which affects many aspects of his life, including his relationship with the only family he has left.

A HESITANT STEP BACK TOWARD REMEMBERING

The assault is not the only event which Anton has repressed. While he is talking with his former neighbor, she mentions a monument erected in honor of Anton's parents and the other hostages who were executed that night. Anton is surprised, exclaiming that he was not aware of its existence, a claim which will prove untrue, or only half true, later on: when he confronts his uncle, the uncle explains that he had told him, but that Anton had refused to attend the unveiling ceremony.

> "I remember exactly what you said." ... "You said they could go to hell with their monument, for all you cared."
>
> "Don't you remember?" asked Van Liempt. Anton shook his head and kept silent. He looked at the white tablecloth and slowly drew four lines in it with his fork. For the first time he felt a kind of fear, something sucking him in, a deep hole into which things fell without reaching the bottom, as when someone throws a stone into a well and never hears it land. (75)

This event portrays a classic example of the symptoms of traumatic amnesia, as well as a hint on Mulisch's part that Anton will not forever succeed in repressing the events of that evening long ago: the reader will later realize that the four lines which Anton draws in the tablecloth with the tines of his fork represent the four houses, and thus that this gesture suggests the "why me?" question: why did Ploeg end up in front of Anton's house?

38   During his visit to Haarlem, Anton rethinks his earlier refusal to have anything to do with the monument erected there, and visits it. The narrator proffers the observation that except for a few photographs, Anton himself, and their names on the monument, nothing was left of Anton's parents. The text reflects the bitter reality of the politics of memory in the immediate postwar period. The narrative speculates on the possibility of a debate concerning the appropriateness of listing the Steenwijks on the monument since they had not died in the same manner as the hostages, who had been put to death by a firing squad in retribution. The Steenwijks had rather been shot in the heat of the moment, "simply murdered like animals". (74) Anton imagines that a compromise must have been struck, that his parents must have been listed on the condition that Peter be excluded, as "[he] belonged, at least in a broader sense, to those who had died as armed resistors, for whom there were other monuments. Hostages, members of the Underground, Jews, Gypsies, homosexuals – they shouldn't just be mixed up together, for God's sake; the end result would be a total mess." (74). The narrative calls attention to an attitude which attempted to weigh and calibrate both the suffering and the involvement of various segments of Dutch society during the war, thus attempting to gauge their value to society, and to determine whether or not they deserved a certain kind of pension, or the respect of the populace. The text emphasizes how detailed and absurd the discussions can become, and what arbitrary distinctions may come into play, when a young boy like Peter can end up in a different category from his parents and have his name excluded from the monument because he had picked up Ploeg's gun in self-defense. The fact of the matter is that such discussions did, and do, take place as part of the process by which a people comes to terms with the memory of the occupation. The narrative of *The Assault* focuses on this issue of evaluating the meaning of the war dead, inducing the reader to reconsider the decisions made in the immediate postwar period.

    This text thus investigates a recently popular appeal to a culture of victimhood, the cult of the occupied. Anton's first postwar visit to Haarlem, the city of his youth, may be read as an index for one important Dutch approach to the meaning of the occupation. The narrator describes Anton's reading of the city of Haarlem as a unique place: "What he saw was not just any city like so many others in the world. It was as different as he himself was from other people." (58) Anton fancies himself unique because of the losses he suffered as a result of the assault. The reader may find this curious; after all, although not every Dutch citizen suffered under the occupation to the degree Anton did, he is certainly not singular in this regard. The exaggeration he makes in considering himself unique is underscored by the text's statement that Haarlem "was as different (from other cities) as he himself was from other people", a proposition which must be either patently false or essentially meaningless on any remotely objective scale. The only sense in which Haarlem's difference (from other cities) resembles Anton's difference (from other people) is the fact of idiosyncrasy, that in Haarlem Anton experienced the events which he – only partially justifiably – feels set him apart from the rest of the population. He projects his sense of being isolated onto the city – a device which undercuts his argument, since the reader knows that Haarlem was not by any means the only city in the Netherlands where exemplary suffering took place, and that even so, Anton was hardly the only person in Haarlem who suffered. If one were to choose a city as a symbol of conspicuous suffering, certainly both Amsterdam and Rotterdam would be strong contenders. Amsterdam serves as an appropriate symbol of the suffering of the Jewish population of the Netherlands and its destruction in the Holocaust, and Rotterdam, the city which had the heart bombed out of its center at the beginning of the war, is a standard icon of the heartlessness and mercilessness of the oppressor.[16] Once again, the narrative reflects a feature of postwar memory of the war: a tendency to attempt to categorize and devise a quantitative analysis of suffering during the occupation, as well as a tendency in some survivors to consider past suffering to be a license for other, possibly self-indulgent, behavior. Though the genesis of such ways of thinking of the past is certainly understandable (particularly in a country where evidence of trauma may lead to financial support), the question remains whether either the community or the individual ultimately benefits in other ways from such categorization.

When dealing with various populations who have suffered, how meaningful or useful is it to determine which group, which individual, has suffered more? If such distinctions are useful, for what purpose? They might be helpful in determining the allocation of the limited resources – financial and otherwise – which can be offered in an attempt to increase the chances that the survivors may heal and perhaps prosper in the postwar era, but one may well argue that that does not make such distinctions meaningful on a moral level. It is a strange ethics indeed which argues in essence that more suffering is better.

Although from a personal point of view, all suffering is horrible and any death is tragic, on a socio-political level the reason for a certain death, or the circumstances under which suffering occurs, may lend a different meaning to otherwise similar events. In the context of the Dutch experience of World War II, such distinctions take on a significance not easily understood unless one takes into account the meaning which the Dutch assigned to their experience of the occupation in light of the history of Dutch responses to war. J.C.H. Blom has argued convincingly that World War II, "the war"[17] in Dutch parlance, has deeply influenced the national consciousness and helped to define notions of ethical behavior because it was during the war that pretenses had been stripped away and individuals had been forced to reveal themselves as either good resisters of the enemy occupation ("goed") or bad collaborators ("fout").[18] In this focus on the events of the occupation, suffering is often viewed as central. Blom shows that this emphasis on suffering as being ethically significant derives from and has been repeatedly affirmed at various points in Dutch history which long precede World War II. Suffering is associated with resisting the enemy – or evil, which is often synonymous – it means being "goed", being faithful in adversity; the risk and sacrifice which were associated with resistance thus were signs of ethical behavior, of faithfulness to the national cause, and therefore also a badge of Dutchness. It is this constellation of values which makes it possible for a fictional character such as Anton to reflect the views of some Dutch citizens when he unthinkingly assumes that there was a hierarchy, a taxonomy, or a calculus of valuable, socially meaningful suffering during the war.

The Third Episode is set in 1956, and gives the reader a first glimpse at the crux of Anton's problems with memory. Repressed memories can affect the subject's life whether or not they resurface. This episode is a reflection on the reactivation of repressed memories – an investigation of the connections between the postwar subject's past and his present. As is typical for this novel, the initial pages of the section prefigure and anticipate the things to come. Anton continues to forget about the events of his childhood, and once again the imagery the narrator employs to explain the process of forgetting is intriguing, drawing, as it does, from the language of relationships. The point is that Anton's relationship to the past is both of central importance to his life, and much more complicated than he thinks.

> The process of putting Haarlem behind him resembled the changes a man goes through when he divorces. He takes a girlfriend to forget his wife, but just doing that prolongs the connection with his wife. Possibly things will work out only with the next girlfriend – although the third one has the best chance. (79)

Setting aside for the moment the sexism in the language, the image of relationships is an interesting way to think of one's connection to the past. Apparently it is easier to replace a companion than to get over the past. The comparison falls short, as the process of forgetting the past in Anton's case is not one of inventing a subsequent reality to replace the one he does not like – which would seem to be the analogous situation to taking a girlfriend to replace a wife – but rather, he simply attempts to forget, and repress the past altogether. Rather than rewriting the past, he attempts to forget there ever was one. Therefore, since nature abhors a vacuum, the past continues to seep in; it intrudes into the past-less life he attempts to construct for himself:

> Boundaries have to be continuously sealed off, but it's a hopeless job, for everything touches everything else in this world. A beginning never disappears, not even with the ending.

> Every few months or so he suffered from a daylong bout of migraine that forced him to lie down in the dark, though it hardly ever made him vomit. He read a lot, but never about the War.... (79)

In Anton's case, the intrusion of the past is marked by migraine headaches, a sign of his unsuccessful forgetfulness. The text mentions several such interludes; at this point in his life, Anton once becomes ill while attending "a splendid performance of Chekhov's Cherry Orchard directed by Charov" (79). The reader who attends to what is happening on stage is not surprised by Anton's response : the scene is strongly reminiscent of the tableau during the assault in Anton's childhood home: "a scene where a man sat at a table with bowed head while a woman outside on a terrace shouted at someone", (79) a painful reminder of the evening when Anton's mother attempted to prevent his brother Peter from suffering the consequences of his impulsive actions while his father sat and endured the shame of his impotent Humanism. That is to say, this connection between the headache and the past should be clear to most readers; Anton, however, does not understand the relationship: "Anton was overcome by a sense of something dreadful, something elusive but so overwhelming that he had to leave at once. Outside in the street ... his symptoms disappeared quickly and completely; a few minutes later he wondered if there had been anything to them." (79-80) The language which describes the evanescence of the experience clearly echoes the earlier description of Anton's attempt to put his experience of the assault behind him, the image of waking up from a dream without being able to remember the content of the dream, but merely the fact that it had been a nightmare.

Anton has attempted to literally put away his memories of the violence of that horrible night in the past – the images used include that of a hermetic seal, of putting something as far away as the moon. He becomes a physician, and the narrative insists that the reader notice his choice of specialty, and the presumptive reasons for this choice:

> And there were not only negative reasons for his choice of anesthesiology. He was fascinated by the delicate equilibrium that must be maintained whenever the butchers planted their knives in someone – this balancing on the edge between life and death, and his responsibility for the poor human being, helpless in unconsciousness. He had, besides, the more or less mystical notion that the narcotics did not make the patient insensitive to pain so much as unable to express that pain, and although the drugs erased the memory of pain, the patient was nevertheless changed by it. When patients woke up, it always seemed evident that they had been suffering. (80)

It should be obvious that anesthesiology is an appropriate career choice for Anton in light of his need to distance himself from the horrible events of that one night which, in a sense, ended his childhood. Significantly the anesthesiologist is the one who silences and controls the patients, making it possible for the "butchers" to do their work, and isolating the patient from any memory of the unpleasant experience. Thus, in this figure of speech, the narrative subliminally suggests that Anton is complicit in the butchery, though he claims explicitly that he is not the one performing the surgery, and feels that this distinction is a meaningful one. As such, this move is emblematic for the position of the many who did not become involved during the occupation; it identifies him as a bystander. For whatever reasons, although they did not help the persecuted, bystanders felt it enough not to participate in the butchery. Although there is a considerable difference between the "butchery" performed by surgeons and the horrors perpetrated by the Nazis, Anton chooses one word to allude to the behavior of both. His experience has sensitized him to violence of all kinds, and he apparently needs to work out a sense of mastery over his past helplessness in his own experience. As he protects his patients from the memory of pain in order that the salutary cutting may take place, he questions his own attitude toward his memory of what happened to him on that night long ago when he was at his most helpless.

Note that in his choice of specialty, Anton had refused the opportunity to become a "butcher". In doing so, he once again explicitly distances himself from those he views as having caused the damage to his life, yet he participates in making it impossible for his patients to voice their pain. Perhaps, in light of the choices he has made in his own life, one might conclude that he considers their silence appropriate and good. The narrative states that "although the drugs erased the memory of pain, the patient was nevertheless changed by it. When patients woke up, it always seemed evident that they had been suffering"; this could as easily be read as a reference to Anton's psychological state after the end of the occupation, as to his patients in the operating room.

Thus the reader must consider the significance of the fact that Anton, the postwar subject, would choose this imagery: perhaps it was an unconscious attempt – despite himself – to give some retrospective meaning to the horrible event. Perhaps, in retrospect, Anton cannot imagine how his life would have been if it had not included the "surgical" removal of his family at such a tender age: his life is forever changed, and Anton has no choice but to construct a meaning for himself and his life out of the historical events which have shaped his existence. Not only does his explanation reflect his need to believe himself in control, but his interpretation of his choice of profession imputes a (perhaps spurious) meaning to this event in his life as well.

Of course the analogy falls short – in contemporary Western society the "butchery" performed by a surgeon is generally considered – and at least intended – to be for the benefit of the patient; thus there would be no shame associated with the participation of the anesthesiologist. If the anesthesiologist makes it possible for the surgeons to do their work, that is a good thing, and not comparable to participating in the Final Solution or other forms of brutality during the Nazi occupation. Although one can not view these two acts – the violence of surgery and the violence of Nazi brutality – as equivalent, it is of interest to the careful reader that Anton somehow mentally connected the two, as evidenced by the narrator's use of the word "butchers" to refer to surgeons. If Anton associates all blood with violence, and all forgetting with brutality, that fact may serve as an index of the severity of his traumatization.

In addition, it must be noted that as the term "bystander" is normally used to denote a person who is to some degree capable of intervening (whether or not there is any reasonable hope of success), the adult Anton, the anesthesiologist, might be analogous to a bystander or even a collaborator in this sense: the anesthesiologist makes it possible for the surgeons/butchers to do their work. As an adult and a colleague to the butchers, he could intervene if he wished. However, the narrator makes an important distinction: the anesthesiologist views his task as that of protecting the helpless patients whose lives have been entrusted to him *while* the butchers do their work – he does not take any responsibility for the actions of the surgeons, but given the existence of surgeons, and accepting as a given their barbaric propensity to cutting, Anton, the anesthesiologist, is the good guy who keeps the patients alive throughout the ordeal.

Once the connection between Anton's trauma and his choice of profession is clear, it is also possible to understand the genesis of his recurrent headaches, and their relationship to his memory of the assault. In an essay by Umberto Eco, he describes an intellectual game he and some friends once engaged in, a game having to do with remembering and forgetting: "The problem was to establish the principles of a technique and of a rhetorical art – and therefore principles of a process that was artificial and institutable at will – that would permit one to forget in a matter of seconds what one knew."[19] Such a line of inquiry is a surprising one for a writer and literary critic like Eco, because at first blush it would appear that the entire notion of narrative is predicated on our ability to *remember* (rather than forget). However, there are clear connections here to the logic of Anton's story and other literary memories of World War II.

In this game, theories of forgetting were predicated on the models of memory used in the ancient memory arts. Eco identifies the impossibility of purposeful forgetting as being related to the memory's relationship with contiguity and similarity. "If object x has been in some way imagined to be in contact with object y, or if object x presents any sort of homology with object y, every time object x is invoked, object y will be as well".[20] Thus, Eco states that a memory, once formed, is almost impossible to erase intentionally, and that the only hope of consciously and intentionally changing the way things are remembered or interpreted lies in emphasizing certain meanings, in hopes of confusing oneself, so that one may remember badly: "It is possible, however, to use a mnemotechnics (and, in general, a semiotics) to confuse memories, even if not to forget."[21] In order to learn to forget or to confuse oneself, one must first clearly understand the process of remembering correctly. One of the standard memory techniques taught by the ancients, and still used by students everywhere, is one in which a new list of objects, words, or concepts is memorized by associating each item with an item on another list which one already knows by heart, such as the alphabet, for instance. This technique only works, however, as long as the would-be learner devises a way to distinguish between various possible referents for each item on the known list. For example, if the familiar list is the alphabet, the learner will need to remember whether "a" stands for "apple" or "apricot", or for "apple" or "artichoke". Note the language used to describe the memory technique:

> Interpreting the expression in context means magnifying certain interpretants and narcotizing others, and narcotizing them means removing them provisionally from our competence, at least for the duration of the interpretation taking place. (260, footnote #2)

It turns out that what Anton does to his patients, or the way he thinks about what he does for and to them, is exactly analogous to what he did to himself in the aftermath of the assault and the loss of his family: he "narcotizes" his patients – he removes their pain from them, hermetically sealed, as far away from their consciousness as if it were on the moon. Anton does to patients what he has already done to himself – he "narcotizes" them, so that their pain is temporally isolated from the rest of their experience. Their (experience of) pain has changed them, but he has placed the pain within certain temporal boundaries, so that they do not consciously remember it.

But the narrator of *The Assault* also reminds us that such "hermetic" seals ultimately do not work. History and memory cannot be denied forever, and they seep into consciousness in the present. In Eco's terms, mnemotechnics (the science of remembering, and forgetting by remembering poorly, by superimposing memory upon memory and association upon association) is a semiotic system, and "every expression determined by a semiotic sign function sets into play a mental response as soon as it is produced, thus making it impossible to use an expression to make its own content disappear." In Anton's case, stones give him headaches, because of the die ("dobbel*steen*") he finds in his pocket after the assault – the only physical object which survived the firebombing of his house – because he had been about to roll it at the exact moment when the assault took place. Like the "symbolon", the symbol of a stone broken in two which his father had described to Peter with such relish just before the assault occurred, stones have become a sign of his trauma for Anton – an unwelcome reminder of his connection to his family – a family which is now gone, and whom he has been attempting to forget, as well as a reminder of the role of fate, which arbitrarily decreed that the murdered Nazi's body be deposited in front of the Steenwijk house, instead of in front of any other house in Haarlem.

The narrative intones: "Boundaries have to be continuously sealed off, but it's a hopeless job, for everything touches everything else in this world. A beginning never disappears, not even with the ending." (79) Boundaries have to be continuously sealed off, for the memory of the pain is still there, and "stones" cannot be avoided in this world; therefore the symbol comes back to haunt Anton again and again. A beginning never disappears, as Eco states so unequivocally, and an association, once learned, cannot be simply set aside: any stone points to the assault, and the undeserved loss of Anton's family; at best one can seal the memory off, narcotize it, place it beyond local or temporal boundaries. As I have pointed out earlier, Anton described his memory of the night of the assault to himself as the memory of a nightmare; not the memory of the *content* of the nightmare, but merely the knowledge upon awaking that one had had a bad dream, just – I may now add – as the surgery patient may know that he has undergone surgery, but not remember the painful details.

Anton's adult interest in anesthesiology is presented not only as the consequence of his strongly vested interest in forgetting, but also as related to an entirely understandable fascination with helplessness: the helplessness of a child whose entire family is wiped out (unfairly, his brother Peter would have said) is projected onto the patient who is powerless under the knives of the "butchers". Note that while the patient is unconscious, it is the anesthesiologist who remains in control – and control is understandably an important quality for this young man, as for many members of the generation which survived and remembers the occupation.

In addition to his choice of career, Anton's social and other interests are indicative of his membership in the generation raised during the occupation. It is perhaps not difficult to understand why he would be uninterested in national politics. It is significant in the context of this study that the narrator indicates that Anton did read the headlines, but then "forgot them at once". (81) The text later indicates that Anton was as interested in politics as the survivor of a plane crash would be in paper airplanes (82); Anton seems to view himself as the survivor of a political calamity; he has not, however, drawn the lesson from his experiences that involvement in politics is important to prevent further catastrophes from occurring. At this point Anton views postwar politics with disdain: to him contemporary politics is merely like a paper airplane, whereas he has survived the equivalent of a plane crash. This view of the unique status which Anton accords to his suffering is further underscored by his response to political demonstrations two pages later: "Somehow he couldn't help thinking that though it was all pretty terrible, it was only child's play, really." (83) Even later in the text, the potentially serious political events in the nuclear age seem to Anton less serious than his own childhood had been. It is in the midst of a political demonstration that Anton's success at distancing himself – his "bystanderhood" – from the reality at hand becomes clear: a panic breaks out among the demonstrators and others on the street, but Anton only feels calmer: "He had felt upset at first, yet now, with shouting and screaming everywhere … he was pervaded by a strange indifference." (84) His failure to come to terms with the past continues to interfere with his behavior in the present; it prevents his having a proper emotional response to the difficulties and dangers of the present. Thus he presents a textbook case of disassociation. This is another dimension of anesthesia, i.e. blocking sensate cognition, "ignoring" that which affects oneself in the present: Anton is the literary paradigm of a new form of bystander.

A further point of entry into Anton's preoccupations is offered in the revelation that he has a special interest in crossword puzzles, which seems to fulfill not only a need for mastery – "it became his ambition to decipher the clue that had stymied the previous person" – but also refers to the mystical aestheticism which had already been evident in his childhood:

> The fact that most letters had a double function in both a horizontal and a vertical word, and that these words were paired in a mysterious way, pleased him no end. It had something to do with poetry. (81)

Control is a significant issue to survivors who experienced and witnessed powerlessness as small children; during their youth these survivors were forced to recognize that even adults, who normally appear to be omnipotent to small children, were often unable to protect their offspring and themselves. Discovering too early in life that parents and guardians are not able to protect the children in their charge can seriously

46   harm a child. It is important to Anton, the child who discovered during the occupa-
       tion that he had absolutely no control over the events in his life, to now prove his
       mastery of crossword puzzles which others cannot complete, by understanding the
       patterns, the relationships between horizontally and vertically organized groups of
       letters which determine the words they spell out. The child's fate was determined by
       a constellation of seemingly unimportant and inscrutable facts and symbols. In his
       case, the political – the decision on the part of strangers to assassinate a dangerous
       and cruel collaborator – had turned out to also have very personal consequences,
       becoming the reason for the death of this child's family, and the fact that the dead
       collaborator was moved by neighbors who he thought liked his family, and then was
       discovered by the Nazis in front of his house, made no sense because he could not
       decipher the reasons for these actions. Thus it should not be surprising that as an
       adult he finds satisfaction in manipulating symbols and patterns, for in completing
       the puzzles, he demonstrates his own mastery of at least the world of puzzles. Puzzles
       have one great advantage over the "real world" for Anton: the conventions of cross-
       word puzzles are such that the act of completing them and the satisfaction found in
       success are generally solitary and private. Anton does not have to involve others –
       human beings are unpredictable – in his pursuits, the need for proof of his ability to
       control the world by way of these puzzles is one which he can fulfill for himself. Of
       course the limitations of such successes are also immediately obvious: his mastery
       over symbols on sheets of paper provides graphic proof of the postwar recognition of
       the limits of human agency. But note also that Anton is completing crossword puz-
       zles which others have begun to solve, but given up on; one aspect of what seems to
       give him pleasure is the thought that he is somehow unique, or at least better than
       others. Having survived exemplary suffering during the occupation, he credits him-
       self with special qualities in which others do not share.

       The fourth episode of *The Assault* is set in 1966, and in the context of the discus-
       sions about the conflict in Vietnam. The time has come for Anton to find a wife, but
       he does not start out decisively: "In love, too, he simply let things happen to him."
       (97) He owns a sextant, which becomes a major prop in his courtship rituals: he is
       fascinated with the instrument, but the women do not understand his lengthy expla-
       nations; although the text clearly indicates that they were attracted to him in the first
       place because his manner aroused their motherly instincts, they certainly cannot be
       expected to understand why he seems so lost that he keeps a navigational instrument
       in his room.

       In fact, the problems he experiences in his relationships with women are closely
       related to his memory problems and their genesis. The text has set Anton up (and
       prepared the reader) for the failure of his first marriage; this description of his
       approach to courtship does not raise expectations for success in the relationships he
       attempts, and the reader does have the quote ringing in his or her ear in which the
       narrator likens the process of forgetting to the process of distancing oneself from a
       wife after divorce, where "Possibly things will work out only with the next girlfriend
       – although the third one has the best chance." (79) When Anton meets the woman
       who will become his first wife in London, the decision is almost instantaneous:

He looked at her, and at that moment everything was decided.

It was her glance, the look in her eyes, and her hair, thick, springy, reddish hair. (99)

If the astute reader is initially surprised by this impulsive response, the reason for it becomes clear to the reader before it does to Anton. Just before he met her, he "dropped in on the dealers in antique navigational instruments behind the British Museum", (98) inducing the careful reader to wonder whether he feels particularly lost. Anton discovers almost immediately that Saskia's father was a hero of the Dutch Resistance during World War II, but does not investigate the history of his wife's family further.

It is not until several years later, when Anton, Saskia and their young daughter attend the funeral of one of Saskia's father's wartime friends, that the inevitable happens. At the reception, when Anton hears someone behind him say: "I shot him first in the back, then in the shoulder, and then in the stomach as I bicycled past him," (108) he is immediately transported back to the evening of the assault. Without considering what the consequences of such a response may turn out to be, Anton questions the man – named Takes – about the number of shots he has described, and there is no going back. If the woman in the cell was both maternal and seductive, Anton perceives this man's attitude of authority as paternal. The narrative space changes when Anton considers the past; there is once again a sense of distancing, of unreality, about the proceedings: "It occurred to Anton...that this was the man who, that evening in the winter of starvation, had killed Ploeg." (110) When Anton banished his knowledge of the assault "to the moon", when he repressed it, it became impossible for the memories of that night to be a part of what he considers his "normal" life; thus, when he comes to realize by a deductive thought process that this man must be the one who assassinated Ploeg, the narrative describes his realization as if occurring "in a fairy tale". When he recognizes – too late – that he is about to break his own code of silence about the events of the past, that talking with Takes will require him to dredge his memories up again, Anton tries to pull back. But this narrative teaches that memories can not always be controlled and that once repressed memories resurface, they no longer belong merely and completely to their initial hosts/owners. Takes is better schooled than Anton in ethical conundrums, particularly as they relate to dealing with the past, and he already knows that there is no going back now. He argues that events are not inevitable, and this conversation could have been avoided if either he or Anton had not spoken as they did, but now that they have spoken, they cannot take back their words.

"I was saying something you shouldn't have heard," said Takes. "But you did hear, and then you said something you didn't mean to say. Those are the facts, and that's why we're sitting here." (110-111)

Anton's and Takes' approaches to the past are contrasted: Anton, who has refused to come to terms with the past, has not even figured out why the events occurred as they did; Takes has ruminated on the particulars of the facts as he knows them so often and so thoroughly that he understands and remembers every detail even years later. Anton still thinks the past can simply be repressed, Takes has a more sophisticated and realistic attitude. Thus Anton and Takes represent the two poles of the continuum of approaches to the memory of the war in the Netherlands in the post-war era; they are representatives of two approaches, two sets of attitudes which are not only present in different individuals, but perspectives between which one finds individuals oscillating from time to time. In this conversation, Anton attempts to take up the position that "time goes on" and that what happened to him must have happened to others, and may in fact be happening somewhere in the world that very moment, and that therefore – and it is just this conclusion with which Takes and many readers would not agree – there is no point in discussing it. He turns on Takes: "You're more upset than I am. It seems to me that you can't leave the War alone, but time goes on. Or do you regret what you did?" (118)

The fact of Anton's own conflict, the fact that he is not wholeheartedly committed to leaving the past behind, or that he is not able to really forget, is indicated immediately following his speech to Takes: "He had spoken fast but calmly, yet with the vague feeling that he must be careful, that he must control himself so as not to hit the other." (118) Anton may succeed most of the time in seeming to be calm, in seeming to have come to terms with his past, but the agitation he feels when someone confronts him with that which he has attempted to forget, suggests clearly that he has neither come to terms with the past, nor completely succeeded in forgetting it. The reader is aware that Anton is contradicting himself when he refers to others who had also suffered during the war, as the narrative has made it clear that in his mind, Anton's suffering is in some way unique.

THE WORK OF MEMORY

Takes protests that he is not just obsessed about the war out of nostalgia, as others are. Thus the narrator allows the reader to consider a distinction between various motivations of those who do not forget the events of the occupation. The Dutch approaches to the memory of World War II which become prominent in the 1980s show that remembering the occupation may serve a number of purposes – and although one must argue that some are healthier than others, and that some are more "legitimate" than others, the variety of purposes which can be served by the memory of the occupation is almost endless. "...Let's just say that she was my girlfriend. But never mind, leave it at that." (119)

Takes' reference to the woman as his girlfriend begins to awaken a repressed memory in Anton. The following passage illustrates what current psychology posits as happening in the case of repression of a memory: in the narrative, time stands still, and

yet the repressed memory somehow continues to control the person who is unable or
unwilling to acknowledge it.

> Anton stared at him, and suddenly all the pent-up emotion washed over him.
> Putting his face in his hands, he turned away and began to sob. She was dying.
> For him she died at this very moment, as if twenty-one years were nothing. Yet
> at the same time she was resurrected together with all she had meant to him,
> hidden there in the darkness. If he had ever thought about her in these twenty-
> one years, he would have wondered whether she were still alive. But just now,
> he realized, he had been looking for her, in the church and later in the café –
> and in fact it was the reason why he had come to this funeral where he had no
> need to be. (119)

As a child, surely Anton must have surmised that the woman in the cell was likely to
die – even if he had not been able to figure this out on his own, she had alluded to
the fact that the end was near. He had, however, put it out of his mind – along with
the memory of flames and shouts – as a way of not having to know. Grief can be postponed, but not denied, and so he grieves for her now, decades after her actual death,
at the point in time where he finally accepts the knowledge that she has died.

And yet his failure to grieve for her in the past, the fact that he has not acknowledged the significance of her life and death before this moment, does not mean that
her death has not influenced him: his unacknowledged quest to find her was his
motive for attending the funeral of a total stranger. And, as the reader already surmises, his quest for her was also the reason for his falling in love at first sight with
Saskia, who is – hardly by any real coincidence – the daughter of a friend of Takes'
from the Resistance.

Thus the text ascribes a very strong and influential role to repressed memories:
they have the power to determine behavior decades after the repression initially took
place. Saskia's father has his own history to live with, and in attempting to comfort
his son-in-law, refers to the beginning of the eruption of repressed memories of the
war, the occupation, and the Resistance in the Netherlands:

> "Yes, but then who's supposed to understand? Never mind; the important
> thing is to keep it under control. Perhaps it was a lucky thing for you that it
> happened this afternoon. We've been suppressing it all these years – and now
> come the problems. I hear it from all sides. Twenty years seems to be a kind of
> incubation period for our disease; all that unrest in Amsterdam must have
> something to do with it."

> "I can't say you give the impression of having any problems." (124)

Thus Takes and Anton relive the assault – Takes explains that his friend and colleague
in the Resistance, Truus, and he, had taken upon themselves the task of assassinating
Ploeg, because he was deemed to be too cruel and too effective and enthusiastic a col-

laborator with the Nazi occupation forces: Ploeg was not only arresting Resistance workers, but also using extreme forms of torture in order to force them to inform on their organizations. Neither of them can explain why the Kortewegs (father and daughter) moved the body toward Anton's house, and not in the other direction. Takes is surprised that Anton has never attempted to discover the reason for their actions. This conversation uncovers a glimpse of how complicated Anton's attitudes toward the events of the assault are. The narrative undermines the notion of a clear distinction between passive victims or bystanders as opposed to active members of the occupation or active members of the Resistance. Just as Anton, the anesthesiologist, is complicit with the cutting the "butchers" perform, so Anton feels affection – though ambivalent – for this man sitting beside him, the man whose commitment to violent acts of resistance (considered heroic, *goed*) was the proximate cause for the death of Anton's family. Anton wonders whether he feels affection for the man because he wishes to participate vicariously in the man's acts of resistance, and thus feel less like a victim. Then he catches himself, and re-adopts the title: yes, of course he is a legitimate victim. But he immediately tells himself it feels as if it had all happened to someone else. (112) His dissociation from the event, signified by the feeling that it had happened to someone else rather than to him, was a move he made in order to narcotize his pain so that he would be able to go on living. Now this psychological device complicates his appropriation of the recognition which Dutch society would gladly give him. The very thing – recognition – which would help to reintegrate him into postwar society, help him feel that he and his past were a part of the whole rather than isolated in some imaginary country or on the moon, is inaccessible to him because the event which brings this recognition has aftereffects on him which prevent his enjoying its benefits. The complexities the Dutch experienced after the end of the occupation as they attempted to sort out the ethical landscape is thus highlighted in this passage.

A DUTY TO REMEMBER?

At the end of the conversation, Takes asks Anton to call him later for further discussion – the reader understands that he hopes that Anton will be able to tell him more about Truus. Anton, indecisive, goes to the beach with his wife and daughter, and falls asleep in the hot sun. Once again, the workings of a repressed memory which is attempting to come to the surface are described in terms of a rift in the space-time continuum: "Something was beginning to pulse underground somewhere, and yet there was no ground. Space itself was pulsing, thumping". (127) Although the reader by now recognizes this cosmic language for what it represents, the narrator continues to present Anton's more materialistic explanations: the splitting headache which Anton notices when he awakens is attributed to the wine he had drunk with his lunch, though the reliability of that conclusion is simultaneously questioned by an appeal to an objective standard – "No doubt the wine at lunch had something to do with it" (128) – which is clearly untenable in view of his knowledge.

As Anton weighs his options, trying to decide whether or not to visit Takes, and there
to attempt to identify Truus from a photograph he surmises Takes will produce, he is
forced to consider a central issue anyone who has faced a traumatic memory has: will
(literally) facing Truus in the form of her photograph transform her from the universal, idealized person she was, into an individual (somewhere deep down he does recognize that she was an individual), and is that what he wants? Is he willing to make
that momentous switch, to trade in the image he has (and since it was dark when he
met her, the image is obviously one filled in by his imagination, fueled by his desire)
and take in return one very concrete and specific set of features – not "woman", his
ideal woman, but one particular one, the one who was Takes' great love? Anton's conflict offers a case study in memory, and its relationship to his erotic history.

"Wouldn't it diminish what she still meant to him?" (129) Taking the abstract –
fill in the blank with whatever you want – and replacing it with the concrete image
of the historical Truus, threatens to undo the significance of the memory. He worries
that it may also diminish the significance of his attachment to his wife, with whom
he thinks he fell in love because he had imagined that she reminded him of the then-
still-nameless Truus. "She had been Takes' girlfriend, his great love, apparently, and
obviously he had the right to a last message from her. Anton couldn't remember anything she had said, only that she had talked a lot and touched his face." (129) Anton
recognizes a moral imperative in Takes' right to be told his love's last words; his hes-
itance to act creates dramatic tension for the reader. The reader knows what Truus
said to him about Takes, and wonders whether Anton will bother to remember in
time to make Takes happy. He looks at a photograph of his wife, Saskia:

> It was not true that he had never imagined what the woman whose name
> seemed to be Truus looked like. From the very beginning he had imagined her
> looking like this and not otherwise – like Saskia. This was what he had recog-
> nized in Saskia at first sight that afternoon at the Stone of Scone. She was the
> embodiment of an image which he must have been carrying about in his head,
> without knowing it, since he was twelve. Her appearance revealed it to him –
> not as something remembered, but as immediate love, immediate certainty
> that she must remain with him and carry his child. (129-130)

Anton imagines that his marriage will be in jeopardy if Saskia turns out to have been
primarily a temporary substitute for an imaginary, idealized, image of Truus – the
breakup of this marriage would be yet another casualty of the unprocessed trauma
which he sustained during the occupation. However, as important as it might be for
him to understand his motives for marrying his wife, he is now replacing a con-
frontation with his memory of the assault – which would constitute appropriate
memory-work – with being obsessed by his reasons for being attracted to Saskia,
which is not exactly the same thing. He then turns the whole argument around: perhaps he is being unfair to Truus by substituting his image of Saskia for the image of
the historical Truus. Although the question is certainly interesting, it is at best an
indirect way to approach his problems with history. Although it feels as if he is court-

ing danger, Anton decides to call Takes and face the concrete image of an abstract version to which he has held on since he was twelve years old.

Takes has not gotten unscathed through the intervening time either; when Anton arrives, it is clear that Takes has been drinking, and he announces to Anton that Willy Lages has been released from prison. Lages, the former head of the Gestapo in the Netherlands, who was responsible for the deportation of one hundred thousand Jews, and for thousands of executions, had initially been condemned to death after the war, but his sentence was commuted, and Takes' worst fears have just become a reality: he has been set free because he is old and ill. For Takes, as for many survivors, this suggests a simple calculus of injustice, as grace is meted out unevenly: mercy is shown to the war criminal, who had shown no mercy to his victims. Takes interprets this show of clemency as a symptom of a pathological attempt on the part of the Dutch to purge society and the self of any tendencies which might be associated with Fascism: "Free the Fascist quickly, for we're no Fascists, our hands are clean." (134) Takes' activities during the occupation, of course, allowed for no such squeamishness: he is a firm believer in decisive action "to further the good cause". He tells Anton that the "anatomical institute", as Takes calls it, where enemies of the Resistance were liquidated, still exists in near-secret. Anton gives voice to the scruples which need to be expressed, but only in an understated way: "'So long as it's for a good cause....' said Anton." (136)

Anton is led down to the basement of the building which Takes inhabits, and the reader is introduced to a portrayal which will recur repeatedly in the works which recall the memories of children of the war, as it does in the informal memory of the occupation for many Dutch survivors: a theme of the occupation as a paradoxically idyllic or bucolic setting.

In some cases, a positive view of the time of the occupation takes the form of a postwar longing for simpler times, when the Dutch were not blessed or cursed (depending on one's perspective) with prosperity, when people were satisfied with the little they had, when they were not choosy about their food or possessions, but shared what they had with their neighbors, and were happy to be together. This sentiment is the basis for the wistful exclamation that the Dutch "stuck together" during the occupation. (Unfortunately, as the rest of my argument illustrates, as people stuck together, they frequently drew their circles in a regrettably small radius).

The version of nostalgia for the occupation which is evident in Takes is a variation of the generic one described above, and quite common in fictional texts about the children of the war. Anton considers the possibility that any nostalgia he notices in Takes might not be primarily aimed at the occupation, or at the prevailing social conditions, but could simply be due to his love for Truus: the World War II-vintage map which Takes has saved all these years has a lipstick "kiss" imprinted on it: a symbol of his beloved's mouth inscribed onto the pictorial representation of military maneuvers of four decades ago. This coincidence of the private and public sphere, and the conflict between the atrocities of the occupation and the solidarity of shared suffering which tempered it, is a surprise to Anton, but a common theme in the narratives of the occupation.

Perhaps the War had become his beloved, and for that reason he could not be
unfaithful to her. Perhaps even as he was talking about its atrocities, he was
really trying to remember Truus Coster and those days when he had been
happy. (137)

Just as Saskia and his idealized Truus have probably become one for Anton, he wonders whether the war and Truus have become one for Takes — it takes one to know
one, and thus the narrator signals to the reader that Anton has understood Takes.

During Anton's visit with Takes, the reality of post-war life intrudes with a
phonecall announcing that a colleague of Takes' from their days in the Resistance has
kept an earlier promise and has committed suicide in response to the release of Willy
Lages. The authorities may see a need to offer clemency, but Dutch society is made
up of various constituent groups, some of whom — for various reasons — do not share
the same experiences, the same value systems, or the same approaches toward guilt
and its satisfaction. That gesture which, if Takes' interpretation is correct, the Dutch
state/people employs to consider itself better than Fascists, may, to Takes' friend, con-
note a cowardly denial of the realities of the crimes against humanity which this old
decrepit man committed in the vigor of his youth.

The dilemma faced by Anton, this novel's figure of the Dutch "bystander", who
wonders about his responsibilities toward Truus and Takes as opposed to those toward
his wife, whom he fears he may have betrayed, or may be about to betray, stands in
stark relief against the more sweeping concerns of the Resistance fighter faced with a
postwar inclination toward clemency. Yet, though the scope of his concerns is more
personal, at this point those concerns are his responsibility, and if he achieves nothing else, he must at least face their implications.

The problem for Anton as a post-occupation survivor is that doing justice to
Takes' love for Truus would require him to remember details of the events from that
awful night which he had so carefully forgotten. Takes shows Anton a photograph of
Truus, and it is up to him to identify the woman in the photograph as the woman
with whom he shared a police holding cell during the night shortly after the assault
had taken place, and to tell Takes everything he remembers about the last hours of
her life. Anton looks at the photograph, and sees Saskia — not because of a physical
resemblance between the two women, "but the expression, in the eyes was Saskia's,
just as it had struck him the first time in Westminster Abbey" (138). Anton does not
have time to consider the implications of the similarities he registers between his
responses to the two women, as Takes is naturally impatient to receive the full report;
memories of the past are as precious to Takes as they are poisonous to Anton. Anton
proves a great disappointment: Takes asks for a report of what Truus said, Anton cannot remember. At this point the reader wants Anton to remember, to give Takes a full
report, because the reader knows that Truus had mentioned to Anton that she loved
a man (whom the reader can now identify as Takes), but that she had convinced him
otherwise because he was married. The reader concludes that knowledge of her love
at this late date, too late to cause any harm, might make the old man happy, and thus
the reader hopes that Anton will somehow manage to face his memories. It seems

cruel when the narrative denies the reader and Takes this pleasure. Anton acknowledges the possibility of participating in "experiments with LSD" which he knew to
be "going on at the University", which might help repressed memories resurface. (139)
Anton recognizes the potential for good outcomes as well as ones he does not wish to
face:

> It was stored somewhere in his brain, of course. Serious candidates for the
> experiment were welcome, and the drug might make it come back... But
> Anton had no desire to; he did not want his past chemically resurrected.
> Besides, there was the risk that none of these memories would be revealed –
> that totally different, unexpected ones would emerge instead, and that he
> would not be able to control them. (139-140)

He considers the risk, his lack of control over the results of such experiments, too
great. Forgetting, that is, his ability to avoid facing memories of the past, is still
important to him. The text juxtaposes the pain of these two men; Takes' pain could
be softened, but this would put Anton at risk, since his equanimity exists at the mercy
of the continued repression of his wartime memories. Anton performs a utilitarian
calculus, and concludes that the possibility that he might have to relinquish control,
because he would put himself in a position where he might be asked to face unpleasant memories (note that he does not consider this outcome a necessary, merely a possible one), outweighs the benefit which might be gained if he could offer Takes a
memory of Truus' state of mind that night in the police cell, and he chooses not to
place himself at risk for Takes' benefit. Note that in drawing up his calculus, Anton
treats Takes and himself as equals, and as individuals; he gives no weight to the sacrifices which Takes has made because of his involvement in the Resistance. History
shows that many members of the Resistance spent the years of the occupation hoping
for a utopia they would bring about at the end of the war, and that they were sorely
disappointed by what often became their exclusion from the ruling classes of postwar
society. As a member of postwar society, Anton does not choose to "remember"
uncomfortable political realities, but holds his right of personal happiness to be self-
evident. Although he does visit Takes, and sees a photograph of Truus, he does not
remember the words Takes most wants to hear, until much later, when he has lost
track of Takes (and even then, one might argue that he does not do his utmost to
locate Takes):

> ...And I'm beautiful too, but only because I'm in love with him, though he
> doesn't know it. He thinks I'm not, but I do love him. Now you're the only
> one who knows it, even though you don't know who I am and who he is. He
> has a wife and two children about your age. They need him, just as you need
> your father and mother...(39)

Although Anton is not able to help Takes, he does come to some resolution by the
end of the novel. As mentioned before, his desire to repress his negative memories of

the occupation is reflected in an unwillingness to involve himself in contemporary political issues.

Although a detailed analysis of this aspect of the text is not the focus of this study, it is worth mentioning in passing that the structure of *The Assault* memorializes various points in the history of political conflict as experienced by the United States and its western Allies: The First Episode is dated 1945, and describes the assault. The Second Episode is set in 1952, and the political context is that of the Korean War. The Third Episode, in 1956, features Anton's first experience of voting (he votes for a social democratic party, because his uncle tells him that's what a pessimist would do), and a number of reasons to think about communism, such as the revolt in Hungary, reprisals by the Soviet Union, and Fidel Castro's landing on Cuba. The Fourth Episode, set in 1966, places Anton's quandary in the context of the Dutch discussions surrounding the Vietnam War. Anton faces the shock of history, and resists shock wave after shock wave, until an absurd event gets through his defenses.[22]

THE LAST EPISODE: THE BEGINNING OF A RESOLUTION

In the last episode – 1981 – Anton becomes politically active; he finds himself marching in a demonstration against the placement of American cruise missiles, an act which Arnold Heumakers identifies as explicitly hopeful and positive,[23] renews his relationship with his children, and talks with his former neighbor Karin Korteweg who tells him the real reason why Ploeg's body was put in front of his house, and not that of the neighbors on the other side.

Anton had, of course, not planned to take part in the peace march, but is forced to due to a toothache. In the fashion typical of Mulisch's authorial control in this novel, the story is brought full circle in the most explicit and overdetermined of ways. Anton, barely forty, has married his second wife, and they have named their son Peter. His migraine headaches have diminished in frequency, but he has other symptoms: nightmares, worries, anxieties. A panic attack in his summer home in Tuscany (a place he is said to like for a number of reasons, in which the fact that it is far removed from Haarlem in 1945 figures prominently), brought on by the ubiquitous presence not only of stones and rocks, but in particular by the sight of a cigarette lighter in the shape of a die ("dobbelsteen", "gambling stone" in Dutch). Anton rips up his physician's prescription for valium, and denial seems to continue to work for him: although the attacks return, their power over him diminishes too.

Anton worries when his age surpasses the age his father was when he died. He accompanies his now-sixteen-year-old daughter Sandra to visit the site of the assault, and in attempting to describe to her what the place (now with a new house built on the plot) had looked like, realizes that she will never be able to understand. When they visit the monument, and he tells his daughter about his conversation with Truus Coster in the police cell, he finally remembers her profession of love for Takes: "he thinks I do not love him", and they decide to visit her grave as well. Anton makes a feeble attempt to contact Takes, and gives up easily without explaining his reticence.

And then, one Saturday, Anton has a toothache. His wife offers the temporary solace of a clove to put on the sore tooth – a remedy she learned as a child in Indonesia. The reader of the novel will probably remember that Anton's mother used a clove to soothe a toothache on the night of the assault, one more reminder that Mulisch is bringing the story full circle.

Anton calls his dentist at home. The dentist makes a deal: he will treat the tooth, if Anton will participate in the peace march with him afterwards. The toothache appears to be caused merely by a raised tooth – the language in which the dentist describes the problem is reminiscent of Anton's repressed memories which also behave like unwanted protuberances, occasionally resurfacing to bother him.

> The miracle had happened. The pain receded behind the horizon and disap-
> peared as if it had never existed. ...
>
> "A slight pressure. It had come to the surface. Often happens with age..." (167)

At the peace march, Anton sees Karin Korteweg, now a middle-aged woman, whom he had known as an attractive young, friendly woman (the first woman in the novel whom Anton had ever noticed as a sexual object) when she was his neighbor, and who, with her father, had deposited Ploeg's body in front of Anton's house. She needs to talk to him. Although Anton is less eager, he relents : "Now, he must know every-thing and then bury it forever, roll a stone over it and never think about it again." (178) Karin explains that it was her father who had decided that the body was to be put in front of Anton's house, that he had emigrated to Australia immediately after the war's end, and committed suicide in 1948, and that she wished that her house had been burned down. Anton is surprised at this; it is clear that he needs to be told by each of the other actors in this story about their side of the story, their suffering – his refusal to remember his own tale has caused him never to think about the others either. Anton, though relieved to hear that his brother's death was avenged years ago, nonetheless does not understand the suicide:

> "Then I still don't understand it. He just wanted our house to go up in flames
> instead of his own: All right, it's not very pretty, but he couldn't know that
> everything would turn out much worse. I can understand that his conscience
> might be bothering him...but suicide?" (181)

Karin is forced to explain that her father's suicide had less to do with what he had done, than with his motivations for his act, which he had later come to despise. His decision to move the body had apparently been motivated by a desire to save his pet lizards from discovery and possibly destruction by the authorities. Karin explains that she had never been able to understand what the lizards had meant to her father: "Something about eternity and immortality, some secret he saw in them." (181)

With wide-eyed disbelief Anton looked out over her head. The lizards...Was it possible? Could everything be blamed on the lizards? Were they the culprits in the end? (181)

At this point, suddenly, after he has haltingly gone through various stages of coming to terms with the past, of which Mulisch gives the reader three intermediate snapshots, after slowly coming to see and admit that there were some aspects to the story which could be evaluated or considered, that there was perhaps some reason to remember, he is confronted with the awful truth that the real reason Ploeg's corpse was dumped onto his family was simply absurd.

> Anton felt sick. The whole story was worse than the partial one he had known. He looked at Karin's face, the tears still on it. He had to get away from her, never see her again. But there was one more thing he must find out. (182)

The question remains why Karin and her father did not move the body in the other direction – toward the Aartses' house. It turns out that Korteweg had had a very good as well as a silly reason for doing what he did: the Aartses were hiding Jews – two parents and a small child – and all of them – the refugees, their hosts, possibly the neighbors (Korteweg), and Korteweg's pet salamanders – would certainly have been killed, had the body been discovered near that house. "In spite of everything, Korteweg had been a good man! So this was why Ploeg's body had landed on the other side, at their own door, so that...Anton couldn't take any more." (183) Here is the final piece to the puzzle which Anton had been so reluctant to complete.

By the utilitarian calculus which Anton and his compatriots took for granted as a normal measure of right and wrong, it "made sense" to dispose of the body in the way it happened. It appears that the adult Anton does in fact take some comfort in knowing the factors which had been taken into account in deciding where to deposit the body; the fact that it was not a random decision, but one involved in not endangering hidden Jews, seems to help. But the text by this point does not suggest that the Jews hidden two doors down provide some sort of alibi that lets fate off the hook: The narration suggests that by the time Anton finally hears of this fact, at the anti-nuclear demonstration in 1981, he rejects any such convenient justification. His memory-work has reached a stage where he has moved beyond needing explanations, and is living in the present with the past behind him.

The narrative emphatically shows that the survivor has a need to come to terms with his own assignment of guilt in the catastrophe. With greater understanding comes a more nuanced view of his calculus of guilt, and its incomprehensible relationship to retribution.

> Was everyone both guilty and not guilty? Was guilt innocent, and innocence guilty? The three Jews...Six million of them had been killed, twelve times as many as there were people marching here. But by being in danger, those three people had unknowingly saved themselves and the lives of two others, and

instead of them, his own father and mother and Peter had died, all because of some lizards... (184)

Thus, in the end, despite Anton's resistance to come to terms with the past, it is clear that he has started on the way to recovery. He has faced his memories, and is beginning to deal with them.

The experiences of this fictional character are typical of those of a significant number of Dutch citizens who repressed the trauma of their experiences during the occupation for several decades after the end of World War II, but finally find they can no longer put off their memory work. Theories about the timing of the attention now being paid to these memories vary. It is clear that the generation that was in its young adulthood during the war is now just past retirement age, a stage in life which allows for more introspection than any other. These same people will also have been more likely to reflect upon their own past while watching their own children go through a very different youth or young adulthood than they themselves had experienced. A third factor was the Vietnam War and the revolution of '68, both of which to a certain degree distracted this generation from its own concerns with the past because they had more pressing issues to deal with in the present. Whatever the reason, Mulisch's character suggests the possibilities of recovery in a way that will ring true to many Dutch readers of the second post-war generation.

The Assault presents an important set of assumptions which are part of the cultural store of the collected memories of the occupation, and further develops them. If resistance fighters and those who hid Jews are celebrated in the post-war Netherlands as exemplars of what it means to be Dutch, and if one of the most important signs of their heroism and high moral character is the risks they took and the suffering they endured, then it seems possible to identify a very similar kind of misery among that part of the population commonly identified as bystanders. Bystanders, as Cynthia Ozick so deftly states in her preface to a book about those exceptional people who did hide Jews, are the norm.

> The bystander stays home, safe enough if compliant enough. The bystander cannot be charged with taking part in any evil act; the bystander only watches as the evil proceeds... The neighbors are decent people – decent enough for ordinary purposes. They cannot be blamed for not being heroes. A hero – like a murderer – is an exception and (to be coarsely correct) an abnormality, a kind of social freak.[24]

Surely it is just a coincidence that Ozick's description of bystanders sounds like a characterization of the Steenwijk and Korteweg families at the beginning of *The Assault*. They are ordinary, even decent, people who fail to alter their response when the circumstances turn extraordinary. Ozick is careful to offer a balanced appraisal in which she does not lose sight of the ethical complexities of an occupied country as a system; she does not boldly indict such people for their lack of heroism, though she is careful not to show approval either. Her description even validates the notion, illustrated in *The Assault,* that minor, apparently random events in the present or past, such as where one is at a given time, or who one's parents were, may contribute to the difference between a bystander and a victim:

> A bystander is like you and me, the ordinary human article – what normal man or woman or adolescent runs to commit public atrocities? The luck of the draw (the odds of finding oneself in the majority) saves the bystander from direct victimhood: the Nuremberg "racial" laws, let us say, are what exempt the bystander from deportation.

It is clear that if, as Anton interpreted history, becoming a victim when you were trying hard to remain a bystander is a matter of fate and of being caught up in apparently random events, then some of the heroes might also have been involved in their work not just because they were brave from the start, but perhaps because they had been shoved in the right direction by experiences as well. Ozick's assessment of the motivations of bystanders is dispassionately fair, and does not take into account the Dutch national myth identified by Blom which wishes that the Dutch nation had without exception been made up of heroes. Such a myth seems to be useful in describing how Dutch responses are distorted on an emotional level and why there is a discrepancy between the reaction of the heart and head when events which took place during the occupation are remembered. This conflict will be shown to recur in other ways and in other contexts in the chapters to come.

At the conclusion of *The Assault,* Anton has completed his own memory-work; he becomes the man mentioned in the preface of the novel whom Anton watched and admired on the water near his home as a child. As Jaap Goedegebuure writes in the *Haagsche Post,* it becomes clear that it was Anton's task "to see a meaning in the wave pattern of his past. Only when he can fathom *his* history and thus *history* (on a large scale) does he have a future and is he capable of maintaining the unity of his personality."[25] While the little boy watched, the man propelled his barge along the river by using a long stick to push it. Standing toward the front of the boat, he would plant the stick in the bottom of the canal, and walk across the deck of his boat toward the back while keeping the stick stable. He was a man "walking backwards to push something forward, while staying in the same place himself. There was something very strange about it, but it was his secret that he didn't mention to anyone."[26] Thus it is with the memory-work being done in the 1980s by the victims of the war, and by their children, who are also victims in their own ways.

3. *Innocent Children*

While *The Assault* is an exemplar of many of the elements which may be found in fiction of the occupation, it is by no means the only text of its kind. Having described and delineated many of these elements in the previous chapter, I will now proceed to consider the child as a protagonist. It will become evident that the narrative structures and features found in *The Assault* are not unique to Mulisch's novel, but also occur in other narratives which engage the post-war consequences of the experience of the occupation by young people. While it may be tempting to view Marga Minco's *The Glass Bridge* [1] and Rudi van Dantzig's *For a Lost Soldier* superficially as variations or even as derivative in some way of *The Assault*, each of them serves to widen and deepen the discourse in its own way. Themes and images of children during wartime belong to the fund of culturally mediated memories in which such novels participate, even as they in turn contribute to the discussion about the effects of the occupation.

While Marga Minco's *De glazen brug*, published in 1986, shows striking thematic similarities to *The Assault*, any discussion of the text or its context must begin with one major difference – that of viewing the memory of the occupation from the perspective of Jewish subjects. In some sense, nearly all of Minco's works from 1957 to the present deal thematically with the occupation and its consequences for post-war

4. Marga Minco, hair bleached, in hiding (ca. 1943). (Letterkundig Museum)

life. Minco's novels as a group might themselves be the basis for an inquiry into how some of the issues discussed in this study are reflected as cultural discourse in ways which change with the point in history at which each of the novels is published, and the time periods in which each of the texts is set.[2]

Seen from within the context of Minco's own writings, *The Glass Bridge* is an interesting case when one compares it with one of her own pre-1980s texts. Her 1957 novel *Het bittere kruid* (*Bitter Herbs*), like the later work, also tells the tale of a young Jewish woman who escapes as her entire family is arrested by the Nazis and deported to concentration camps.[3] But what marks *The Glass Bridge* as a work that falls solidly into the cultural and conceptual landscape of World War II novels of the 1980s is that the narrative does not end at the close of the war. Where the earlier story concludes just after the end of the war as it becomes clear that the main character is indeed the sole survivor in her family (deliberately exploiting the child's perspective[4]), *The Glass Bridge* adopts two new narrative strategies: First, it shifts to the experiences of a protagonist as someone who, although still young, is on the threshold of adulthood during the war. Second, Minco's 1986 text extends the tale to include not only the horrific wartime events leading up to the deportation of the protagonist's family and her experience of hiding during the occupation, but additionally provides a study of the ramifications of these experiences for her later life in the decades after the end of the war. The text illustrates the ways in which her wartime experiences (as a Jew) – living through exceptional peril – change her and investigates the ramifications for the rest of her life of the experience as a lone survivor of a family decimated in the Holocaust in a postwar Dutch culture largely oblivious to both her experiences and her grief.[5]

Since Minco's young protagonist Stella is Dutch-Jewish, the novel is clearly set in the context of the experience of the primary group of those persecuted and exterminated under the Nazi regime. It is understood from the very first that Stella is in danger because of who she is, as opposed to young Anton in *The Assault* – a purportedly "normal", apolitical child protagonist within the circle of his ethnically entirely Dutch family. As a Dutch-Jewish child, Stella is commonly understood to be a likely target for violence and persecution during the occupation, as opposed to Anton's more conventional family becoming "unfairly" and unexpectedly caught up in and destroyed by the random violence and mayhem of war.

The title of Minco's text itself is an indirect reference to the fact that the occupation was catastrophic for Jews in the Netherlands,[6] derived as it is from the expression "op het glazen bruggetje geweest zijn", which literally means "to have been on the (little) glass bridge", or, in other words: "to have been in mortal danger". Minco's elimination of the diminutive suffix of "bridge" ("bruggetje" in the expression becomes the "brug" of the title) suggests a longer and more general period of danger; the title rejects the initial impression implied by the source phrase that the period of danger was an isolated, random or unlikely incident. The "bridge" in the title also appears in the context of one of Stella's memories of her father: she describes him standing alone on a bridge. She has been momentarily forgotten and in essence abandoned, a scene which becomes a prefiguration of her father's death.

Apart from the decisive ethnic differences between the two main characters in Mulisch and Minco's texts, both *The Assault* and *The Glass Bridge* exhibit striking conceptual similarities which allow for productive comparison. Both novels feature single child protagonists who escape death at the hand of the Nazis while their entire families perish. For both main characters, the experience of love and comfort in the midst of tragedy is mediated through members of the Resistance – a love which will indelibly mark their respective future romantic entanglements by virtue of the subsequent loss of these lovers. Finally, the notion of the significant function of the memory of childhood events remains central to the lives of the protagonists after the war has ended. I will briefly consider each of these similarities in order to describe the similar notions they express, and to examine how their differences may serve different purposes.

In Marga Minco's novel *The Glass Bridge,* the catastrophic events endured during the war are presented as a part of life which derives from the protagonist's identity and from historical factors which the characters understand; by virtue of being Jews in a country under Nazi occupation, any claim to "ordinary" existence the family might have is out of the question. Stella, the Jewish first-person narrator of *The Glass Bridge,* is aware at the beginning of the story that Jews are being deported and she is critical of relatives who, as members of the Jewish Council, believe they will be saved because they have cooperated with the Nazis.[7] This constellation contrasts with the studied ordinariness of Anton's family in *The Assault*; the Steenwijk family had counted on not becoming involved in the occupation or the resistance in any direct way. At the time of the assault, Anton's mother exclaims that all had gone well for so long and expresses disappointment that this pattern was broken so close to the end of the occupation.

Although the fates of separation and loss which befall both children are ostensibly similar, the main characters in each respective novel begin their tales from quite different positions: while Anton figures as someone who is unwillingly propelled into the conflict which will forever mark his life as an accident of history, Stella's peril is an inescapable fact of a history in which she cannot participate by virtue of her ethnicity. In this respect, neither child can be said to be anything other than "innocent" of what befalls them. But the calculus of suffering for each of the two innocent protagonists is quite different, and readers are expected to read them differently. Since Anton is as ordinary as the average contemporary reader (who is, presumably, engaged by the narrative and is changed by the act of reading in the same way that Anton's ordinary existence is changed by some event he witnesses), his story serves as a meditation on grief, memory, closure and forgiveness from within the circle of ordinary readers. With Stella's story, the readers begin from a decidedly extraordinary position of peril quite removed from ordinary existence. By virtue of reading, one is invited to construct an unimaginable fate (as Stella will construct an identity for herself in the course of the narrative) and to imagine the results for Stella's childhood and adulthood. By virtue of her Jewishness, Stella's grief as a sole survivor is different from Anton's; it is a sorrow that the reader in the period following World War II under-

SOLE SURVIVORS

The fact that Marga Minco's character Stella is a "sole survivor" coincides with both the biographical facts of Minco's life[8] and with the historical reality for Dutch Jews as a whole. The fictional narrative thus embodies/recapitulates what Dresden describes as the historical facts which inadvertently created the space in which Holocaust narratives (fictional or non-fictional) are told.

> Now that the intention [to kill all Jews] did not quite succeed, however, we find therein the opportunity for written or oral transmission. The *almost*, that is to say the void that exists between (a series of) actions and their intended but unreached results, leaves room for the irreplaceable expressions of the victims, which within the perspective of the perpetrators would not have had any right to exist. [9]

Stella is a young woman who survives the very difficult times of the occupation, only to find herself the only member of her family who has survived the war. Unlike Anton Steenwijk in *The Assault*, Stella is suddenly entirely alone; there are no other relatives who could fill the roles of surrogate parents assumed by Anton's aunt and uncle. Although she is older than Anton at the time of the catastrophes which forever change their respective lives, she is by no means at an age when she would have been expected to be completely independent under more normal circumstances. Therefore, although their actual ages differ, Stella and Anton both fit the paradigm of a young person forced to grow up too suddenly; they are both images of a youth truncated by the vicissitudes of historical accident. But Stella, unlike Anton Steenwijk, is forced to invent the life which will sustain her through the peril of the war, and then to enter adulthood bearing both the identity of her birth and the one she assumes in hiding. It is this feature of her survivorhood which distinguishes her from Anton, and which will redirect the focus of *The Glass Bridge* to another sort of perspective on memory and grief.

Stella survives because she has avoided arrest twice – first with her parents and again later when the rest of her extended family is deported. She naturally falls prey to survivor's guilt as she mourns the loss of her family. Jacques Presser has shown that all survivors survived by – in some sense – "betraying" others, if by doing nothing worse than simply leaving them behind.[10] In addition to Minco's fictional illustration of this point, she adds the inspired plot device of having Stella extend both her guilt and her emotional work to include not only the circle of her "real" family, but also to include the woman whose name is on the new, well-crafted, false identity card which Carlo, the member of the Resistance, brings her and whose identity she assumes – "Maria Roselier".

In accordance with Presser's formulation, Stella's guilt about her survival has two distinct parts. The first results from the kind of passive betrayal centered around the circumstances of the capture and deportation of her immediate and "real" family. Stella, like all survivors, abandoned her family in this sense. As her parents were being deported, she kept away from her street because she had been forewarned; when the rest of her extended family was arrested, she coolly climbed the stairs in her house and hid on the roof. Although the text registers her concern, it is clear that there was nothing she could have done to save her parents or other family members from deportation, and that she nevertheless felt great conflict concerning their different fate: "Not until I was up on the roof did it occur to me that I should have warned them, that I should at least have called out, and given them an opportunity to prepare."[11] In addition, the postwar Stella is sensitive to the fact that in her case, the calculus of life and death was even more complicated: she survived because a stranger named Maria Roselier had died earlier, giving up an identity which the Resistance then lent to Stella.

LIFE-CHANGING LOVE

Stella, using the name of her borrowed identity, is old enough to come of age as a woman during the occupation. Like Anton Steenwijk in *The Assault*, she experiences a life-changing love in perilous times. But unlike Anton's brief encounter with Truus Coster in a dark cell, Stella's relationship is more adult in both the sexual sense and because the love that changes her life extends beyond mere momentary comfort to the context of her safety. In the first pages of the novel, the text places in the foreground her beloved and the good fortune his involvement in her "case" means for her. It is said of the man later called Carlo that "all he wanted from her was a photograph..." (for the new false identity card he would acquire for her, thus giving her her new pseudonym). Her lover and benefactor's appropriate behavior is later depicted in clear contrast to that of other people who had been supposed to "help" Stella in the past. The narrative describes two abusers in particular. The first is Mr. Koerts, who sells Stella's family outrageously expensive but poorly made (and thus dangerous) false ID cards whose high price necessitates the sale of her mother's heirloom jewelry. The second is the Resistance courier who is supposed to protect Stella and take her to her next safe house, but who sexually harasses her at every turn, aware that she is at his mercy. Stella manages to rebuff him, but naturally finds the situation unsettling and threatening. The text underscores the irony of the situation: a person is in such a vulnerable position that it is precisely the people whom she has no choice but to trust who endanger her.

Compared to such unethical behavior and incompetence, Carlo is a dream come true. Rather than the life-changing love that Anton experiences as comfort in his childhood's darkest hour, Stella's relationship with Carlo occurs in the "daylight" of her everyday survival; he is someone assigned to help Stella whom she can safely trust and with whom she feels comfortable. In a move which one could call typical in occupation narratives, she eventually falls in love with him. As Augustinus P. Dierick has also shown, coming-of-age is a common theme of narratives set during the war, and (first) sexual experiences often complete this thematic circle.

> A persistent motif in fiction dealing with war is war's association with the discovery of one's individuality and moral character. Adolescence, of course, is at the same time a period of discovery of one's sexuality.[12]

MEMORY AND CHILDHOOD EVENTS IN POSTWAR LIFE

Of course, Carlo is not Stella's lover's real name – he is defined by his behavior and his role. Likewise, Stella does not use her original given name during that period. The transformations of identity which "Stella" must perform in her quest to survive the occupation serve as a major theme of the text, along with the transformations of identity associated with her relationship with Carlo. Carlo's betrayal by a traitor in the Resistance and subsequent death deprive Stella of the chance to know the identity of the person she loves, but she is also left with the legacy of the persona who loved Carlo. To provide some closure and abandon that identity is, to some extent, also to abandon her great love. The question of the identity of the person whose name Stella adopts is important not only for her affections, but to the central questions of memory and grief in the text.

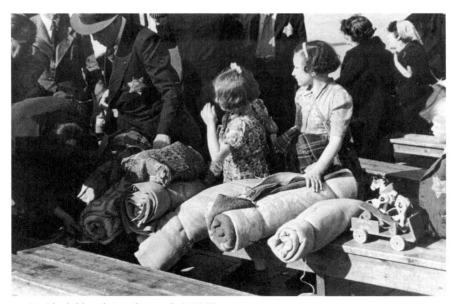

5. Jewish children being deported. (RIOD)

INNOCENT CHILDREN

66   The narrator tells us that Stella knows nothing about Maria when she takes on her identity except for her date of birth and the village where she lived – a village that Stella has neither heard of nor visited. As the reader learns, it will be twenty years after the end of the occupation before she finds the time (or rather, before she is ready) to visit Maria's home village of Avezeel.

The text alludes to her taking on the "Maria Roselier" identity in the very first line of the novel. Then the reader has to wait for quite a while before finding out who the main character is, other than "Maria Roselier". In the meantime, the text emphasizes the main character's (i.e., Stella's) role in inventing a new identity for herself: the Jewish identity is erased, and another is constructed. The new identity is also one of an almost-outsider; to cover for the lack of appropriate accent and dialect, Stella/Maria states that although she came from the far southern part of the country near the Belgian border, she has lived in other parts of the country long enough to lose the traces in her speech which would have identified her as a Southerner.

In section II of the book, which covers the postwar period, the narrative changes from a first- to a third-person narrator; as if Maria Roselier is the narrator of the whole thing, and Stella (the name to which the protagonist eventually reverts at the end of the occupation) is a persona somewhat removed from the narrating persona.

WARTIME EXPERIENCES AS DEFINING MOMENTS

The emotional involvement during Stella's period of hiding proves to be not only a defining moment for her at that time, but is to color and transform all of her future attachments. Stella's coming of age and love affair with the man who provides her with her identity card, the raw material from which she must manufacture her new identity, are presented as though it is clear that their relationship would presumably have continued after the end of the war. However, her lover is betrayed and dies at the hands of the Nazis. Although Stella marries after the war, she subsequently begins a series of affairs which function first to provide her with the excitement which accompanies illicit relationships (presumably fulfilling a need for excitement created during the war when she enjoyed going outside despite – or perhaps because of, in defiance of – the real danger of discovery by the Nazis), and more importantly, to reassure herself that the relationship with Carlo – which she has been denied by history but retains in memory – had indeed been better. A similar pattern also appears in *The Assault* – Anton's marriage begins its disintegration when he discovers that he has married his wife in a move which he suddenly understands to have been an attempt at substitution; he had needed her to replace the unknown woman whom he met in the jail cell and thus tie himself to a past he has later come to reject.

Although Stella's life is presented paradoxically both as a continuation of the life she led during the war and as a reaction to the traumas of the occupation, the narrator presents her wartime experiences as preferred in her mind to the later ones. This pattern also appears in *The Assault* in the figure of Takes, a former member of the Resistance who spends the rest of his life mired in his memories of his activities in wartime, and in particular remembering his love for his fellow resistance fighter Truus Coster. The irony in this tale is the fact that Anton might have been able to tell him that Truus reciprocated his love for her, but somehow does not do so. The reader ponders the question what the psychological effects of such a disclosure would have been for Takes. As Anton says to him, he needs the war; it is not clear that hearing a confirmation of the dead woman's love for him would have helped him. Such knowledge might only have provided yet another screen on which to project the past, or worse, a too sudden sense of closure. For Minco's protagonist Stella, it is clear that there is no one to provide her with such information. In a sense, the novel is about her attempt to discover for herself or deny the information which would make such closure possible. Since she cannot do this with Carlo, she looks for such resolution as she finally begins to search for the life of the real "Maria."

The element of loss found in these narratives reflects a very real feature of the memory of the occupation for a certain segment of the population of the Netherlands. There are those who claim that the post-war prosperity which the Netherlands enjoys coincides with a loss of social cohesiveness, and lament the loss of solidarity represented by recent developments. References to a culture of solidarity recur again and again in stories people tell of life under the occupation: we had no material goods, but at least we were close to our neighbors, and we shared a common hope for a better future. Thus an oral history of the reconstruction of the country in the immediate postwar era is entitled "How beautiful peace looked while we were still at war."[13] An article about Piet Calis' dissertation, a study of illegal literary journals during the occupation,[14] entitled "We were happy only in the midst of the fire. Writers and journals during a wonderful time behind bars",[15] formulates a sentiment still occasional-

6. Grade six of the Jewish school at Bezemstraat 3 in The Hague. (RIOD)

INNOCENT CHILDREN

7. Westerbork Transit Camp in the Netherlands. (RIOD)

ly expressed by Dutch citizens who survived the occupation. Fortunately, their bluff has not been called in recent decades.

For Minco's narrator, excitement in the generic sense – whether derived from an illicit affair or from the experience of war – is the generalized symbol of that which Stella seeks, as she attempts – or so it appears on the surface – to recreate a past in which she was happy. She is, in fact, actually searching for proof that the "good old days" will never be matched by the present or future. It is clear to the reader that Carlo is lost forever, and that she will have to go on without him. Her reluctance to find the last pieces of the puzzle by going to Avezeel to discover the identity of the woman whose ID card she had carried during the occupation, the identity of "Carlo", and the relationship between these two people who between them had saved her life, and thus to provide closure to the history of the occupation, seems remarkably similar to Anton's resistance to confronting the past. Even more salient is the fact that the missing piece of information in both cases is closely related to the lost and anonymous loved one. However, it is not at all clear from the conclusion of *The Glass Bridge* that having the missing piece of information will "heal" Stella in the way that Anton's final piece of information brings him the closure he has avoided for so long. For Anton, the missing piece may be understood to somehow balance the equation in the calculus of suffering. Stella/Maria remains a Jewish child who has escaped to adulthood, carrying her ID card in the way that Anton Steenwijk carries a pair of dice.

Nostalgia for the "better" times experienced during the occupation might at first seem to be an oxymoron, but is a familiar theme in texts which memorialize that period of history and the times which followed it. Minco certainly has spoken frankly about the disappointed expectations which followed on the heels of the liberation, of the dissolution of happy groups of people in hiding who find postwar life a lot less satisfying than they had expected:

> You did not know what to expect. You had a cozy and pleasant life. It was romantic, and you were looking forward to a paradise. Because you thought: later on, when the war is over, it will be good. We used to live in the Kloveniersburgwal with a lot of people in hiding above us and below us and next to us. There was a quality of friendship among people which no longer exists. You would really do anything for someone else. [16]

It is one thing to hear such nostalgia for the war expressed by more standard "bystanders", ethnically Dutch citizens of the Netherlands who were not in any exceptional danger during the occupation, but quite another notion when it comes from a Jewish survivor who has lost just about her whole family. Sera Anstadt, whose novel *Een eigen plek*,[17] tells a story very similar to that recounted in *The Glass Bridge,* confesses to having experienced the same letdown: "The most horrible time was the period when peace had just begun. All of a sudden, the group context was lost." She describes that most of her acquaintances emigrated shortly after the war – to America or Israel; her boyfriend was gone, her parents had been killed: "The most difficult time. Not to be compared with the war. During that war you had to actively work at surviving. After the war you stayed behind, lonely. Because everyone around you was dead."[18] This reality of a young Jewish woman left behind as a lonely[19] survivor is reflected in the last chapter of the novel, which describes the main character's reluctance to return to Amsterdam and give up her daily pilgrimages to Eindhoven, where she can stand and look through a gate to watch Jewish camp survivors who have recently returned from the East, hoping to see her parents. After several weeks, she returns to Amsterdam, to an empty house which she senses will remain empty.

> I wondered why I had returned... Only a few months ago, there had been people here who paid attention to each other. Was this what we had been waiting for?[20]

Unlike Stella, Mulisch's Anton considers both his postwar experiences and the world which had preceded the Assault to be radically discontinuous from the events surrounding the Assault. Anton thinks of the events of that night as singular, presenting a mysterious and perplexing puzzle which he refuses to or is reluctant to solve.[21] However, the Present in the form of rocks and stones, fire, smoke and ashes intrudes upon his hermetically sealed Past, and reminds him of several missing pieces.

The reader knows what Anton really means: that the responsibility to report on a past which he has tried to forget threatens to bring it into the present from which he has sealed his memories away. Due to Anton's successful strategy of forgetting, the events of the past lack a sense of reality, and Anton refuses to make them real.

Both of the texts I have discussed thus far (*The Assault* and *The Glass Bridge*) are exemplary recent novels which use both the "history" and personal history of World War II in the Low Countries as their setting. This chapter will conclude with an analysis of a third exemplary text which continues and extends the discussions of the treatment of childhood and memory. Rudi van Dantzig's novel *Voor een verloren soldaat (For a Lost Soldier)* shares a number of similarities with both the Minco and Mulisch texts. All three focus on a single child protagonist who is the offspring of parents who are understood to be "normal" in the sense of being apolitical, each presents separation from these parents as a direct or indirect result of war-related activities, and the memories of these events play a central role in the life of the protagonist after the end of the war. While these three novels share a number of similarities, it can also be said that what distinguishes them may provide us with some insight about the ways these stories participate in the construction of the history of the time. Rudi van Dantzig, the artistic director of the National Ballet of the Netherlands, uses similar narrative strategies, but alters and expands them in a way that addresses the questions of the suffering and otherness of the dislocated or relocated child in terms of sexual identity and cultural difference. It is, in some respects, the most radical of the three texts in that it depends upon the existing cultural expectations about children in the war and some of the existing stories in order to tell its story of dislocation, occupation, and liberation of an entirely different sort. With this in mind, I will take a closer look at *For a Lost Soldier*, focusing on the role of memory and its relationship to the development of the subject.

The history of children's lives during World War II featured several possible kinds of dislocation which would subsequently be taken up in fictional and nonfictional narratives. The child removed from the family circle by acts of war or wartime retribution represents one of these; it is the single event which sets the story of Anton in *The Assault* in motion. The removal of Dutch children who were "rescued" by being separated from their families for the purposes of being hidden provides the defining moment of Marga Minco's protagonist Stella's life. But there is a third way in which Dutch children were separated from their families during the end of World War II – the practice of "farming out" children. During the closing months of the Second World War, many Dutch children – particularly those children in urban areas or those thought to be old enough for involuntary conscription into the forces of the Nazi occupation – were sent to live in the countryside for safety.

The "farming out" of children is a well-known theme of the Dutch cultural history of World War II, and it is to this familiar event that *For a Lost Soldier* refers in setting the scene for this story about the occupation. The young protagonist, Jeroen, is taken from his familiar surroundings and exposed to unfamiliar and uncomfortable circumstances in order to enhance not only his chances of survival, but also those of his younger brother. His separation is understood not as a flight from imminent danger or the result of acts of aggression in wartime, but as a prudent and precautionary move.

Because the text's narrative perspective is emphatically that of a terrified child (though it is maintained less consistently later on in the text), what is less clear here – but which most Dutch readers would understand – is that Jeroen is really one of the lucky ones. However frightened he may be to leave Amsterdam and his family, he is likely to survive the end of the occupation out on the farm; children who remained in the cities in the western part of the Netherlands suffered severe malnutrition in the closing months of the war, and in many cases did not survive.

Although *For a Lost Soldier* is set in the same time period as *The Assault* and *The Glass Bridge* and makes use of the common fund of images about the occupation that any Dutch reader would bring to the text, it nonetheless varies considerably from both the Mulisch and Minco stories in that the occupation is not explicitly seen as the moral or historical stage on which the action of the text occurs. The narrative does not detail the deportation of Jews to concentration and extermination camps. It does not refer to the raids in which Dutch citizens were rounded up in order to be deported to Germany as slave labor in the war industry or as hostages. It makes no mention of brave Resistance fighters who put their lives on the line to steal ration cards so that they can feed hidden Jews. This narrative concentrates on a subject too young to be aware of such things. This difference in the child's age introduces an intriguing

8. Children from Rotterdam traveling to the countryside, where food is more plentiful (1941). (RIOD)

change in the location and identification of the suffering of its child protagonist. Like *The Assault,* Rudi van Dantzig's novel *For a Lost Soldier* deals both with a character's wartime experience and with the relationship between memory and that subject's attempt to come to terms with his experience – or, to avoid doing so. Diny Schouten comments that the title "*For a Lost Soldier*" leaves out a noun: "a complaint, a monument, a farewell letter, or *what*?"[22] Of course it is all of those.

Van Dantzig's protagonist Jeroen is presented as a small boy at the outset of the narrative. His world is one of a sheltered child whose worst fear is that he may have head lice, in which case his hair would have to be shaved, an event which would invite teasing by his classmates at school. The narration also emphasizes in its language the character's smallness when it signals to the reader that "today" is a big day for Jeroen: "So, this is the day." (13)[23] Jeroen decides the timing is perfect: he has to leave his little brother and his parents, his familiar surroundings, in order to go somewhere far away in Friesland – a place he has only heard of – but at least it will happen "just in time" so he will not have to worry about having head lice. But that fact is only a slight comfort – the suitcase waiting packed and ready in the hallway near the door is described as "threatening and inescapable". (14) He has not had much time to prepare for this trip – he had not been informed of the travel plans until the day before when his father signaled the approach of scary news by doing something unusual – he put his arm around him. The news seemed bad to the boy: Jeroen was being sent off to the countryside because food was more abundant there than in the city. The narrative communicates the parent's dilemma in this regard – the difficulty of convincing the little boy to be happy about going (because going might be necessary for the boy's survival and possibly for the whole family's) without seeming too happy about the impending separation.

While Jeroen's departure from Amsterdam and his family may be all for the best, the narrative does not for a moment allow the reader to think that this is an enjoyable adventure; his mother is not even at home to say good-bye to him. She and her sister have gone off to attempt to find food for sale or barter from farmers miles outside the city, another element of the culture of life during the winter of starvation familiar to Dutch readers. Jeroen's father drops him off early in order to get back to the house by the time the younger brother will need him, and the child is left alone in a nearly empty truck. The departure is postponed even long after the other children have arrived while they and their one adult guide sit and wait for permission to leave. Jeroen goes to sleep in order to forget about the frightening reality in which he finds himself: "This car does not exist, the children do not exist, I myself do not exist..." (18), but does not succeed in filtering out the sounds – he can still hear the others, though as if at a distance. If childhood is a time when one is cared for and feels safe and at home, this day marks the end of his childhood. Jeroen is yet another child forced to grow up too soon by the vicissitudes of life under the occupation.

This sense of Jeroen's separation stands in sharp contrast to that of Anton in *The Assault.* At the beginning of Anton's story, the narrative signals clearly that he is still a young boy by the way in which he is playing a board game with his family. He is particularly thought to be very young by his older brother, who thinks Anton naive and superstitious because he believes having the green game pieces will help him win the board game, and by the childlike interest he shows in the Greek "symbolon" described by his father. His brother Peter is older and too blasé for such childishness. The image of the child as presented in the first pages of the first chapter of *The Assault* is of someone who is protected inside his house, where it may be chilly, but it at least is warmer than it is outside where the "winter of starvation" reigns.

Jeroen's exile to a place of relative safety by his prudent parents is seen not only in contrast to Anton Steenwijk's circumstances, but – as is the case in *The Glass Bridge* – provides the narrative's author with a chance to shift the story to the themes of identity and assimilation. Jeroen's culture shock and subsequent responses to it are not seen as the necessary requirements of survival as in *The Glass Bridge,* but rather as an aspect of the much younger child's sense of developing identity. By locating this emerging identity in a much younger protagonist, the author engages our sympathies in quite another way than Minco does with Stella in *The Glass Bridge;* one sees the much younger Jeroen not as someone who makes the choices which will define his later identity as a young adult (thus a free moral agent), but as an impressionable child.

Once Jeroen has borne the initial pain of separation from family and surroundings, his suffering is not immediately abated when he reaches Friesland. On the contrary, he is a case study in culture shock. Understandably, his first impulse is to attempt to escape and return to Amsterdam. In what may seem to be a mild echo of more adult considerations, he regrets having cooperated with his father and with the various adults who led the transport at each stage of the journey and temporarily decides he should have resisted way back in Amsterdam. He is shocked and wonders whether the whole thing may well have been a plot by his family to send him to distant Friesland in order to let him starve to death. The reader shares the point of view of a child who feels truly abandoned and endangered; he concludes that apparently even his father must have been in on a devious plan to do away with him.

Once established in his foster home, Jeroen's insecurity and fear of abandonment are evident in an excessive desire to please his host family and to fit in. When his foster mother – in a move which an adult reader would interpret as an attempt to put him at ease – asks Jeroen whether his mother cooks on a stove just like she is doing, he lies: "I nod, afraid that she would otherwise send me away after all. I have resolved to agree with her, whatever she says." (31)

Thus the beginning passages of *For a Lost Soldier* present a main character similar to that of *The Assault*; a young boy from a Dutch family who has no direct political involvement with the forces of occupation or the Resistance. These young children are the offspring of parents who are merely "minding their own business" and taking simple and by no means excessive precautions to keep their children alive. They have neither allied themselves with the occupation, as did some parents who saw in such connections an opportunity to improve the chances of survival for their offspring, nor have they engaged in any particularly brave acts of resistance which might have been a source of danger to their families. In the context of an occupation many initially thought would not last for nearly as long as it did, Anton's and Jeroen's parents' strategy of noninvolvement was cautious and prudent. Since many assumed that Hitler would soon fall, adopting a strategy focused on surviving a temporarily unpleasant situation was one common response. Documents recently republished illustrate clearly that the German occupiers of the Netherlands consciously elicited and encouraged such quiescence as part of their strategy to control the civilian population; one bilingual – German and Dutch – sign posted in public places on May 10, 1940 unambiguously delineated the alternatives: individuals who cooperated would be left unharmed, whereas acts of resistance would be severely punished:

I. The German Armed Forces guarantee the citizens complete personal safety and the security of their possessions. Whoever behaves calmly and peacefully has nothing to fear.

II. Violent behavior and acts of sabotage will be met with the severest punishments. The following are considered sabotage: any damage or withholding of harvest products, supplies or installations of any kind which are of interest to the occupying army, as are the removal or damage of posters or announcements. The following are under special protection of the German Armed Forces: gas-, water-, and electricity plants, railways and waterways[24] as well as works of art. [25]

But where Anton Steenwijk's life is forever altered by an act specifically outlawed by the above proclamation, the younger protagonist of *For a Lost Soldier* is changed by virtue of having been removed from danger. The removal itself sets the stage for the act that alters Jeroen's existence far away from the front lines. In a sense, what is at the center of this story is young Jeroen himself; he is fleshed out as a character by reference to the common fund of images and the cultural history of the time. The consequence of his exile is the early experience of otherness – presented from the point of view of a child who is gradually learning to "pass".

THE OCCUPATION IMPOSES CULTURAL ADJUSTMENTS

Jeroen, despite himself, gradually adjusts to life in Friesland. The family treats him well. At his first meal, he behaves as one would expect: he eats generous portions of potatoes and meat, and – as every Dutch reader familiar with war stories can predict, but Jeroen does not know – his stomach, unaccustomed to such excesses, rebels. Jeroen's memories of home are tied to touch and smell; he thinks about finding his suitcase, taking his city clothes out and holding them in his hands, then putting them away in order to prevent anyone else from touching them.

This narrative shares with *The Assault* and other stories of occupation a notion of the inconsistent passage of time: although Jeroen has not yet been completely integrated into the new Frisian culture, he starts to feel at home in his new environment, and develops a fear that he may have forgotten his parents and his home.

I wander about in a deceptive no man's land, a kaleidoscope of coldly changing formations... How much longer will the war last, I have no idea. For
months, or years, or maybe it will stay like this for the rest of my life...(85)

As Jeroen attempts to imagine the end of the war, and tries to think about his family and his home, he enlists the help of scent stimuli: he feels and smells his city
clothes, expecting the scent of the bedroom, "the closet where our clothes were and
the sweetish smell of Mommy's slip" (86), and discovers to his chagrin that either the
scent has become faint, or that perhaps his memory has faded. He may have somehow forgotten what home smells like. This passage is worth noting not only because
it contributes to the overwhelming evidence that memory is an important concern in
narratives of the occupation, but also because it suggests the importance of scent for
memory retrieval in this text.

As expected, exposure to a "foreign" culture becomes an opportunity for growth
and an educational experience for Jeroen, who learns about himself and about the
world. He learns to negotiate cultural differences, and comes to understand the difficulties of adjusting to a different (sub)culture without giving up the self. He discovers that some aspects of a culture are easily "put on" and that some others are, on
the other hand, less easily borrowed. He has been transplanted from an atheist home
to a religious one. He finds he can certainly fold his hands when the others pray, but
that doing so makes him feel like a liar. (47) This issue is not emphasized in *The Glass
Bridge,* but the difficulties of Jewish children whose lives had been saved only because
they appeared to deny, attempted to ignore, or were even forced to shed,[26] their ethnic and/or religious identity, is a well-known fact. The fact that Jeroen's literal survival is not dependent on his submerging an identity which would threaten his life if
revealed (as with Stella's Jewishness) further problematizes the notion of the child's
identity; but the result of his experience in Friesland is nothing in comparison with
the identity he acquires in his own coming of age.

For a Lost Soldier is also a coming-of-age story, and the young Jeroen starts to learn
about sex in conjunction with his acculturation. Since he is on a farm, he will of
course be exposed to certain aspects of reproduction in animals, although the experience initially falls under the category of events which make him feel like an outsider:
during mating season, the Frisian children demonstrate a much better understanding
of what it is they are observing than he has, and he is afraid to ask for clarification.
His ignorance is particularly awkward since he has serious questions about his own
sexuality which he would like to ask, but he already senses he might not receive the
answer he would like. The narrative also presents a situation in which Jeroen discovers that – unlike one of the local boys – he is relatively uninterested in a girl's body,
but later on he finds a male friend much more intriguing. However, since he has no
understanding of the meaning of such things, he is merely confused. The adult reader presumably does not share his confusion. With these scenes, Rudi van Dantzig
introduces into the entirely traditionally located narrative the somewhat less typical
story of Jeroen's coming of age as a gay person. In this regard, van Dantzig's text uses
the "frame story" of the occupation and liberation and the Dutch reader's pre-exist-

ing fund of cultural associations to interrogate notions of gay cultural and sexual identity.

At the time of the liberation, Allied (Canadian or American) soldiers come through the village to "set" the area "free." They do so rather unnecessarily, since it had never actually been occupied in the literal sense, and there are no German troops in residence. Jeroen is once again reminded that he is still an outsider: the other children decide to send him back to the farm to tell the parents the good news, rather than allow him to stay with them to explore the new sights. Though initially outraged at their logic, he nevertheless assents: "my things are in Amsterdam". (94)

A SEXUAL OCCUPATION

Soon, however, Jeroen will feel accepted, but by a different group: a soldier in the army of the Liberators, a hero, chooses Jeroen to accompany him. Jeroen, who does not understand the soldier's intentions, but senses danger, complies nevertheless:

> The arm around me is warm and comfortable, as if I were sitting in a chair which encloses me. I let it all happen, almost with pleasure. "This is liberation," I think, "this is how it ought to be, different from other days. This is a celebration." (110)

The novelty of the situation – the liberation, and the fact that this man is a "Liberator" ("Bevrijder," as the Dutch called the Allied soldiers) – induces in Jeroen a reluctant willingness to do things he would probably not agree to under other circumstances – as it did in the rest of the newly freed populace; this, too, is an

9. Children are fascinated with a Canadian tank. (RIOD)

important piece of the folklore about the occupation. Images of Allied soldiers danc-
ing with European women are common symbols of the exuberant celebrations at the
liberation. Images of soldiers with little boys are less familiar. The child narrator suggests there is a sense of destiny in his choosing to comply with this soldier's wishes,
or rather: a larger force outside him which takes control.

> Wolt, a strange name, just like Popke or Meint.[27] Foreign. It's a miracle that
> he has chosen me, it must have something to do with God, this sudden change
> in everything for me. (110)

This child has adjusted to so many changes in recent months that change has ceased
to surprise him. His hesitant compliance serves as a reminder that the Dutch people
had been helpless to determine their own fate during the occupation, that this fictional character Jeroen is a figure of this powerlessness, and, moreover, that Jeroen
and the whole nation, in their various spheres of influence, found that the period of
time immediately following the liberation failed to live up to the dreams they had
entertained during the occupation, dreams of an endless freedom. The liberation did
not turn out as expected. Jeroen finds himself in over his head: the soldier is more
powerful than he, he speaks with more authority, and Jeroen does not dare to refuse.
His big friend may be generous with chewing gum (as the stereotypical image of
Allied soldiers has it) but he also has demands which he expects Jeroen to comply
with as a matter of course, and – naturally, since he speaks English and Jeroen Dutch
– without any explanation. Although Jeroen is proud to be driven around in an army
vehicle, he vacillates between this sense of accomplishment and a profound ambivalence about his behavior. "Wolt", as Jeroen calls his big friend, is probably a misunderstood "Walt". This minor misunderstanding is only a small symptom of the enormous gap between their worlds, their expectations and the unequal measure of
authority each of them exercises in the "relationship". Jan Brokken points to themes
which he considers similar to those of van Dantzig's ballets, where he sees "childlike
innocence cruelly disturbed. The desire for perfection and purity has become an
obsession for him."[28] Aad Nuis suggests three interpretations: that Wolt introduces
Jeroen to homosexual love, or, secondly and thirdly "You could also call it a rape: reality appears to be a confusing middle between those two."[29] The metaphorical point
concerning the emotional, psychological and cultural cost of being liberated by a
stronger "other" is in any case clear.

   Although there are many similarities between Jeroen of *For a Lost Soldier* and
Anton in *The Assault*, at least one major distinction must be made: the narrative
about Anton is in one sense a "case study" of post-traumatic stress disorder, a reflection on how one traumatic event can change an entire life, while not really coming
to the foreground until much later. *For a Lost Soldier*, on the other hand, uses the
occupation as a stage for self-discovery, a different kind of coming-of-age story:
although trauma is certainly present in the forced separation of Jeroen from his family, by virtue of this distance the narrative creates a much greater space in which to
display Jeroen's sexual self-discovery through his relationship with and subsequent

loss of an Allied Soldier. Though perhaps less traumatic in the traditional sense than Anton's experience of the assault, Jeroen's life is changed forever by events associated with (the end of) the occupation. This coming-of-age was forced at a time before the child was developmentally ready for it; one may indeed argue that this aspect reflects the historical reality of what happens with children in wartime, or under an occupation. Truncated childhoods are a common consequence of the experience of wars. In this case, an adult sexual experience is forced on the boy, in a manner that may safely be called rape by codes of conduct which pertain in the US in the 1980s. Much is made of Jeroen's level of unpreparedness for the sexual experiences which Wolt encourages him to have:

> Kissing people means that you love them: Wolt had held me in his arms tightly as if he wanted to crush me. Why did he do that? He did not even know me...I close my eyes tight and try to sleep. Don't think about "that"... Diet says it is a sin to talk about those things, but if it is an American, it can't be sinful, can it; they only do good things, don't they? (147)

Jeroen's position is a tenuous one – his feelings toward Wolt and the relationship with him are fundamentally ambivalent. He is anxious about the physical desires Wolt exposes to him, but also very proud that a "Liberator" would choose him. The relationship is complicated by the fact of its necessary secrecy, after all: since Jeroen cannot tell his foster parent, his foster siblings or his school teacher about this relationship, he cannot use it to gain the social status he so fervently craves with them, or even to explain his behavior (such as when he disappears to go and meet Wolt), which he feels must seem decidedly odd, suspicious, and utterly transparent to the others.

ASPECTS OF MEMORY: LANGUAGE AND SENSE EXPERIENCE

Jeroen's outsider status is painfully underscored in a scene at school, where the teacher has assigned an essay on the topic of the liberation. Jeroen is finding it difficult to write the essay – his last meeting with Wolt had ended in disappointment, because Wolt did not after all ask him to stay with him forever, as Jeroen had expected – and Jeroen finds that the letter "W" which he has scratched into the corner of his desktop sums up the meaning of the liberation for him. The complexity of his relationship with Wolt renders him mute. He cannot describe or even allude to the relationship in a school essay, and compared with the powerful and conflicted emotional responses which the relationship evokes in him, the commonplaces about the liberation which his teacher expects him to expound upon in his assignment are so colorless that he cannot bring himself to write them. The teacher announces that the Liberators will be leaving the area, and that the children are to write down their memories for future reading. The insensitive teacher misinterprets Jeroen's inability to write about his experiences – confusing, and forcefully inscribed as they are on his twelve-year old body by a much older man – as a lack of appreciation on Jeroen's part of the greatness of the event. As it is impossible to divulge the truth, Jeroen is forced to give up in shameful defeat. The teacher, unsympathetic, chides Jeroen:

"Later on you will comprehend what a wonderful thing happened during these days – then you will be ashamed that you had so little to say about it."

I look at the dry hand which closes my notebook. "Too bad," he says, "really sad for you." (170)

The child's repression of his trauma – not unlike that of Mulisch's character Anton – is presented as muteness, a refusal or inability to speak. The silence of the child is interpreted by the adults as a symptom of a failure to understand the significance of the events associated with "liberation", but their reading directly contradicts the child's experience. Although the adults are unable to see it, this liberation has – and will have – much more far-reaching consequences for him than for any of the others.

Jeroen slowly begins to understand that his "lost soldier" has left the area with his unit, but hopes against hope that Wolt will contact him. When he receives a letter, he fears it may be bad news from Amsterdam – a letter from a neighbor telling him his family has perished – but hopes for a letter from Wolt, although that prospect introduces yet another concern. He fears that his foster mother can read English and might thus discover his secret. (The fact that he himself knows almost no English is of less concern for the moment). But the letter is from his parents, and his only connection to Wolt are his sensory experience and the place which, as the letter announces, he will soon leave:

I want to stay here and wait, stand here until the scent of the earth penetrates me, until I have become of the same material as the ground under my feet, shot through by the roots of the grass, by the wriggling and digging of insects. I want to remain part of this area, of the ground upon which I lay with him, felt his skin, breathed in his scent, felt the warmth of another man's existence run over in(to) me, knocking, banging and taking custody of me. (201)

This narrative emphatically presents the sensuous aspects and sensual components of memory, memory embodied in senses of taste and scent; but it is the lament, the fear that one may fail to remember, which this subject has in common with others who attempt to memorialize the past. Just as Jeroen had tried to remember his home by the scent of the clothing he had brought with him from Amsterdam (and which remained in his suitcase, because city clothing would have been inappropriate attire on the farm), so now he attempts to remember by using his sense of smell. "If only I don't forget what Wolt tastes like, I must continue to remember his breath and the taste of his spit in my mouth. But how do you do that, remember taste, and smell?" (205)

The sense of smell is necessarily fleeting, but his visual sense – a more traditional vessel for memory in literature – will prove highly unreliable as well. When he leaves

Friesland with his mother after the liberation to return home to Amsterdam, Jeroen has a photograph of Wolt in his shirt pocket. Naturally, after he returns home, his mother washes his clothes, which ruins the photograph – his last and only sign of Wolt – and effectively effaces Wolt's image.

Back in Amsterdam, Jeroen performs his memory-work: using a map of the city, he carefully plans a route which will allow him to search every street of the city in turn. What appears to be childlike optimism – that Jeroen could hope by this method to find a soldier who is unlikely to even be in the city, who is (the reader knows) likely to move around from place to place – is actually a sign of the despair of someone abandoned by a loved one. The survivor must plod along the streets, in a kind of parody of memory-work; whatever the child may think he is doing, the attempt to find the loved one who has been taken away (by the war, or at least that's what the child may need to believe) functions as an exercise in making the absence real to the boy. The work of memory is necessary because it enacts the survivor's process of grieving; the child has to convince himself that his loved one will not return by trudging the streets until he is ready to accept the reality of his abandonment. Little Jeroen – a child, and thus relatively free of responsibilities – can find the time to do this work; many adults who might have been willing to join him by performing their own memory-work may have been constrained by the responsibilities associated with physical survival.

In Rudi van Dantzig's *For a Lost Soldier*, the events endured in the course – and particularly toward the end – of the war are presented in an attempt to reconstruct the sudden end of the protagonist's childhood, and the subsequent loss not only of his relationship to his family, but of his entire understanding of the world. The fact that he cannot write an essay assigned in school about his wartime experiences is compensated for by his receiving a photograph of his soldier. The fact that soon afterward his mother washes his shirt with the photo still in the pocket should come as no surprise to an experienced reader of fiction – but it does confirm the view that the construction of memory is a central theme in this work.

If silence is the symptom of memories not yet assimilated, then language – narrative – must be the vehicle through which one reconciles the past and (re)appropriates one's history. Language does indeed perform this pivotal function in this text. The narrator uses adult language self-consciously to create a control over the events which he lacked as they were actually occurring. However, more importantly, one can show that for the narrator language explicitly mediates the experience and becomes the key to remembering. History is a language-bound process, and can only be retraced (if imperfectly) by way of and in language.

In *The Assault*, memories of the events of warfare (at least in part) are based on a linguistic object, namely the word "stone" with which the protagonist is repeatedly confronted despite his efforts to repress it. Since Jeroen, on the other hand, has tied his memory of the soldier primarily to such elements as the specific places where they were together (the country house, the spot behind the dike, the tent and the place in the grass where it stood – places which he is later unable to locate – places which are not available to him after his return to his parents' home in Amsterdam), and to scent, the referents which would jog his memory evaporate of their own accord. Although it is possible for him to relive the memories of this important period of his life in the present tense – a stylistic device which impresses upon the reader the continued deep influence of the past upon the present – thirty-five years later, Jeroen is found frantically attempting to relocate them only days after the formative events have come to an end.

As the child Anton banishes his memories of events which had taken place in plain sight to a place not unlike the moon, that is to say, a virtually inaccessible region of his memory, Jeroen's memories originate from a place of secrecy and silence. Because the events he associates with this period of his life and his experience of the end of the war are sexual acts (and particularly since they are forced homosexual acts, and he was a young boy), they are necessarily relegated to realms of secrecy and muteness.

For Jeroen, the sense referent – scent, landscape – is removed against his will when he is forced to accompany his mother back to their home in Amsterdam – he is only a child, after all – and he presents his work of memory as exactly that: as work. Using a map, he deliberately plots excursions through the city which will allow him to survey the entire area in hopes of locating his soldier. At least for a while, he carries out his plans with diligence.

Thirty-five years later, an adult Jeroen explicitly acknowledges his childhood acts of forgetting, and then chooses to remember. His childish (intentional) remembering – his work of memory – had allowed him to exercise some control over the grieving process, but failed to bring back his soldier. And so, many years after the fact, he remembers again – alone by choice this time. Jeroen's memory is visualized and put into a different perspective through the medium of television, where he watches a group of Canadian soldiers returning for an anniversary reunion. As the images are flat, he sits directly in front of the television, pressing his nose onto the screen as if to retain the memory of tactile detail.

Van Dantzig's protagonist Jeroen only partially experiences the end of the war as a liberation from the German occupation; one of his "liberators" forces an erotic relationship on him which the boy experiences as fundamentally confusing. And as the soldiers are forced to move on, the boy also strongly associates his liberation with the loss of his – however ambivalently perceived – loved one. Where Mulisch's construction of memory revolves around repression – a forgetting which is only gradually and reluctantly overcome – van Dantzig presents a character who demonstratively accepts his "liberation" many years after the fact.

Like Jeroen, Stella also has good reason to mourn the end of the occupation, as for her the liberation brings with it the news of Carlo's death. Unlike Jeroen, Stella had a more appropriate relationship with her "Liberator", one based on approximate equality – since, unlike some others, Carlo did not chose to take advantage of her situation – and thus a relationship which might have had a chance of succeeding after the end of the occupation. In any case, she was denied the opportunity to pursue this avenue.

Stella waits for several decades before confronting the historical reality of her wartime experiences, the loss of her identity, and the reality of Carlo's and Maria's identities. As was the case with Anton, it appears that it is not until she has acquired a certain amount of life experience that she can face the literal facts related to her past which she did not know at the time. For whatever reason, her response, the time lag she requires, appears to be a fairly typical one for victims, and – as will become clear – others affected by the war as well. Unlike Anton, she chooses freely – after repeatedly resisting suggestions that she do so – to discover the necessary facts and confront realities which may lead to a resolution of her past.

Once she has undertaken the process, Stella takes more of a responsibility to move her memory-work along than Anton does. This phenomenon shows a characteristic of Mulisch's writing which Hugo Bousset, writing about the novel *De elementen*[30] calls "His master's voice": Mulisch's preference for omniscient, omnipresent – and, one would be tempted to add: omnipotent – narrators. As Bousset describes the phenomenon: "Mulisch controls his novel as the gods control the universe." (194) According to Bousset, Mulisch's view of these "gods" to which Bousset compares him is a deistic one, and Mulisch has a mechanistic view of the novel: "it is like an alarm clock which he winds up, and of which he decides when it will ring." (194) But the narrator is everywhere, and directly addresses both the main character and the reader. However, Bousset adds, *The Assault* is an exception to this tendency.

Gary Saul Morson's[31] terminology is helpful in discussing this distinction. Mulisch's narrative creates a teleological universe, in which it is foreordained that the secret will be revealed. The reader is prepared for this outcome from the first page by repeated foreshadowing, a literary device which reinforces the reader's expectation that fate will win out.

As Morson puts it, authors who do not believe in fate are more likely to employ sideshadowing as a technique in order to underscore for the reader the fact that the events of the text could have been different, therefore that they were not preordained. Stella discovered the truth about the past belonging to the actual person whose identity she had put on, and which she had in fact reinvented when she chose to, when in the contingent events of her life, she was finally able to find the time and energy she needed to face the past. This narrative, which shows that the events could have been different, or that the timing need not have been what it was, restores to the character the responsibility for taking steps to uncover and face the past. Unlike in *The Assault*, in *The Glass Bridge* history would not reveal itself to characters uninvited. Though repressed history – as long as it remains hidden – haunts the characters in both texts, Stella in *The Glass Bridge* chooses to confront the past, and thus is able to perform her memory-work.

Mulisch , on the other hand, has been criticized for the many coincidental meetings required to bring Anton to the point where he completes the puzzle of his family's history. In an interview with *Die Zeit*,[32] he parries that unplanned meetings between acquaintances in such a densely populated country as the Netherlands are not so unusual as citizens of larger countries might imagine.

Whatever the reasons for their engagement with the past, the main characters of *The Assault, The Glass Bridge,* and *For a Lost Soldier* all experience a time decades after the end of the occupation when they are able to consider the past and the effect this past has had upon their present life. The three share a number of characteristics. All three were fundamentally influenced by their experiences and memory of the occupation in ways that continued to affect their lives after the occupation. All three find that a new level of understanding or acceptance may be achieved during middle age or late middle age. The reason for this "delay" is a combination of various factors, such as the coincidence of new information, a growing readiness to understand a painful past, their having reached a point in their life cycles where they have more leisure than before. They have achieved a certain self-knowledge, in some cases a stable marriage, their children are no longer small, and for the first time in their lives, they can afford to spend time and emotional energy allowing themselves to begin to dwell on, deal with, grieve over the past – to do the memory-work they have postponed for so long.[33]

However, these three subjects of the occupation present an anything-but-simplistic picture of how one comes to terms with the emotional, historical, and social fallout of the war: to know all is not to understand all, nor is it to forgive all, and it is certainly not an opportunity to suddenly and wholly integrate one's personality and to deal with the memory of the occupation once and for all. The process of remembering and of integrating that memory, requires work. *The Assault, The Glass Bridge* and *For a Lost Soldier* each reflect this process, and may – for some readers – offer a fictional world in which such work will proceed.

INNOCENT CHILDREN

4. *Language is the Landscape of History* Armando and the History of Enmity

Given that the conventions we use for our calendar are cyclical, there is a moment every year when we are thought to find ourselves close to the end of World War II. In the minds of some readers, this imagined closeness can even be invoked to explain the periodic recurrence of texts related to the commemorated events of the war. On the surface of it, this answer may seem preferable to imagining that such texts appear because they may be more marketable on the occasion of some major anniversary. In similar fashion, the recurrent discussions in the press about how to celebrate an anniversary of a wartime event seems to suggest that the occasion somehow places us "close" to the event or even to the memory of it. In fact, we are not close at all; our choice of certain dates as the appropriate time for commemoration of various events of World War II is a cultural construct based on nothing more than the arbitrary linguistic sign of the date (e.g., June for the commemoration of D-Day, August for the observance of the anniversary of the first use of the atomic bomb). We are in fact at a greater remove from the event with every commemoration.

To a certain extent, the commemorative exercise underscores our distance even as it is used in an attempt to help us remember. It is at once an appeal to common memory and an implicit statement of difference about those who experience the event as

10. Illegal scout troupe in Arnhem. (RIOD)

remembered experience and those who do not. This sense of the duality of a central event seen in retrospect is similar to the phrase I commonly heard in the Netherlands as I was growing up in the postwar period – "Jij hebt de oorlog niet meegemaakt", ("You haven't been through the war"). As I came to understand it, it was a phrase which, in some cases, despite the speaker's conscious intentions, had the effect of distancing two people – usually a parent and child – by emphasizing the two very different sets of experiences which populate their memories. With this old truism the speaker intends to communicate to the listener: "If this had happened to you, you would understand me." The notion implicit in the phrase is the assumption that shared experience tends to lead to shared understanding and automatic acceptance and – perhaps – even shared memory. Language (such as in the form of the phrase "Jij hebt de oorlog niet meegemaakt,"[1]) may impose distance while still suggesting what you have to do – that is, it may be taken to mean something like, "You must finish your vegetables, but you will never really be able to understand how important it is to me that you do so."

Some Dutch literature may also function as another kind of instantiation of a cultural truism; it is a story which we tell each other in an attempt to remember or to remind the reader of specific experiences of World War II. In some sense, that literature has behind it a set of cultural constructions and assumptions which are evoked in the same ways as one does in reminding a child, "Jij hebt de oorlog niet meegemaakt" – the use of the phrase does not necessarily involve a complete accounting of the speaker's actual experiences as such. It carries its own weight. In this study, I am suggesting that these literary texts have not been produced and published consistently and in the same way throughout the last five decades. While remaining mindful of the danger of oversimplification and watchful to locate those texts which seem to run "against the grain" of general trends, I believe that as a matter of fact the memory of the war in the last five decades as reflected in Dutch literary texts has changed several times – from a memory of an experience viewed in a fairly unambiguously way which readers during the late forties and early fifties would know firsthand, to a period of silence and lack of writing/publishing on the topic during the early sixties, to a renaissance of literary production starting in the late 70s and blossoming during the 80s.

The decade of the 1980s[2] saw a new group of texts which tie themselves thematically to World War II. It should not come as a great surprise that the stories we have chosen to tell ourselves may have changed over time. In fact, many of these texts engage issues of the idea of memory in general as well as specific memories, and also shift to an emphasis on various forms of memory by "children of the war" born just before, during, or even after the war – those too young to have actively participated in the war but who nevertheless find themselves "remembering" or facing the "memory" of the war in various ways: in family dynamics, political choices, attitudes toward national identity, the state of their emotional health, and in ambivalent relationships to the past and present.

Thus, texts which appeared in the 1950s such as those of Simon Vestdijk (e.g. *Bevrijdingsfeest, Pastorale 43*) dealt with the immediate past and the views of the meaning of the war current at the time while raising questions about some overly simplistic assumptions about who had been good *("goed")* or bad *("fout")* which were prevalent at the time. But these issues are addressed in the context of a society consisting of adults who were understood to have been present during the period of a "recent" past as (presumably) reliable adult witnesses.

In addition to the shift of emphasis in the 1980s to the notion of memory itself (and particularly the memories of "children of the war"), the literature of this decade introduces some new notions which may be seen as involving a more nuanced view of the period. The insights of the literature of the 1980s includes some new truisms such as the insight that it was possible to recognize a potential lack of justice in the punishment of perpetrators and to also acknowledge the particular possibility that the children of perpetrators had been treated with great unfairness. These developments co-exist and are developed alongside the more traditional understandings of the suffering of those thought of as victims[3] and their children. It is in this period that the use of terms such as "oorlogsgetroffenen" (those affected by the war) and "kinderen van de oorlog" (children of the war) come into use as a kind of response to the recognition that adults who survived the war (either as collaborators or victims) were affected by it, and that their children and even grandchildren in turn were affected by the results of a trauma[4] visited unto several generations.

Finally, there is a newfound recognition in the texts of the 1980s that even the children of those who had neither been clear victims nor obvious perpetrators ("by-standers") were emotionally affected by the occupation, because even their bystander parents had not survived the war untouched or unscathed. Thus, the reminder/accusation which takes the form "Jij hebt de oorlog niet meegemaakt", actually masks the fact that those not directly involved in warfare do experience its effects;[5] its language both distances those addressed from shared experiences and posits an "expected" result: you cannot understand because your experiences do not coincide with mine.

I remember that admonition well from my childhood, but the intervening years also remind me that I no longer experience that old phrase in the same way. Those collections of attitudes about the (perceived) authority of adults, the use of language, and the tools of logic I acquired in the course of growing up not only serve my present, but also color and alter the past. I react quite differently to that admonition when I hear it today; in some measure, my involvement with texts can be seen as my adult answer to the admonition – reading and listening to stories is the way in which I strive to understand the experiences which do not coincide with my own. In some sense, stories and the language that is used to tell them has become the way that one learns to examine memory.

As I approach the painter and author Armando (born Herman Dirk van Dodeweerd, in Amsterdam in 1929; his chosen name is translated "he who arms himself"),[6] it is helpful to view his work in the context of what other writers of the 1980s have done with the theme of the war. His work offers a very different approach which allows him and the reader to examine aspects of the problems of memory, culpability and the function of language more directly than most of the other fiction written about the war and occupation.

As I previously suggested, Harry Mulisch's *The Assault* elaborates on the effect years later on the child of a bystander family who unexpectedly becomes a victim of the war. It also offers the surprise of a sidelong recognition that the child of a collaborator may have shared some similar suffering in the post-war period. In *The Glass Bridge*, Marga Minco investigates the emotional effects years later on a Jewish child who escaped extermination. It, too, clearly presents some challenges to the standard tropes of Dutch wartime and postwar experience by depicting the impure motivations and occasional outright bumbling on the part of members of the resistance. And Rudi van Dantzig, in *Voor een verloren soldaat*, profiles the ambiguity of the relationship between the Dutch people and the American "liberators" (it can be read as either a case study in which an individual liberator is abusive toward an individual Dutch child, or (somewhat more cautiously) as a parable of what happened to the Netherlands culturally in the postwar years – or both).

These texts are not just "about the war." They are also "about" memory and different perspectives on culpability and innocence. They are about varieties of motivation (which range from altruistic to fairly selfish) among workers in the Resistance. They are also about the postwar consequences of one's status as a survivor – even decades later. Of course, this summation is not intended to obscure the fact that each of these three novels show some differences from the others and from other examples of literature about the war; they are, however, representatives of a range of similar texts written in approximately the same time period about the impact of the war and memories of it on survivors. Taken together, they offer a look at various ways in which Dutch writers and their reading public participate in discussions about the meaning of the memories of World War II among various factions in the "second generation".

While Armando's "novel" *De straat en het struikgewas* [7] ("Street and Foliage"), which I consider here, may be seen to share some narrative strategies with the novels described thus far, his literary work (and, indeed, the body of his work as a whole) offers a completely different approach. In the realm of Dutch-language texts which deal with the memory of World War II, the work of Armando inhabits a unique and unusual space in the way that it uses language itself to examine the notions of history, memory, language, and responsibility more directly than most of the other fiction written about the war and occupation.

As with Harry Mulisch and Marga Minco, Armando's own history of producing texts involves a body of work which could serve on its own terms as the basis of a study of the shifts in the image of the Dutch wartime. But the body of Armando's work is not merely linked by thematic concerns of the sort which connect Minco's *Bitter Herbs* and *The Glass Bridge;* it also shares a set of formal approaches and an interest in enmity and otherness which combine with the autobiographical urge in "Street and Foliage". I would thus be remiss not to touch briefly on the ways in which his quintessential 1980s' work is consistent with the history of his interventions in the worlds of literature and the visual arts. Armando has been on the Dutch literary scene since 1954 with his poetry debut in *Podium*, and more generally since 1959 when he began editing the literary journal *Gard Sivik*. He was also the arts editor for the *Haagsche Post* from 1958 until the end of the 1960s.

As Pieter de Nijs[8] mentions, Armando's literary work was criticized early on because it was viewed as a glorification of violence,[9] and because his use of "ready-mades" was not universally appreciated around 1960. Armando described his technique as "annexing and isolating fragments from reality", a technique which clearly applies to his "Agrarian" poem cycle, in which he quotes brochures for farm equipment. Other cycles include "Boxers" and "Fighters", both of which reflect an interest on Armando's part in texts in which the surface banality both hides and reveals reality. In the 1960s, Armando not only watched boxing matches, but trained as a boxer himself. The importance of machinery and (implied threats of) violence found in his poetry are clearly reminiscent of Futurism and its aestheticization of violence. However, as the subtitle of De Nijs' article, "Armando's Tough Sensitivity", suggests, Armando's interest in these topics is highly complex and represents a point of view formed with the admittedly dubious benefit of the experience of World War II. It thus reflects a different sensibility.

Armando's body of literary work combines the formal device of the "ready-mades" or "found text" [quotes from conversations overheard in public places, popular literature (such as Karl May novels), sports commentators (in "Boxers" and "Fighters"), and brochures for farm machinery] with a thematic concern with everyday expressions of enmity, power, and violence; it is built around an internal paradox encompassing beauty and an apparent aesthetic of violence, the banal and the sublime. While both sets of these poles are inextricably connected in Armando's work, it is important to note that Armando's point of view is much less distanced from a human perspective than that of the Futurists. It would not be inaccurate to describe his work as a literary sociology or psychology of enmity or, in the literary sense, as an archaeology of enmity.

This point may be demonstrated by an analysis of his own representation of his work. In *Krijgsgewoel* ("The Turmoil of Battle", 1986), Armando makes the following observations about his book *Aantekeningen over de vijand*[10] ("Notes Concerning the Enemy") of 1981.

> What's that book about. It's difficult to say. In my opinion, it's about goings on.[11] About human goings on/actions. They say it has something to do with "the war". I'm not so sure about that, I actually thought that it has more to do with people, but I've been wrong before.[12]

This statement lends support to the view that human behavior during wartime is simply a subspecies of human behavior in general, that it is consistent with other patterns of human behavior, rather than unique.

Although one should not take Armando's word for it in this case (*Aantekeningen over de vijand* most certainly is, in some sense, about war), it is important to recognize that, if so, war is not to be viewed as discontinuous from everyday life but rather as a variety of life – or as an (admittedly) exceptional or extreme form which life may take. The reader must not miss the – ironic – connection he makes between the war and people while facetiously asserting a dichotomy: "They say it has something to do with "the war". I'm not really sure about that, I actually thought that it has more to do with *people*, but I've been wrong before." A view of war which recognizes it as a part of life sees that, in times of peace, war is anticipated, and its influence also continues after peace has once again been declared. It would not occur in a world in which society and its inhabitants did not allow for enmity.

It is in the context of Armando's apparent intent to fathom the psychosocial genesis of enmity and violence in combination with a fascination with mechanisms of inclusion and exclusion that his most controversial book should be viewed. In 1967, Armando and Hans Sleutelaar were greeted with calls of outrage when they published *De SS'ers,* a book consisting of interviews with eight Dutch men who had been members of the Waffen-SS. Readers' responses diverged sharply, with some calling it an impressively revealing portrait of inhuman(e) beings, others criticizing it as immoral, because it gave the interviewees an opportunity to speak freely and reveal the motivations for their actions – thus, some critics felt, justifying them in certain readers' eyes. The review of *De SS'ers* in *Trouw* (July 20, 1967) was entitled "A Dangerous Book Without Contradiction", and stated that it was dangerous to allow SS-ers "the opportunity to vent all the excuses which they have invented in the course of time, without a response from the other side. In the hands of someone who is unfamiliar with the actual deeds of the SS-ers and their boss, this book is just plain Nazi propaganda." Some readers thus thought the publication of these texts irresponsible to the extent that they could be seen to give voice to a perceived potential fascist threat to democracy. The innocuous surface of the text was that of a simple oral history, and the discomfort of some readers with the work should be attributed to a lack of authorial intervention in the interviews, as suggested in the *Eindhovens Dagblad:* [13]

It is full of simplifications: One can not really blame these voluntary SS'ers. Such political views were probably forced on them [bij hen ingehamerd]. One can, however, blame the editors that they felt a need to present it as a not-yet-available essential historical witness. Admittedly, a clear representation (image) is offered of the spirit which predominated in the Waffen-SS (to soften the horror on their side, they constantly refer to the not-so-decent things others did and the number of six million murdered Jews is repeatedly questioned, as if numbers are really what's at issue) the lack of any commentary allows them to get away with too many retrospective excuses ("bewijst al dit nakaarten al te veel eer").

The reviewer's anger is most clearly apparent in the language, and particularly in the structure, of his writing. His outrage is revealed in the placement of the most offensive evidence he can muster of the collaborators' infamy, their lack of having learned anything during or after the war: the fact that they would be so callous as to quibble, to count their guilt as only relative in light of the "not-so-decent things others did" and to question the famous number of the murdered. Their squabbling is proof positive of their lack of political and social education, as he states elsewhere in this text: "Each of them expresses himself in a politically naive kindergartner's language." It is clear that the book has struck a nerve.

Despite the understandable discomfort of many readers, one can easily recognize the consistency of this project with Armando's other aesthetic and sociological interests; it is consonant on a formal level with his interest in the ready-made, and the thematic content makes sense in the context of his long-standing fascination with (the) war and the concomitant concepts of enmity and violence. Recording the interviews without comment was in accordance with the mainstream of the *Nieuwe Stijl,* the style of journalism prevalent at the time. Thus this project fits comfortably into the spectrum of Armando's projects rather than being a call for an overly kind look at fascists. It fits within a productive vein of research intended to ask the recurrent question about how the war or occupation could have happened as it did. Ian Buruma formulates a similar point of view in the words: "And yet the frightened man who betrayed to save his life, who looked the other way, who grasped the wrong horn of a hideous moral dilemma, interested me more than the hero... partly because, to me, failure is more typical of the human condition than heroism."[14] Jaap Goedegebuure comments: "Presenting SS-ers as normal people was not a shocking device, it was – for many, a rather shocking – reality."[15]

Since the publication of *De SS'ers,* Armando has turned toward texts which have more prominent fictional or poetic aspects and have thus been generally received as more "literary". Nevertheless, many critics commonly identify apparent "autobiographical elements" in his works. What has remained consistent in Armando's oeuvre, however, has been a careful attention to the genesis and social roles of violence and enmity, expressed with a brilliant sensitivity to language. His writings in the 1980s engaged these issues in an explicit way in the context of memory and autobiography. Armando's birth in 1929 places him as a boy of ten to fifteen during the occupation, just like the unnamed protagonist of *De straat en het struikgewas.*

It is worth attending to the form of "Street and Foliage."[16] It should be noted at the outset before the novel is discussed in detail that much of the language and many of the ideas contained therein also appeared in different form in Armando's earlier books, except that these earlier works were structurally more fragmentary. I focus on "Street and Foliage" not only because its date of publication sets it squarely within the time period of which the texts discussed in this book are representative, but particularly because Armando himself has called this work his definitive text about the war. This text, perhaps more than any other of Armando's, may also be read as a novel. In an interview, Armando very nearly endorses this view:

"I do not consider *De straat en het struikgewas* a volume of stories, either. That book has something more of a novel, the form of one. It's not a novel in the sense of a beginning and an end, and maybe that too. That I leave to the readers. I do not really care about it one way or the other."[17]

Thus the form means that a more appropriate and fruitful comparison is possible with the other texts which illustrate the history of the children of the war. As one thoughtful reader, Ernst van Alphen, describes the structure:

> The short chapters of which this work consists on one hand follow the chronology of the narrator's life. On the other hand, each brief chapter is simultaneously a repetition of the same themes: heroism, a fascination with violence. Armando presents each moment of his pre-war youth as a prefiguration [vooruitwijzing] of the war, while the postwar period functions as a "post-figurement" [terugwijzing].[18]

In an interview in the *Revisor* in 1989,[19] Armando stated that there had been personal issues which had had their genesis during the war which he needed to work through before he could complete "Street and Foliage". He explained not only that the process of writing the text had functioned as part of his memory-work, but also that it represents a milestone in the progress he made in working through, absorbing, and reconciling his childhood experiences of the occupation. Interestingly, it is significant in this context that he refers to one of the standard indicators within postwar Dutch culture of having experienced the occupation – a commitment to eating all the food on one's plate:

> De *straat en het struikgewas* is the completion of that theme of war, violence, guilt, complicity, enemy, perpetrator and victim. It was not until I had finished that book that I first dared to not finish all the food on my plate....[20]

Armando's autobiographical statements about his eating habits permit the reader to speculate about the process of healing: did the process of writing this book provide an opportunity for Armando to synthesize his reactions to the occupation? Is that the reason why this book takes the form of a novel – however fragmentary?

In describing the significance of this work as representing a psychosocial stage, or rather a point, in his experience of the postwar period, Armando refers to a favorite sign of the meaning and consequences of survivorship – finishing all the food on one's plate – in order to show that for him the writing of "Street and Foliage" coincided with his at last having resolved some key social and psychological issues held over from his childhood experience of the occupation.

It is in this context that the narrative "contents" of Armando's "novel" "Street and Foliage" takes on signal importance. It is useful to pay particular attention to the roles of language and landscape in Armando's study of violence. He describes the landscape as "guilty", and by his use of language, demonstrates that the language bears witness to the violence done to others during the occupation, and still bears the marks of this violence. It is an aggression which persists into the present. In "Street and Foliage", the "main character" may be – it is not entirely clear – a boy who likes to play with his friends in a wooded area near his house, though this boy is never named, and the narrative (as evident in the pronouns used) occasionally moves from third to first person and back.

THE QUESTION OF AUTOBIOGRAPHY

As is the case with the other texts I discuss, some readers of "Street and Foliage" have interpreted the work as an autobiographical account.[21] As Holocaust revisionism and the German *Historikerstreit* each illustrate, it is important for the writing of history that one is able to distinguish between metaphor and outright falsehood, such as establishing the historical veracity of some detail of the Shoah, or that a young woman named Anne Frank did, in fact, write the documents which have since been published as her *Diary*. But such issues do not constitute my primary focus; rather than considering it a priority to make such distinctions, I argue that these are not the only aspects of our responses which are worth investigating. It is possible to approach texts at a different level and from a different and more productive point of view when one focuses not primarily on the presence or absence of "literal truth" but rather (after granting that some subjective aspects are likely to always be present in such texts) on wording, choice of topic, or the decision to include or exclude certain material. One investigates the possible reasons for selecting certain issues and not others for discussion when one asks why we frame the questions as we do. In short: it is important to consider what is at stake and to what end the members of a certain community or (sub)culture become involved in these dialogues rather than others. One must consider how our concerns are reflected in the selection of issues and topics, the choice of materials included in books, or the choice of vocabulary. Although it is important to know the difference between historical facts and falsification, as a number of thinkers have suggested, discovering why we find certain issues rather than others worthy of debate can be as telling as selecting for factuality.

Just as it is important to know the difference between historical truth and falsification, so it is essential to discuss why it is that we find certain issues rather than others worthy of attention. As is the case with a number of the other texts which I consider in some detail, Armando engages the collected memories of bystanders and the issues surrounding them. This text has in common with those discussed in the preceding chapters the fact that the main characters, "children of the war", are not directly involved in the war: they are not part of the occupying forces, nor do they collaborate with them; they are not active in the resistance, and they do not belong to a minority which was specifically targeted for persecution and destruction by the Nazis. Besides the fact that he does not belong to any of these groups, the main character of this text has in common with other protagonists who are children of the war the important fact that he was a child during the occupation, and too young to be held responsible for either collaborating or resisting. Nevertheless, even though he was young at the time, and his family appears not to have suffered any direct persecution, it is clear that the war/occupation has inexorably altered his life. This text is a study in the ways the lives of young boys who watched the occupation from their perspective were changed by their early experiences, and the implications of those alterations for not only the persons they became, but for the language and memories they brought to adulthood.

The author locates the impact of these life-changing experiences particularly clearly in the language itself – treating it as an index of other cultural practices – and in the presentation of landscape and place, each of which has local practices associated with it. Armando does not stop at description; he presses the issue and pushes for an understanding of the basic issues in play. In the first place, note that all the characters in the work are essentially bystanders: they are the children of civilians who live in a rural area which happens to be the place where a camp will be built during the occupation. The text, however, starts at a much earlier, much more (apparently) innocent moment before the war, establishing what counts as the "normal" condition of the area and its (male children's) society: with boys as Cub Scouts. The text shows that even among Cub Scouts, members of an organization explicitly intended to foster unity and "brotherhood", distinctions exist; there are distinctions among boys of differing socio-economic status, between the in-crowd and unpopular boys.

Young scouts were called "cubs". There were distinguished cubs too.

"No" said the distinguished cub. "I'm afraid I'll tumble."

I looked around, surprised, but no one stirred. What should you say instead. I'm afraid that I'll fall.[22] Or just (normally): I am afraid that I will fall. But you don't say: I am afraid that I'll topple, you don't say that.

As if distinguished boys can't be nice.

But who on earth is afraid of falling. Do people ever fall. Yes, plenty. But not yet back then.[23]

Armando, with his talent for teasing out very complicated situations and cultural constructs using the simplest of language, simultaneously reminds the reader here of the utopian place which childhood holds in our culture and appropriately questions an overly simplistic image of the society of youth as essentially different from that of adults. This move enables him to show the damage sustained by young children of the war during the occupation. It also affords him the latitude needed to extrapolate the effects of this impairment from young to more adult bystanders.

The mediation in this passage starts with the memory of the name given to the youngest boy scouts: welpen, "cubs", expressed in four words: "Jonge padvinders heetten 'welpen'". ("Young boy scouts were called 'cubs'".) The narrator does not delineate what the reader is to think of this name, thus leaving open interpretations or associations such as "small", "dependent", even "cute", (which might be the first associations) but significantly without excluding notions of "young wolf-to-be" which might present themselves later on; in any case the reference is to a wild member of the animal kingdom – as the Boy Scout movement clearly must have intended it to be. Thus the reader is set up for a critique of any utopian notions he or she might hold of childhood as a time when the individual is free of the claims of human adult society. The narrator brings the core of this critique to mind in five words; reminding the reader of the importance of class in childhood as well: "There were distinguished (upper-crust) cubs too." Since there are not enough bicycles to go around, the den mother asks one of the "upper-crust cubs" to give another cub scout a ride on the back of his bicycle. Riding two to a bicycle is a common experience of Dutch life, and learning the twin skills of giving and accepting rides an important part of childhood; a set of skills which a Boy Scout would want to prove he had mastered. The cub's answer ("'Nee', zei de deftige welp, 'ik ben bang dat ik duvel.'") is perceived as odd by the narrator; first, presumably, because of the boy's refusal to prove his mettle, and secondly because of the language used: "duvel" is slang, of a variety unfamiliar to the narrator. The narrator makes a list of other possible words and expressions which might have been chosen, from somewhat coarse to unmarked, and returns to the thought that "duvel" is not said. ("As if distinguished boys can't be nice.") Then the text pursues the meaning of what was in fact said:

"Who would be afraid of falling anyway? Is there such a thing as people who fall? Oh, yes, plenty of them. But not yet back then." The reference to the passage of time, the time which is to follow "back then," removes the focus from the time of childhood when being able to ride a bicycle was a new skill of paramount importance, to a later time when one had more important issues to face. As the thought is pursued, the reader follows the narrator from his childish utopian notion that people don't fall off bicycles to the adult view, the voice of experience, that people do, in fact, "fall". One remembers that World War II became proof positive to many otherwise optimistic people of the capacity of humankind for falling.

The question of class remains at issue throughout the book; it is alluded to again[24] later at a point where a distinction is made between boys "of the street", and boys who did not participate in the activities on the street, and in an ominous remark to the effect that the main character would later end up being involved with those very boys who "had been (sitting) at home", the boys of higher classes, who as teenagers spent their time on school activities and on homework rather than on the life of the street. This refers to the main character's "rise" in social ranks by virtue of his education: he will become an artist "despite" his lower-class background.

Starting from this point, the reader is poised to recognize the various aspects of Dutch culture which Armando's text presents as important factors in the history of the occupation and in civilian responses to that history, as well as the impact of various historical moments on future memories of this period. As has already been signaled by the reference to the Cub Scouts, this text appeals to the fundamental influence of culture early on. Even small children have a culture by which they are influenced and influence others in various ways; their views and behavior are culture-bound. The narrator studies and reports on the subculture of children: "You didn't want to wear gloves as a child. Occasionally you would die of cold, for instance when throwing snowballs, but you did not want to wear gloves. You also did not want to have a hat on. Never. No matter how cold it was. You never wanted to cooperate at all."[25] The adult narrator presents the memory of his childhood culture in a voice reminiscent of a child's; a stylistic device which underscores the normalcy of children who resist adult culture and the imposition of their parents' "civilizing" will in little ways, and thus – by implicit contrast – opens the door to a recognition that the larger issues of war and occupation which certainly do confront these children later on should not really have been their concern.

In the same vein, the language in which the introduction of the war into the children's world is represented makes it sound inevitable, as if reflecting a child's magical view of the world, and connects the genesis of the camp built near the narrator's home town with the children's ball game: "On the spot where the ball kept returning, less than a year later 'the camp' arose."[26] It starts as barracks (30), in the calm before the storm: "We were waiting for the surprise attack and the conquest and the show of strength"[27] and then, during the occupation, it becomes a camp.

Because the camp is built in the woods near where the narrator lives, it constitutes the children's contact with the occupation. He and his friends are confronted on a regular basis with the soldiers associated with the camp; in fact, the site of the camp in the novel is the place in the woods where the boy's favorite climbing tree stood. The "occupation" in fact means the occupation of the children's favorite "playground" by the enemy. Nevertheless, the image of the occupying forces is ambiguous and the people's feelings are ambivalent, where an unremittingly negative view might have been expected. The narrator presents quite a few different glimpses of the enemy, of which some are negative and others quite positive. Usually, these images are mediated through monologue or dialogue; the reader listens in on discussions among the bystanders, who are talking about the soldiers. The language used is an index of their attitudes. Thus, in a discussion about the commander of the concentration camp, who has been quartered in the home of one of the locals, she declares him a decent man: "Oh, a fine man, not a thing to find fault with."

Although some, such as the commander of the concentration camp, surprise the local citizens by behaving as decent or civilized people, others break all the rules. A story is told of a Dutch officer, "a teacher, a Christian one", who had "surprised himself by taking a German officer and three soldiers prisoner."[28] As the tale has it, the Dutch officer disarms the Germans; but the German officer convinces him to return his pistol "on his word of honor". Of course the enemy officer uses the pistol to shoot the man who had taken him prisoner and regain his freedom. After the telling of the tale, which had been passed on by a Dutch survivor of the event, a discussion ensues among the civilians on the question whether or not the German had been in the right. Some discussants justify his behavior in light of the fact that it occurred in the context of a war, but the narrator (or the last speaker quoted) does not agree: the principle of one's "word of honor" ought to be respected, even in wartime. Thus a good deal of discussion is apparently taking place within the community about what the enemy soldiers are like, and the narrator reports on the behavior of the soldiers in various passages. In one instance, he reports that the soldiers sometimes behaved roughly. In this case he refers to their having painted a dog black and their having behaved in a rowdy manner while they cut down a tree.[29] One should note, of course, that the fact that these events are considered remarkable implies that the soldiers usually did "behave" themselves.[30] Since the boy watches them so closely, it is clear that the soldiers have become role models, examples of foreign adult males and the ways in which they act.

SOLDIERS FASCINATE THE CIVILIANS

The boys do indeed pay close attention to the soldiers and their activities: thus the boys cycle after the soldiers when they go marching. In this passage, the narrator tries to remember whether the soldiers took cover during sudden rainstorms. When he cannot remember it, he takes this as a reminder that he was not one of these boys. Again, the need to have this distinction clarified is an indication of the fact that a child will think of the conditions of his childhood as "normal". He states that they could easily have sought shelter during the rain, that it would have been all right for soldiers to do that.[31] The point of this train of thought seems to start with a discussion and perhaps questioning of a macho image – the boys are learning what it means to be a man – which ends by demystifying this somewhat: the soldiers whom the narrator observes are occupying forces who are in comfortable control, and not fighting at the front; and therefore different standards of behavior apply to them. Life seems less dangerous here. Such thoughts are readily recognized as likely for a young boy in the narrator's position; what is of interest to me is the fact that the text brings to the reader's attention how far-reaching and basic the influence of the wartime constellation was for the children who lived during that time. "The enemy was openly visible from the moment the fighting was over."[32] The enemy talks and moves like a human being; the narrator states that he observed him as often as possible, and that he had no choice. "It turned out that he spoke and moved: the enemy evidenced human characteristics. He just walked through the street, in a group or alone. Sometimes he even entered a store."[33] In its insistence that these are human beings, the description renders the neutral designation "the enemy" absurd. Another snatch of conversation presents a different strand of a well-worn argument about the military: the question whether or not soldiers are human, in conjunction with a fascination about what they look like. Most important of all, the presentation of various arguments about soldiers

– "They are normal young men dressed up," versus "They aren't human at all" – underscores the natural, but embarrassing, curiosity the civilian population – and particularly the young boys – felt for the occupying forces.

> They spoke of "our" soldiers, of "our boys."
>
> By the time the enemy had moved in "our soldiers" ceased to exist. They had to take off their uniforms, and when a soldier takes off his uniform, and changes into everyday clothes, then he isn't a soldier anymore.
>
> Actually it was one big dress-up party.[34]

Historical accounts of the days following the German attack concur with this description. Upon capitulation, it was to the advantage of Dutch soldiers to change into civilian clothes and head home. If the Dutch soldiers are only soldiers because of what they are wearing, that fact raises crucial issues about identity for the young boys who are participating in or listening to these discussions. Could the boys become soldiers by wearing different clothing? Does that mean that they could behave like military personnel: behave in a brave manner, have authority over others, and perhaps kill someone? In raising these questions, the narrator prepares the reader for passages later on where such issues are more explicitly identified as central to the development of the (male) psyche of survivors of the occupation.

11. School yard: a teacher checks to see if children are carrying around any shells they may have found (1940). (RIOD)

98   Quite apart from the content of the arguments, the mere fact that the civilians watch
and discuss the soldiers with such rapt attention reinforces a sense of community,
which is engendered by and experienced with a newfound poignancy during the war
days. The narrator refers to the use of the plural first-person pronoun: "we".[35]

The boys are fascinated with uniforms: military clothes make the soldier. The SS-
ers, however, are described as soldiers whose status as feared warriors does not wholly depend on their attire.

> There they were, that's what they looked like: gray and dusty. They were wear-
> ing short boots. They were soldiers. Not people. Not dressed-up young men.
> No: soldiers.
>
> I saw it myself, I took a good look at them.[36]

Of course, since the civilian population and the soldiers live in such close proximity,
the child is confronted with some "ethical" issues which he must consider quite seriously. When someone waves at a soldier, he asks: "Was that allowed? Could you just
wave to the enemy? I did not think so. I was shocked."[37] It appears that the little boys
like the war, but find their delight complicated by cultural expectations that one does
not fraternize with the enemy; in their conversations, they show that they have a clear
sense of what is and what is not acceptable:

> As they rode back, the one boy said: "I like war," and he blushed.
>
> Of course he was right, but you can't say something like that. He knew it too,
> or he wouldn't have blushed.[38]

The sense of ideological complexity and ambivalence which arises because the civilian population and the enemy soldiers live in such close proximity and under circumstances which take on an appearance of "normalcy" in the course of time is further complicated by the fact that the soldiers who have moved into the camp seem in
many instances to behave like decent human beings, as normal and likable in their
interactions with the children as they had seemed to the adults. A few anecdotes are
mentioned, such as one in which an SS-er gently plays with a boy and his scooter:
"He did it very carefully, on the toes of his right boot, must have been afraid that he
would make it collapse. The soldiers laughed. That was permitted. Laughing was
allowed in a case like this."[39] A 10-year old child is confused by this scene which
might appear fairly routine to an adult with a better-developed sense of ambiguity:

> I still remember that the ten-year old boy, who watched the tableau, was star-
> tled. It did not add up. How is that possible, how can such a man joke around
> with a child, they were murderers, weren't they? They had skulls on their hats.

Back then he did not know yet that they were not murderers, but obedient soldiers, who were given orders and obeyed them.[40]

The statement with its attendant irony about orders and obedience does not obscure
the problem, but rather serves to intensify it. Children are not known for their ability to entertain moral ambiguity or even subtlety, and this child has been socialized
to believe that members of the SS are "bad guys", dangerous enemies. Yet he is being
confronted with the fact that the adults do not mind that a soldier with a skull on his
cap, an SS-er, would play a gentle game with a young child. Armando takes a well-
known difficult ethical and psychological problem and reduces it to its essential elements.

The fact that the "normally decent" behavior exhibited in this event was found to
be confusing is further reinforced by language incorporated in the chapter entitled
"The enemy". The text offers both sides of the argument concerning the humanity
and, perhaps, "normalcy" of the young soldiers. For example:

They smelled different, they walked differently, they wore different clothing,
they spoke a different language. "That sums it up…"

Yet they were not strangers, they were the enemy; they were enemy soldiers.
That was the deal.[41]

The last sentence offers an explicit reference to the cultural construction of the roles
of enemies which had come to be accepted. Because these roles were taken for granted, the adults could not fully accept the fact – reflected in much of their conversation – that the soldiers were "just" young men; and when they did notice this fact, it
caused great cognitive dissonance. After all, they wore uniforms, so they were the
enemy. This new view is incomprehensible to the narrator:

Now people try to convince us that they were just normal people, young people, but how could we have known that? Once in a while you would hear
someone say: they're just young guys, but you did not pay attention to that.
After all, they were wearing uniforms!

It was the enemy.

I don't understand it at all.[42]

How could the narrator and his friends have known at the time that the enemy was
young men? They were caught between their fascination for the soldiers' way of life
on one hand, and cultural expectations on the other which prescribed how they as
"good" Dutch citizens should behave; that they must reject any overtures by the
enemy. They were expected to hate the soldiers because their enemies were members

of the SS who had occupied the children's nation, and yet the boys found it tempting to watch them closely as potential role models. After all, they were the victors.

SOLDIERS AND CAMP GUARDS, VIEWED WITH AMBIVALENCE

Not many adult readers in the 1980s or thereafter will share the child's difficulty in believing that an enemy soldier could also behave with normal decency toward a child in a non-combat situation. Nevertheless, readers will most likely not take the statement that they were "not murderers, but obedient soldiers", at face value, but will rather recognize the irony in the phrase. By presenting such an obviously innocent example, Armando pushes to an extreme the question the generations after the war have had to ask: how is it that people who were good and decent parents to their own children could behave in such criminal and cruel ways in other situations? Does "following orders" constitute an adequate alibi for one who has committed war crimes? The most extreme example of such questions belongs to the children of camp guards and torturers whose childhood memories tell of wonderfully kind and loving fathers, people who – upon reflection – realize that one oddity of their memories of childhood is that their fathers came home from work with blood on their shoes. If "following orders" does not cover the commission of war crimes, does it perhaps excuse compliance by young men conscripted into their nation's armed forces, even if that nation's goals included the occupation of other nation states? The text, in emphasizing the youth of the soldiers, in recognizing their status as human beings who at times wear uniforms, in presenting scenarios in which these soldiers exhibit positive aspects of normal human behavior, puts in the foreground this important question. The inhabitants of this small town – both adults and children – struggle with the resolution of this problem in their own minds.

The reader may note the fact that the arguments in the text are usually implied rather than clearly articulated. In this feature of its style, Armando's text is true to two aspects of the historical experience of the occupation. First, it is a fact that in informal conversation, people tend not to discuss important matters by employing propositional logic, but rather by implication and innuendo, and while claiming – or assuming – the veracity of assumptions they simply accept as common or even universal without actual proof. Secondly, the implied or unfounded element of the arguments reported in the text reflects the reality of life during the occupation when dissent with the occupation forces was dangerous. Explicit dissent was subject to severe punishment; further, one rarely knew whom one could trust because individuals were encouraged to report criticism of the regime to the authorities.

The ten-year-old goes home, tells the story of the soldier playing with the child, and raises the obvious question: how is it possible that an enemy can behave in a friendly manner? His parents explain that the two things are not incompatible. The reader must recognize, however, that the child's expectations reflect what he has (over)heard; if he expects the soldier to be cruel, it is because he has been taught to fear enemy soldiers, especially SS-ers.[43]

While the boys may have been taught to and certainly do fear the enemy soldiers, it has already become clear that they are also fascinated by them. One of a number of activities in which the soldiers engage and which interest the children, is their singing. The soldiers sing as soldiers are wont to do. The adults dislike this singing, and their distaste is described in language which exposes the traits perceived as "German" which are most commonly disliked by the Dutch:

> And the enemy sang. They sang constantly... Sometimes you heard them far away...

> No matter how brief the snatch was, I recognized it immediately: it was their language, it was their sound.

> "Hideous, that singing of theirs. So loud. And those truncated sentences. Terrible."

> The boys did like it, even though they hated to, they had to admit that they liked it, they admitted openly that it was beautiful.[44]

The attitude of the boys to the soldiers' singing, which they had initially adopted from their elders, has worn thin; they have experienced a change of heart in this respect. Of course, the adults found the loud singing – in the hated foreign language – unpleasant, just as they found the "clipped tones" of the spoken language to be a sign of the barbarism of the enemy. The text reflects a shift in the boys' attitude: it first echoes the received wisdom, touches on the cultural barriers which must be overcome before such admissions can be made, and describes the new consensus – the boys later come to admit that they like the singing.

As this and other parts of the text show clearly, the war and subsequent occupation form a watershed in the memories of the narrator and his friends, i.e. the civilian population of the area around the camp.

Memory is infused with a sense of "hindsight" – the sense that the perceived meaning or interpretation of events changes in light of their context. In retrospect, a person's life and the town's history is divided into "after the war" versus "a point when the war was yet to begin". The latter may sound unexpected, but it is a fair index of how important the war proved for a person's life and for that of the community. Thus one hears different voices in the text say: "The war had not come yet, this was just before the war came. Something might happen any minute now." Or: "Whatever happened to that man: the war had not yet started. You don't know, do you."[45] This theme of anticipation in retrospect is repeated – sometimes with an even stronger sense of eagerness associated with it. It is as if people were sitting around waiting for "the attack and occupation and show of strength".[46] The words "show of strength" reinforce the suggestion of a creeping, though reluctant, respect for the superior military strength of the foreign occupation force.

The text emphasizes the informal communality which arises between the soldiers and civilians and the normalcy of everyday contact between the enemy and the population.

> The streets were paved. There was a pavement. You could walk there. The enemy walked there too. But what do you mean by that. Well, that you ran into each other.

> "Greetings, dear enemy."[47]

In a manner so indirect as to seduce the reader to face facts, this passage indirectly raises many issues connected with the position of the bystander: if you had walked on the same streets as the occupying forces, would or should you have resisted, or would you – by force of habit – have come to see their presence as a normal part of daily reality?

During the occupation, soldiers take possession of the land on which the boys used to play, and build barracks on it, so that it becomes "the camp" (that is, the camp known as "Amersfoort").[48] The boys' favorite climbing tree is no longer accessible to them and the landscape is ruined by its association with the terrible acts which take place there.

The language of the text effectively represents this sense of defilement. Just as one uses the term "bystander" to refer to members of the population of an occupied country who did not agree with the measures taken by the Nazis but did not resist them either, so in Armando's text the landscape is quite literally presented as a bystander. Speaking of the place, in a section entitled "Ter plekke", "On the spot", the narrator refers to the boys' favorite climbing tree and the place where it grew.

> A year later it was no longer possible. There was barbed wire around this area. It was a camp. It was *the* camp. One spoke of "the camp".

> The tree was in the camp.

> Gave a lot of thought to the tree while the camp was there. What a lot that tree must have had to see.

> When there was no longer a camp there, I quickly went to check if the tree was still there. The tree was no longer there. No trace left of the tree.[49]

> However, there was another tree. "It is still there. What happened to that other tree?"[50]

Armando creates the trees[51] to reflect or stand for the realities of the history of the Dutch population – some of whom remained, while others perished. It is standard practice in the postwar period that those human beings who survived find themselves interrogated by their own consciences: What did you see? What did you tolerate in order to survive? Armando's text will surprise many readers by raising such questions with reference to trees: What did the trees see? What did they tolerate in order to survive? Later on, the narrator raises the ante: the reader was not wrong to see a parallel between trees and people. In fact, the bystander tree is guiltier than previously thought. Armando is a master at showing how small the differences between the "good guys" and the bad ("*fout*") ones are. Here the narrator shows the reader exactly how slippery the slope can be for bystanders:

> They often speak so condescendingly of the people who put themselves in the service of the enemy. Fine, but what do you think of the pine and spruce trees, which completely submitted and still submit to any old enemy. Look at the depictions in which the enemy is at work: there they stand, the trees, they are standing in the background, laughing. And not just the pine and spruce trees, the other trees too.

> Shouldn't someone say something about that?[52]

> I should think so, for in some cases they are still standing there, the trees, the edge of the forest and the trees, on the same spot where they used to stand; don't think that they moved away to go stand elsewhere, they are still standing there like uninterested witnesses. I examine them, I look at them, and then something nasty happens: they are beautiful, I find them beautiful.[53]

Some readers may wish to find fault with Armando's text at this point on two grounds. First, the insight that many bystanders are ethically not much better than actual petty collaborators (and therefore the clear distinctions commonly made during and right after the war between "goed" and "fout" are spurious) is hardly new. Secondly, one might judge the narrator's finding fault with trees for not having moved during or following the abominations they observed to strain the analogy or to be unfair: Unlike human beings, trees cannot walk away. But even while crystallizing the objection, the reader recognizes that perhaps many people are or *were* tree-like in some cases: getting up and moving out of the way of evil may be costly and difficult, even for human beings who are (presumably) capable of purposeful mobility. And intervening in order to attempt to thwart evil is even more difficult and much more dangerous, as it involves hideous moral dilemmas.

One of the striking issues one confronts when reading this text is the offense against common sense of walking trees: clearly, Armando is not playing with trees as symbols here, but rather with what we expect trees to do. Everyone knows that a tree cannot get up and move. So what advantages does this method offer? What does this use of language allow him to get at that is inaccessible to the authors of the other novels "about the war" which I have mentioned – novels with plausible plots and realistic characters? The advantage of Armando's approach over the techniques used in those other novels is that he problematizes language in such a way that he is free to bracket the reader's "common-sense" assumptions about the world. Armando's narrative strategy is to show landscape as history, and to use language to do so: the most basic fact about Armando's landscape is that it shows us how the world changes because of the way the narrator has observed and described it. (Nice scenery. – Don't climb that tree – the camp used to be there. – I ought not to like that spot after all. Sure is beautiful though!)

In his writing on Armando, R.L.K. Fokkema adopts Charles Sanders Peirce's semiotic schema, wherein one distinguishes three different types of signs or semiotic relationships: iconic, indexical and symbolic signs. Ernst van Alphen[54] takes issue with Fokkema's interpretation and argues that the semiotic relationship Armando uses (e.g., in the connection between trees and the history of the place where they grew during the war) is indexical – the most salient aspect of this relationship is contiguity. The trees were present, were adjacent to the events that occurred, they were "there". If Van Alphen is right, the meaning Armando imputes to the trees (which were on the spot during the atrocities which occurred in the camp) is similar to the reason visitors to the Holocaust Memorial Museum find it particularly poignant to view a large pile of shoes taken from extermination camps. The shoes derive their meaning from the realization of the visitor to the museum that they are the very shoes which Holocaust victims wore and in which they walked until their deaths. While the size of the pile is also significant as a visual representation of the number of victims killed, it is only relevant because the principle of contiguity provides significance to the shoes. Just as the piles of shoes are important primarily because they had once been on the feet of Holocaust victims, so Armando's trees are worth attending to because they are the very trees which "witnessed" the atrocities in the camp.

There are differences between the two symbols, however. One distinction which is of primary significance concerns the notion of the symbol as a static object. The shoes, never worn again after their owners were killed, will not change. They thus remain as stable evidence of or witnesses to the events of the past. Their static quality serves to help visitors remember.

As living things, the trees do change – and in the process erase the traces of the atrocities. In the text, Armando loudly bewails this fact and accuses the trees of inconstancy.

As living beings which change and grow, however, the trees can symbolically represent the experiences and the anxiety of the survivor who needs to grieve, later let go, and eventually in some sense move on – though without forgetting or giving up on the memory of the victims – in order to avoid becoming a strange parody of a perpetrator herself.

We often use inanimate objects such as relics, photographs, and other personal items to help us remember the departed. Such objects have the advantage of being (somewhat)[55] immutable, holding out the promise that the dead, or the events in question, will be remembered. The static quality of these immutable objects and their very resistance to change seems by analogy to demand that the survivor remain equally unchanged, thus reinforcing a natural but unhealthy tendency among survivors to feel and act as if they had become frozen in time. Such a response is neither possible nor desirable.

While Armando's trees in their non-specificity have some disadvantages as symbols for victims, they provide a more useful function as signs of the survivors or bystanders. Survivors who wish to grieve or express their sorrow or regret, or even apologize for not having saved more victims, might wish to do so by remaining on the scene of the crime, by not changing. However, remaining or remaining unchanged is not possible. The moment has passed, life and time go on. What is left, what forms the connection between the present and the past, is memory.

THE PERIL OF BEAUTY

At the point where the reader sees the words "they are still standing there like uninterested witnesses", which indict the rooted, unmoving trees, the narrator is explicitly present, and his gaze precipitates the discovery of a terrible fact: he finds them beautiful. The recognition of this fact cuts him to the quick – if the narrator places harsh requirements on the trees, he treats himself equally sternly. Here the narrator is indicted for recognizing beauty in nature, and consistency requires him to accept that if one wishes to be strict with collaborators, then some bystanders may also be guilty, and if bystanders are not free from responsibility, then the narrator's aesthetic impulse is suspect as well. The text does not go easy on beauty:

Beauty ought to be ashamed of itself.

Especially the beauty of the places where the enemy perished. Beauty is so crazed it doesn't know what to do. Beauty has been thrown off balance.[56]

Note that the narrator specifies the beauty of the spot where the enemy perished rather than a more conventional place of mourning – the place where the victims died. The normal dichotomy is between enemy or perpetrator and victim (such as Jew or other Holocaust victim, Resistance fighter, or bereaved family member of same, or member of the silent majority of the occupied population). Thus, while this passage can be read as an allusion to Adorno's dictum, he reinvigorates and expands the message.

In the context of a culture which has for centuries admired beauty for its own sake, Armando proclaims the shame of beauty: the word has lost its meaning. The loss of innocence in the landscape mirrors the effect on language of the occupation and the Holocaust. It is a truism in the postwar period that certain expressions have been forever tainted and thus can no longer be used; after Auschwitz, poetry is problematic. Is this because the poet's pursuit of the aesthetic qualities of poetry henceforth embodies a beauty which is an affront to the memory of the murdered, or is it because language itself has been corrupted, has become suspect? "Street and Foliage" allows for both readings. In Armando's text, the landscape which "hosted" the atrocities of the occupation during World War II is a landscape which is thus always occupied and bears a responsibility for the horrendous events which it has witnessed. And the language which was involved in allowing history to reach the point where such atrocities could occur is fundamentally complicit. Influence functions in two directions at once. Since it is impossible to function without that language, it is interesting to follow along as the text investigates what the language used says about those who speak as well as about its effect on them.

> The beauty of the places where the enemy was, where the enemy was located, where the enemy lived and ran amok, where the enemy conducted his reign of terror, and where the traces of the enemy's reign of terror are still present. There of all places.[57]

> I have said it before and again and again, but I can't repeat it enough: beauty is worthless, beauty doesn't care about anything.[58]

Beauty is useless because its presence is irrelevant in ethical situations. The beauty of nature does not disappear in a place where horrendous crimes are committed, and its persistence mocks the narrator's sense of justice and decency. The expectation that natural beauty be associated with goodness leads to the narrator's disappointment that the trees did not move away when an offense against nature occurred. While commenting earlier on the narrator's anger at trees which had not moved away in response to the atrocities they had witnessed among themselves, I alluded to the concept of "fairness", the knowledge that it is a good deal more difficult for trees to move than it is for human beings. Knowing that not many human beings were able to respond in any significant way to the crimes perpetrated among them, how can one expect trees to take action?

The effect of this comparison implicit in the text is to create a mental or emotional space in which the reader is invited to consider the ethical implications of evil for the bystander. In light of this passage about beauty, a central aspect of the narrator's view of trees comes to light. Trees, as part of nature, are associated not just with humans, but with beauty as well, and beauty is often assumed to be related to goodness. This text sets up the facile correlation as a trap, and then explodes it: why do we feel that evil cannot (have) occur(red) in a beautiful place? Would that be equivalent to assuming that enemy soldiers, SS-ers, cannot be friendly to a child? Apparently, beauty cannot be used as an index for goodness. The narrator, an artist, now professes shock – beauty is suspect.

> There is really something going on with beauty, it can't be denied. It must be clear that beauty is no good. But here's the rub: I have dedicated my life to beauty itself. I am in thrall to it. I serve it.

If "beauty is no good", and the narrator is an artist who supposedly serves beauty, then that raises the difficult question of complicity. Art is often presumed to give succor where interaction with other humans cannot, but it is now clear that art cannot be the answer. Nature, another traditional source of comfort, is not what the narrator had hitherto assumed: nature is implicated in violence. And then comes the step where the pretenses are peeled away, and one can recognize the aesthetics of violence which underlies the whole. The reason nature is beautiful is because of its relationship with violence.

AN AESTHETICS OF VIOLENCE

> Where can you find comfort? Not with others, you seem to have ruined that for yourself. Where else, then. [60] If not with other people, then with what they have made: art. Sometimes you can find comfort in nature. Nature looks peaceful, but isn't. That's why nature is very beautiful.

> But is comfort really necessary? Can't you do without it?[61]

Armando's depictions of the soldiers, the children and the landscape together function to challenge traditional assumptions about innocence and guilt. Just as the silent landscape is guilty, so the ferocious enemy does not fit the stereotype: in a passage of "Street and Foliage", to the outrage of the people of the town near the camp one of the "enemies" is friendly to a local child. When the enemies take off their uniforms, they are just naked men. Armando subtly identifies a generational difference among the Dutch civilian population in the way the soldiers are perceived: when the enemies march around singing, the adults find this barbaric, but the little boys enjoy and admire the spectacle. The little boys form a connection between the two worlds: the world of violence, aggression, and enmity on the one hand, and the normal, quiet, innocuous world of the bystanders on the other. The connection presented in this text is mediated through the memory of language, in that it can only be recognized when one pays careful attention to the language, even the vocabulary, used in the acts of speech isolated and presented by this text.

In their play, the local boys mirror the violence which takes place in the camp. They are enamored with knives; they lovingly repeat a rumor that German children have truly wonderful knives, with a groove for the blood in the blade. This kind of talk reinforces the notion of Germany as a combative culture – more brutal than that of the Dutch bystander – which prepares even young children to fight effectively. By contrast, the Dutch seem to themselves to be mild-mannered; even the Dutch armed forces had not been able to put up much of a fight when the Germans attacked, so that the implied comparison becomes one between German children and the Dutch military, with the German children "winning" this imaginary contest, proving themselves braver, better prepared for battle by the sheer fact that they possess better and more serious knives. This segment of the text thus intensifies the impression created by the tale discussed earlier of the Dutch officer who so foolishly let a German talk him into returning his weapon, and paid for his trust in a shared code of honor – be it military or personal – with his life and the lives of his compatriots. In the passage where the boys talk about German children's knives, Armando sets their language aside and plays it back, in order that one may hear it clearly, thus questioning the assumption of Dutch innocence, even that of children. The reader sees the seeds of the same aggression which is at the heart of the war in these presumably innocent children.

The notion of innocence is further qualified when the child-narrator confesses to the reader that he killed one of the "enemies", then hid his knife, and continued his life for decades without ever being suspected. Thus any simplistically clear distinctions between enemies and innocent victims are undermined, and the dangers lurking in the banality of language and landscape are exposed. It is particularly interesting that a number of readers have taken the story of the murder to be (possibly) autobiographical, and even more significant that in interviews where he is asked about this tale, Armando has consistently taken a deliberately ambiguous position ("implausible deniabilty"). He implies that he did not do it while very purposefully leaving open the possibility that he might have done so. (Or vice versa.)[62] In fact, he gives at best a psychological alibi, but does not even follow through on it. If trees are faulted for not having walked away, the important fact for Armando's reader is that he or the narrator of "Street and Foliage" or some other character in the novel could have killed the soldier in the way described. He had a sharp knife. He had been taught to hate the enemy. He had come to assume it was his right to defend himself. He had absorbed the notion of heroic deeds and admired German children for their skill at warlike behavior. Thus, it is possible that the act of killing might have come naturally to him. The ambiguity Armando preserves by not definitively identifying the perpetrator mirrors the effect of the functions of language and landscape in the text as a whole: Soldiers may be nice guys. Trees may be guilty. The perpetrator might have been anyone. The hero might have been anyone. The slope of culpability is more slippery than we often realize; language contains within itself the seeds of indeterminacy, and the landscape may change even as I attempt to describe it.

HISTORY'S TRACES

A similar problem pertains when the narrator looks back upon history and attempts to give an accounting of what its connection is to the present. The context for Armando's discussion is a passage in which the narrator wonders what happens to old clothing. In essence, it is a question about the trace of history: after a period of time or a specific event passes, what is left of it? What happens to events after they occur? Do they leave a trace? They appear not to: things wear out, they decay, they dissolve.

The narrator voices his disapproval of this state of affairs, of the way material history fades. If the physical artifacts which were present at a historic event simply disappear afterwards, this leaves the human survivors in an awkward position. Has the reality of the past faded with the dissolution of these objects? What difficulties does such a view pose for those whose lives have inexorably been changed by their experiences with these historical conditions? And if the material trappings of those days have already worn away, is it surprising or inappropriate that the memories have not?

> How were those people dressed, those people who sat in those carriages? I wonder what happened to those clothes? What happens to something like that. Does anything ever remain? Very little, I would think. It wears out, it dissolves. I don't always approve of that.[63]

The narrator has in his possession a significant object which constitutes a trace by which to remember his father.

> The father's notebook with the addresses of his friends from back then. They had once laughed and talked; do you still remember so-and-so: that kind of conversation.[64]

The book contains a record of friends' names and addresses which remind the narrator of the relationships the father had with other people – their laughter, conversation and reminiscing. Memory is a central factor in relationships:[65] These apparently innocent events which can be remembered provide a foil to the boy's memories of a favorite climbing tree which became a memorial to the atrocities which occurred in the camp.

The sense of the disruption caused by the war is reinforced by references to the weather which remind the reader that the pathetic fallacy does not pertain: although there is a war on, nevertheless the weather is beautiful – something which some memoirs of World War II mention as well.

> The father called to the mother, his wife: it's war.

> There was a man standing around on the street who was yelling "It's war." Yet it was lovely weather.[66]

The word "yet" in the last sentence serves to underscore the character's sense of surprise at the incongruity between the radical change which his world had undergone with the onset of the war and good weather, which seemed unthinkable under the circumstances. Brakman presents a sense of unreality as typical of the experience of the early days of the war:

> When I reflect on the war, two important aspects stand out. First, I consider it very important that that time was so unreal [irreëel]. When I look at myself

off in the distance walking around in that war, it is hard to realize: that's me. Another fact which occurs to me is a sense of shame.[67]

Whereas the weather is remembered as having been so consistently fine as to seem out of sync with reality, the conquest resulted in many other more typical visible signs: "Items of clothing, (human) limbs, papers. Junk." which are promptly cleaned up "and everything looked as if nothing had happened."[68] The scraps which remind the citizens of the war and which symbolize the memories of the invasion are quickly swept up after the occupation becomes a fact. After the war, the traces which have been so quickly erased will turn out not to have disappeared completely. The memory of rags, parts of bodies and other trash on the street must return in some way to haunt the narrator – or else one would not read about them in this text. But at times, it was "too easy" – shockingly possible – to forget the fact that the occupation had begun, even for those who lived through it. Normalcy eventually set in:

> Something has happened. Something has happened – what was it. Oh, yes, the enemy is here. I'm going to look at him again today.[69]

The confusion of the population is aptly illustrated, as is the potential moral ambiguity and the invitation to be a bystander which result from it. This is embodied in a quote which describes this lack of immediate recognition of the change which has occurred:

> The occupier was already there. I was walking along a quiet road, near what would be the camp a month later, the camp.[70]

Armando positions the reader as a citizen of the occupied country. One does not stop going out and walking around because the "occupier" is present, and (the text implies) one is thus implicitly getting ready to also accept the next "steps" – the building of a camp nearby and impromptu meetings with soldiers along the road. The italics provide the emphasis on what interests Armando in such passages: the language and vocabulary which represents the concepts which constitute the world experienced during the occupation, or (more specifically) the world remembered years later.

ROUGH TRANSITIONS

The language of this text also illustrates the difficulty experienced by those who must attempt to adjust to the sudden change in their environment engendered by the occupation. As an illustration of this difficulty, the narrator recalls the familiar game often played by children in which a word is repeated out loud again and again until it sounds funny:

– War, I think it's such a weird word, war, war, war, war, if you say it often, it
becomes even stranger, don't you think?

– Well, you get used to it.[71]

In its ambiguity (does the phrase refer to the odd-sounding word "war" or to life during the occupation?), the laconic comment: "Well, you get used to it", reminds the
reader that the populace adjusts to the new circumstances to a certain extent. After a
brief burst of excitement, life returns to some semblance of normalcy for many, and
most Dutch citizens attempt to live quietly and stay out of trouble. During the occupation, the initial assumption that the Germans would soon lose the war and the later
realization that the occupation would last for a very long time each in turn contributed to a general acceptance by degrees of the need to adjust to the new regime.

After the adjustment to the occupation, the transition to peace will in turn prove
challenging.[72] The text emphasizes that peacetime means that changes must be made
all over again. This is particularly difficult for a "child of the war" – someone young
enough not to remember the prewar period clearly; the adults' easy judgments about
those who behaved either well or incorrectly during the occupation were unexpected
and seemed inappropriate to the child who had seen the ambiguities firsthand.

I really had to get used to peace. All that chatter about good and bad, about
black and white.[73]

One can envision a number of reasons why a transition from the occupation to peacetime might be stressful for a child. First, after five years, the psychosocial environment experienced during the occupation would seem normal to the child. Secondly,
in the sentences quoted here, the child narrator expresses a dislike for the adults' habit
of categorizing people as being "good" (Resistance fighters) or "bad" (collaborators,
members of the National Socialist Party) based on factors which the child may not
understand and may have instinctively come to recognize as questionable, if not arbitrary. The young narrator's experience has shown him the complications – reflected
in passages discussed above – of attempting to evaluate others along unambiguous
parameters during wartime, and taught him to distrust choices offered in black-and-
white terms. This sophistication is reflected in a discussion in which certain perpetrators are referred to as inhuman(e), which the narrator counters with his view based
on more direct experience: "It is *because* they are human that they were capable of
doing such [terrible] things."[74]

Another voice presented to the reader questions the tendency of the populace to
appropriate the meaning of the war for one's own purposes. It asks: "Does the war
really belong to you?"[75] The text elaborates on this theme throughout the work, later
issuing in a rhetorical question which calls attention to the longevity of the psychosocial effects or social "meaning" of the occupation: "So, don't you know that the
war has been over for a long time?"[76] This text signals and addresses various issues
concerning the long-term effects of surviving the occupation on the individual and

society. As noted above, survivors of the war were forced to make painful adjustments to their expectations at the start of the occupation. But in the case of the "children of the war" it is the transition from the occupation to peacetime which is especially difficult. These experiences and difficult adjustments deeply influenced the generations which survived the war. They left their stamp on their world view, their politics, and their personal ethics. In addition, the experiences caused these generations to share a profound sense of cohesion which set them apart from those who came after them, those who had not "experienced the war".

And there are people who did not experience the war because they were born after the war had ended. There are more and more of that sort. They have to

12. Dutch children enjoying a snowball fight with U.S. officers. (RIOD)

be rebuked. They need to be watched, for it is now their turn to plan the bat-
tles of the future. Yes, it does keep you busy. [77]

The experience of the occupation comes to be viewed as a basic formative event, essential for the crystallization of opinions and the development of values which make individuals into participants in the community's identity – without which one cannot understand survivors or be a full-fledged member of society. Since the shared experience of the occupation created a sense of cohesion (be it an illusion or not), those who survived this experience were tempted not to trust those who had not. This dynamic is illustrated by the fate of others, such as Dutch citizens repatriated from Indonesia after the war, who were frequently isolated and alienated from Dutch society. Although they had also suffered greatly, these survivors and children of the war from the East did not gain the acceptance they had hoped for from the people who had survived the war on Dutch soil.[78]

PLACES

After the end of the war, the child of the war who will be the narrator of this text begins a process which involves sorting, absorbing and integrating memories of what happened and how – and why – the adults responded to those occurrences during and after the occupation. The text suggests that clarity and understanding are achieved only after a period of time: "No, I did not understand his uneasiness and his aversion. I could not understand them yet back then."[79] The text underscores the fact that coming to terms with wartime occurrences is an active process. The narrator reports going to view places which he considers significant in his experience: a "re"-visiting of his experiences from a different perspective – that of a tourist or archaeologist. Essentially, his travel is a form of memory-work, just as purposive, investigative "travel" around Amsterdam was for Jeroen, the protagonist of *For a Lost Soldier*.[80]

> Heard a countless number of voices during the war. Including voices which the occupier did not want people to hear, voices from across the sea.

> Later I went and looked at the spot where those voices came from, from which rooms, from which little rooms.[81]

Note that the narrator's quest to visit the site in London from which Radio Orange was broadcast is not just physical or geographical, but a journey into memory. It is a journey that simultaneously connects to and has implications for, the future:

> So. This is it. From here they spoke to us.

> But what next? How are we supposed to go on from here? Do I really need to go on? Hasn't this been enough?

The memories. Memories with almost nothing to them, and yet they make your head buzz.[82]

The point of memory-work is to resolve issues in the past in order to loosen their grasp on the individual so that one can be free of them in the present and the future. This process allows one to answer the question "Should I go on? Hasn't this been enough?" in such a way that the present and future become possible and are not determined by unresolved experiences of the past.

The complexity of sorting out the continuity or discontinuity of history and place is variously represented in this text. It is clear from the discussion above that the narrative creates an ample space to accommodate the requirements of memory-work, a process intended to eventually release the hold of destructive memories. The survivor's relationship to the physical space where the atrocities occurred necessarily differs from that of the subjective interior. The choice between continuity and discontinuity here may be resolved in another way – by the traditional cultural practice of making memorials on or of places where significant good or evil events have occurred.

The narrator in this passage is stating his opposition to the decision to build a new subdivision on the site of the former camp:

I don't think they have any right to be there, but they are of the opinion that they live there.

Buildings have been built there. They should not do that. They ought to leave it the way it was. I don't think it looks nice the way it is now.[83]

And the present? It does not exist. It will appear later in the shape of the past. It will disguise itself as the past. You'd better watch out.[84]

"I am a survivor," said the man, "I am so ashamed, I could die."[85]

At a certain point in the narrative, the narrator states explicitly that the time has come to examine the place where the atrocities occurred. The stated goal for this exercise is to draw a connection from the physical site to those things which had happened in that place in the past. But such a research project is deemed to be senseless. The reason: the physical place has been altered, and thus cannot be examined for traces of the past. One might ask why, since the traces of the past reside in memory/human emotion, what difference it really makes whether the pavement is still made up of the very same stones or bricks or not. It is not as if the narrator were suggesting that they look for blood on the stones; they were looking at them in order to be able to talk about their memories of what had happened on the surface formed by those stones. If so, the question presents itself as to whether the attempt to remember really requires the literal presence of exactly the same stones as had been there during the occupation, or whether some of the memories can become available without them.

Then comes the surprising move: the narrator announces that the paving stones have been replaced. As with the guilty trees already discussed, the responsibility for their removal is assigned to the stones themselves. They were impatient. Apparently, the stones did not stick around long enough to participate in the memory-work. Do they stand for human beings who wish to move on too swiftly or want to get on with their lives without looking back?

James E. Young offers a thorough analysis of the consequences of the fact that most (Holocaust) memorials are immutable; Armando's changeable place of memory has the advantage that thought and memory are explicitly required in order for the narrator to hold on to the meaning of the place: "In this age of mass memory production and consumption, in fact, there seems to be an inverse proportion between the memorialization of the past and its contemplation and study. For once we assign monumental form to memory, we have to some degree divested ourselves of the obligation to remember. In shouldering the memory-work, monuments may relieve viewers of their memory burden... To the extent that we encourage monuments to do our memory-work for us we become that much more forgetful. In effect, the initial impulse to memorialize events like the Holocaust *may actually spring from an opposite and equal desire to forget them.*" [my emphasis][86] As Young argues, there are distinct advantages to immutable memorials. Armando's place of memory is mutable. It has not been officially designated a shrine. The uses to which the land, the *place*, were put will be remembered only as long as they are, well, remembered. A text such as Armando's promotes and allows the process of memory to take place. Even a reader who did not know the place firsthand when it was a camp can now consider what happened there and why. Whereas, as Young argues, a monument might have the opposite effect of what it is generally thought to do: to permit forgetting. Since Armando's text, on the other hand, induces the process of reflection, it stimulates remembering, and encourages the reader to consider the causes of wartime events.

> It's about time to look at the paving bricks and the clinkers,[87] to examine every spot in order to be able to say: look, this woman walked here, so-and-so walked here and over there such-and-such occurred.

> Such an investigation is senseless.

> The paving bricks and the clinkers are no longer there, they have been replaced, they have disappeared. Something else has been laid[88] there now.

> They were rather impatient, the paving bricks and the clinkers.

> I love it the way it was, and not as it is. This is an aberration.[89]

The simple image of a stretch of pavement which has been redone illustrates the passage of time and its effacing of the traces of the past, the fact that the past cannot always be revisited. It expresses skepticism about the ability of the community and culture to properly deal with the past. The text also issues a warning about the difficulty of living in the present if the past has not been dealt with:

> So how can you be happy if you're living in the present. What good is the present. It's to be hoped that the present will be over soon.[90]

This passage also illustrates the generous and witty use of rhetorical questions which Armando makes in this text. The frequent omission of question marks, a signal feature of Armando's style, reinforces the illusion created by the non-literary style of this text, a reminder that this is intended to appear to be a "found text", a text which gains its credibility from the impression that it reflects spontaneous speech by "regular folks". As a ready-made, a found textual "object", the text takes on an aura of authenticity, it constitutes a plumb line of informal convention, the "common-sense view" assumed to be typical of the culture.

The complicated issues of continuity/discontinuity before and after the occupation are further problematized in a series of propositions regarding the meaning of physical space and its role in human experience through its relationship to time and memory. On one level, what is at issue is the question of qualities which adhere to the physical place which are remembered by the narrator upon his return. In the case of someone's first visit to that place, the narrator notes that the physical surroundings and their apparent meaning would necessarily be taken at face value. A visitor would have no experience with which to compare it and thus it would have to seem acceptable. A first-time visitor would likewise not know what to expect of the site and would not be able to distinguish between various traces of various pasts and would not therefore be struck by any incongruity between past experiences and the appearance of the site in the present. Therefore, the real issue becomes the problem of memory – a quality which resides in the human observer who bears within memories of what it used to be like.

> You would do better not to return.

> It would be better if you did not know what this place looked like, what it was like. The worst possible thing is to know what it was like. When you go to a place for the first time, you don't know any better. If you don't know what it was like, this place looks pretty good. But if you know what it was like, you won't like it one bit. I don't like it at all, because I know what it was like, what it looked like. That's the disadvantage of getting a little older. It's better not to.[91]

This conflict between the present and past reality influences and complicates one's view of the present situation and sometimes ruins it. Either the present is sufficient (if disappointing) in comparison to the past, or the present is tainted by association with a past which occurred in the same place: "Don't you know that the war has already been over for a long time?"[92] The incongruity sensed by the narrator is between the narrator's memory of aspects of the landscape on one hand and, on the other, the way the landscape presents itself to him in its postwar guise. Thus, the landscapes and individual features thereof are associated with guilt for the crimes perpetrated on its canvas, a background which is thought to bear a trace of these bad/ "fout" deeds; it functioned as a bystander, as it observed the deeds while they occurred, but did not prevent them from happening.

Even worse, the landscape is doubly guilty not only because it is a witness to atrocities, but also because it subsequently erases the traces of these events in the processes of growth and decay which are part of its "natural" cycles. Thus for Armando, the landscape is implicated just as language may be said to be. The text is not "just" an aesthetic object or event: it is also a means by which one can examine the language which, like the landscape, bears the marks of aggression, but also erases the traces of the violence which once took place, and still continues to.

So "Street and Foliage" demonstrates thematic concerns similar to the fictional works discussed in earlier chapters with protagonists who are children-as-victims. As do the other texts, "Street and Foliage" convincingly shows that children of the war are forever marked by their early experiences; it displays the world of their youth and the psychosocial standard which it set for them, and which they felt compelled to reject wholesale at the start of the postwar era. Only much later did it become clear that one cannot simply "turn off" the experiences of childhood and the generalized expectations for life based on them. It is also difficult for outsiders to understand the seductive pull which led to some of the choices made by bystanders in the occupation. One of the strengths of Armando's text is first, that it paints such a vivid picture of the world of the child bystander that one born later can more easily recognize its deceptive lure. Secondly, in presenting the temptations of the past, Armando's text shows them accurately and cannily in such a way that parallels to the present repeatedly present themselves. The reader is invited to recognize that persons and human culture have not essentially changed, that our language still socializes us in dangerous ways and gives us away, exposing our fecklessness, our lack of defense against the evils of a cleverly devised hideous dilemma.

Armando moves toward explicit honesty about the role and emotions of children raised in World War II, who see soldiers and admire them, who have experienced the cognitive dissonance between ideologies expressed by the adults and what the children experienced first-hand. This same topic is addressed tangentially in *The Assault*. At approximately the moment when Anton's parents are being shot, he is enjoying his very first ride in an automobile, and shortly thereafter, he is transported in a truck and on a motorcycle, exciting events in his young life. The lure of the slightest of collaborations – not consciously or even freely chosen, yet so seductive – is clear. In contrast, the other option chosen by Dutch citizens is exemplified by his uncle who, having come to pick up the boy and take him home with him, leaves behind the warm

German military coat he had been given. His goal is to hurry to take the boy home, leaving the German post as soon as possible.

Van Dantzig's text also illustrates the danger of being seduced by the superior possessions and technical expertise of the military: Jeroen, the main character in *For a Lost Soldier,* also is privileged to ride in a car and expects to enjoy the reflected glory of being with a soldier in a military vehicle – except, of course, that his relationship with the soldier is illicit and therefore he will never be able to boast of it. The fact that "his" soldier belongs to the Allies, not the enemy, does not help his cause. His dilemma becomes clear in the ironic scene with the teacher who thinks he does not appreciate the importance of the liberation because he cannot write a superficial essay, a hagiography of the soldiers, glorifying it. The theme is repeated in the other bitterly ironic scenes of the liberation feasts in Amsterdam where the women are throwing themselves at the American and Canadian soldiers and the boy protagonist is unable to take his place and enjoy what he thought should have been his moment of triumph.

Minco's text *The Glass Bridge* presents a wiser protagonist. Several minor characters, members of her family, however, allow themselves to be taken in by false promises – in this case, illusions of safety in exchange for small acts of collusion or merely a lack of resistance, rather than adventure or fame – and lose their lives. It is not the intent here to assign responsibility to such persons or characters for their own deaths; there is no guarantee that different choices on their part would have saved their lives. On the other hand, in hindsight it is painfully clear that their willingness to cooperate with the occupation's policies only made the killers' job easier.

Armando's text echoes all the concerns alluded to in the other, more traditionally novelistic treatments featured in previous chapters, but in attending to the specifics of language as an (archaeological) index and vehicle of cultural constructs, it allows for a more thoroughgoing critique while avoiding the pitfall of simplification. If the reader does not have a clear sense of how one should have acted during the occupation at the end of Armando's text, this is in part due to the author's refusal to reduce the complexities of the excruciating ethical dilemmas faced in that period to a simple calculus of good or bad, "goed" versus "fout."

The questions concerning memory addressed in this text are investigated in the historical and fictional landscape. Two of the central elements in this landscape on which the narrative focuses are trees and paving stones. Both trees and stones have a relationship of contiguity with the atrocities which occurred in and around the camp during the occupation; both trees and the pavement were present when people were imprisoned, mistreated, and – in some cases – killed. Of course they were also present when a German soldier (an SS-er) treated a small Dutch boy with common decency. They were also present when another soldier observed by the young narrator rode his motorcycle in a tight circle for the sheer joy of it. They were also present when the soldiers marched and sang and changed their clothes (looking vulnerable and "normal" after removing their uniforms) and went swimming.

Thus, Armando's work may be viewed as presenting an archaeology of language, which focuses the reader's attention on the cultural memory of the occupation, which is embedded and reflected in language, just as language in turn influences the memories held by various groups which make up the populace and influences the meaning we attribute to such memories.

It then becomes possible to look at the language used to recall or expose the memory, and the events of which the memory exists. Also, as one examines the memory, the language is a clue to emotional and ethical aspects of the memory; one should pay attention not only to the things people say, but also to the way in which they say them, the language in which the thoughts are couched. Upon careful excavation, one can expose buried memory, just as certain rocks can bear the imprint of prehistoric organisms. It is on this evidence that we can know them, so that the language people use or used during a certain time can tell us what people used to think and assume, and allow us to gain an understanding of what their attitudes were, and how these attitudes and cultural values affected their historical experiences, the memories of the same, and the way in which people lived with their memories. We may know these things with this difference: that the language, with its imprint of formerly held views, in turn stamps impressions on the present, and thus – if left unexamined and uncriticized – will tend to help perpetuate old views. As the therapeutic community has it, the negative effects of unprocessed traumatic experiences are passed down through generations.

In conclusion, it is clear that memory is centrally important in this text. Armando approaches memory by way of language, which functions as a memorial for and of the past. In addition, when one attends to language – the language spoken in the past as compared to the language which is still spoken – one is able to recognize the remarkable persistence of certain attitudes. The language quoted illustrates some attitudes and assumptions which were possibly factors in the genesis of the war, attitudes which allowed certain events to take place because of society's preconceptions.

The text of "Street and Foliage" inevitably calls attention to the fact that certain ways of relating have persisted into the present, just as they were already present during the period which preceded the occupation, and that therefore the current generation bears the stamp of the war, as did its parents, and is also no less immune to being occupied by that past, or being "occupied" by similar events in the future, than was the war generation.

5. *Judgment, Justice,*
and other Collaborations[1]

If one is able to entertain the possibility that knowledge is "a social product, a matter of dialogue between different versions of the world",[2] it is incumbent upon a reader who takes literature seriously to engage in that dialogue, to examine a given construct of our understanding of "our" realities, past and present, and how they are reflected and molded by our modes of representation. If the body of texts produced by a community can be said to constitute an ongoing dialogue about certain cultural practices, then an interesting question arises whenever a flurry of new texts and discussions appears or older discussions appear again in a different form or a new context: what kinds of events or shifts in interest on the part of a community provide the occasion for such a convergence of activity? In those situations where the activity involves radical reformulations of common cultural practice or the breaking of old silences or social strictures, the question is more complex: How has the topic in question made its way from the margins of discourse to the center?

This study is an attempt to consider a practical form of this question about the interaction between what has been said and what can be said concerning the texts which take World War II as their setting, and (as I have shown) do so with particular attention to the memory of children of the war.

In some sense, it is incorrect to view the shifts away from the simple cultural truisms of "goed" and "fout" as completely discontinuous events. In the case of Dutch fiction of the 1940s and 1950s, it is possible to identify certain individual strands and voices which dissent from the conventional wisdom of the time or formulate a more complex reality in opposition to this wisdom. I will mention two of the major ones briefly in this chapter; they are largely exceptions to the rule. A subtler formulation of the question might well inquire about what sort of cultural "permission" would allow for the appearance of topics which were previously not discussed. Does this sudden freedom to speak about something one has been silent about (or repressed or avoided) arise from a constituency which coalesces at a given time, or does the appearance of a single dissenting voice provide the "seed" around which some ongoing cultural debate suddenly seems to crystallize?

One could argue that the fictional texts discussed in the previous chapters may be understood as providing examples of both of these tendencies in action. Put in its simplest terms, the new constituencies represented in the wide variety of texts published in the 1980s appear precisely because they come into their own in this decade and lend their voices in turn to the ongoing construction of the history of World War II. But there also seems to be a general recognition of a broadening of the subject matter of these texts – particularly the appearance of texts which consider the fates of those who collaborated with the Nazi occupation and their children. In his lecture for the 1985 conference which commemorated the fortieth anniversary of the end of World War II in The Netherlands, A.G.H. Anbeek van der Meijden signals that the subject of collaboration – heretofore not necessarily a central theme in Dutch writing – has begun to occupy an important position in Dutch literary discourse when he states: "as many as three literary texts appeared in 1982 which touched on the problematics [of collaboration]..."[3] He proceeds to mention that this interest in approaches to the problem of collaboration in fiction is accompanied by the emergence of a nonfictional genre which he describes as "getuigenisboeken," testimony books. As an example, Van der Meijden mentions Rinnes Rijke's *Niet de schuld, wel de straf. Herinneringen van een NSB-kind* (an untranslatable title which one might loosely render: "Not Guilty, but punished all the same. Memories of a child of a member of the N.S.B.")[4] as an example of this nonfictional genre from the same year as the three fictional works on that same topic.

By the late 1980s, it is no longer necessary to merely suggest that the subject of collaboration has begun to occupy the Dutch reading public; the bookstores and literary columns are full of evidence that it is a subject whose time has come.[5] The decade of the 1980s saw a convergence of developments where different groups of the children of the war (Jewish survivors and their children, the children of those not explicitly politically engaged, and – as I will show in the next chapter – the children of families repatriated after the war from Indonesia) each begin to tell their separate stories, and to identify and describe the effect of their different experiences during the same period of history on themselves and their families. As their texts appear alongside one another, some interesting patterns of similarity and difference begin to emerge – yet another consequence of their personal histories.

In this chapter, I focus on several representative texts which consider the history and memory of the war produced by or about the children of collaborators. One feature of the group of texts about World War II which appeared in the 1980s is that the negative consequences of a family's wartime past become an allowable subject for discussion – a newfound freedom which particularly applies to children of those parents labeled "fout" during and after the occupation. As Peter Romijn asserts: "In the Netherlands, fifty years after the liberation, reputations and careers can still be destroyed by revelations of past National Socialist affiliations."[6] Although former collaborators still mostly attempt to hide the fact, some of their children find that they cannot.

As I noted in my discussion of *The Assault*, Harry Mulisch provides an indication of the dynamics involved in being the child of a collaborator in the context of a postwar chance encounter between the protagonist Anton and Fake Ploeg, the son of the collaborator whose death precipitates the destruction of Anton's ordered life. Fake Ploeg the younger confronts Anton with the fact that Anton has always felt like a victim because his parents were killed. But Fake, now a young adult, points to an incontrovertible fact: despite Anton's childhood suffering, he has become a doctor. Fake the younger bears his own suffering as the son of a collaborator; his mother was unable to find any other kind of job but menial labor and was thus unable to educate Fake, so that he has not risen to the social level he might otherwise have expected to reach.

Fake's indictment of Anton might be said to mirror the larger experience of the children of collaborators: while he remembered Anton's suffering, it is clear that Anton was oblivious to the hardships which young Fake and his family experienced.

Several other cultural developments also contributed to the freedom to discuss the issue of collaboration in the Netherlands: The publication of a sociological study by Inge Spruit[7] of the child of a Dutch "fout" person, *Onder de vleugels van de partij: Kind van de Führer* was published as early as 1983. Research on the lives and memories of the children of German perpetrators by the Israeli psychologist Dan Bar-On appears in the 1980s,[8] and suggests some clinically identifiable similarities in the childhood experiences of the children of both victims and perpetrators. A book about the experience and memory-work of the Dutch daughter of a member of the N.S.B. (the Dutch National Socialist organization) writing under the pen name Hanna Visser also appears.[9] She is also active in the "Werkgroep Herkenning" ["Recognition"], the Dutch self-help group for the children of collaborators founded in 1981. Bar-On and Visser meet and eventually cooperate to bring together children of Holocaust victims and children of collaborators.

These writers and their texts provide examples of persons who face the moral, psychological and historical aspects of the complex issues affecting the children of the war thoroughly and honestly. There is evidence in the 1980s of these issues being discussed within the popular discourse as well – as demonstrated in the person of Rinnes Rijke (pseud.), the child of a collaborator and the author of two "memoirs" of the difficulties he experienced after the war. Finally, Adriaan Venema's *Het dagboek*[10] ("The Diary") is worth noting for the significance of Venema's decision to write a novel – Venema, who is well known toward the end of the 1980s and at the beginning of the 1990s for his four-volume history of the collaboration committed by members of the Dutch publishing world.[11] His stated reasons for doing so address his perceptions of the traditional differences between fiction and non-fiction which are closely associated with the Dutch investigation of memory and history in the 1980s.

COMPLEX RELATIONSHIPS

It should hardly be surprising that the Dutch showed no great affection for the Germans in the decades immediately following the end of the war. What may be less well-known outside the Netherlands is the fact that this ill-will (considered entirely understandable at the end of the occupation) persists in some form even to the present day. A second fact worth noting is that at least part of the Dutch population does not make a distinction between "Germans" and "Nazis" in this regard; their resentment is directed at Germans in general, not just a specific segment of the population.

This observation might be productively thought of as a kind of unpleasant "family secret". As most Dutch are aware of the questionable logic in such an attitude, they will rarely admit to it; it is difficult to "prove" in any real sense that this unacknowledged subterranean strain of bitterness toward Germans and Germany exists in Dutch culture. The negative response at issue here is unreflective: The moment the mind is engaged, most Dutch citizens fall into line, reminding themselves that "German" and "Nazi" are not synonymous and that, secondly, the generation which perpetrated war crimes has either passed into old age or died, so that it is incumbent upon the present generation to rethink and reject old prejudices. Such pragmatic approaches succeed most of the time. What is of interest is the persistence of the old stereotype in the face of conscious efforts of people of good will. Its survival as an unfair characterization – immediately rejected once recognized in oneself – suggests that it is fed by deep subconscious cultural needs.

Although it has not been proven to exist by a survey of the population,[12] this pattern is illustrated lucidly by the Dutch writer (and, it must be said, hardly an ethnocentrist or xenophobe) Ian Buruma in the introduction to the book *The Wages of Guilt. Memories of War in Germany and Japan.* Buruma describes and analyzes just this attitude with reference to his childhood in the Netherlands.

> There was never any doubt, where I grew up, who our enemies were. ...

> No, the enemies were the Germans. They were the comic book villains of my childhood. When I say Germans, I mean just that – not Nazis, but Germans. The occupation between 1940 and 1945 and the animosity that followed were seen in national, not political terms. The Germans had conquered our country. They had forced my father to work in their factories.[13]

Buruma is in a position to report on regrettable phenomena such as the misconstruing of national identity as political choice more frankly than most. In the introduction to *The Wages of Guilt,* Buruma precedes his examination of German and Japanese cultural practice by turning his analytical skills on the culture of his childhood. He writes about these experiences in the past tense; he is referring to events which he remembers from his youth, a stage in his life to which he can admit because he has since outgrown its temptations. His memories of the images which were presented, the attitudes which were inculcated, and the cultural mechanisms which drove this acculturation, speak not only of Dutch attitudes toward Germans, but also of the attitudes of some Dutch survivors of the occupation, often presumed to constitute the majority view, toward other Dutch citizens.

> Our teachers told us stories of German wickedness and their own acts of bravery. Every member of the older generation, it appeared, had been in the Resistance. That is to say, everybody except for the butcher on the corner of the high street, who had been a collaborator; one didn't go shopping there. And then there was the woman at the tobacconist; she had had a German lover. One didn't go there either.

Buruma relates that the children's "comic book prejudices" changed into "moral outrage" as they discovered historical facts about the Holocaust.[14] He points to at least one important reason why intolerance toward Germans would be acceptable among people who have long prided themselves on their tolerant attitudes and behaviors: it is convenient when attempting to explain the genesis of evil acts to be able to separate human beings into groups which are good and those who are evil, and it is opportune to draw the moral line of demarcation along the geographical border: "It was comforting to know that a border divided us from a nation that personified evil. They were bad, so we must be good."[15] However, the question whether this goodness extended to all Dutch citizens was of more practical consequence in the postwar years, and Buruma indicates that collaborators and those who had had German lovers were shunned after the war.[16] In the previous chapter Armando's approaches to the issue of how the Dutch, including collaborators and those who failed to oppose them, perceived themselves and were viewed by others after the end of the occupation[17] echo some of Buruma's insights. Buruma further identifies the overwhelming similarities between Dutch and German cultures as one reason why it is so tempting and (surprisingly) important to the Dutch to make a clear distinction between "good Dutch" and "evil Germans", rather than to distinguish between good and bad behavior among members of each nationality.[18]

This understanding of clear distinctions is echoed by the writer Michael Ignatieff, who argues that drawing overly clear lines between nations or ethnic populations is a common impulse among European ethnic groups that are culturally similar but not quite the same and consider their distinctiveness important for one reason or another. In Ignatieff's book, *Blood and Belonging. Journeys into the New Nationalism,* he rehearses the implications of various aspects of nationalism, such as notions of identity and how they sometimes lead to bloodshed. Describing the need to emphasize and reinforce a distinctiveness between two groups that appear all but indistinguishable to outsiders, he borrows an apt term from Freud, who, in Ignatieff's words, "argued that the smaller the real difference between two peoples, the larger it was bound to loom in their imagination". Freud names this phenomenon the "narcissism of minor difference".[19] It also follows, as Ignatieff points out, that enemies need each other in order to define their own identities. This insight is certainly in harmony with Buruma's description of the childish comfort gained from the knowledge that one was a citizen of a victim, rather than a perpetrator country.

This victimhood appears on the face of it to allow one to evade culpability for the atrocities of war and occupation. But Buruma points out that this is double-edged: occupation is "always a humiliating business, [...] because it dramatically shows up human weakness".[20] As he phrases it, as someone who did not live through that war, in attempting to decide what one "would have" done,

> ... only a fool would put himself or herself among the imaginary heroes. It is easier to understand the ugly little compromises people make to save their own skins, the furtive services rendered to the uniformed masters, the looking away when the Gestapo kicks in the neighbor's door. (6)

Thus it is easy to understand that, however unfair or ungrounded in fact such responses might be, some Dutch survivors of the occupation found it important to mark the borders between themselves and Germans in indelible ink. Second, one may understand that the desire for a clear calculus of right versus wrong made it particularly difficult to deal with the ambiguities of how to behave under the occupation which were experienced during the war itself. In light of the high emotional stakes created by the pain endured during the occupation, survivors of the war felt a strong need to distinguish between good citizens (presumably including themselves) and those called "fout": traitors, a group which comprised collaborators, those Dutch citizens who had love relationships with Germans (particularly members of the occupation force), those who did business with the occupation government (whether willingly or under duress), those who joined the occupation force by serving in the government or various branches of the military, such as the Dutch division of the *Waffen-SS*, those who betrayed hidden Jews or members of the Resistance, and so on.

As will be clear from this list, it is difficult to define the borders of this group clearly. Buruma indicates the reason for these fuzzy definitions in his phrase "the frightened man who betrayed to save his life, who looked the other way, who grasped the wrong horn of a hideous moral dilemma."[21] The wartime occupation of a country which had hoped to remain neutral creates great conflict in the population, puts any ambivalence toward the enemy in a harsh light, and thus causes enormous resentment among citizens who resolved their dilemmas in different ways. The cultural similarities between the Dutch and the Germans only complicated the issue; since – as Buruma notes – the Dutch, who more closely resembled the Nazi ideal of a "Nordic race", were treated more humanely on the surface and thus did not suffer as much under the occupation as the Poles or the Russians. Yet this similarity only underscored their sense of betrayal at the German disregard for the country's political neutrality and sovereignty. If the Dutch felt betrayed by the Germans, how much more resentment might a "loyal" ('goed') Dutch citizen feel toward an alleged collaborator (someone labeled "fout")?

A fear of being deceived about an individual's political commitments was certainly reasonable during the occupation, as there were traitors at work and individuals who pretended to be part of the underground in order to flush out real members of the Resistance and then turn them over to the occupation forces. The relative lack of organization, or the at best decentralized structure of the Resistance certainly added confusion. The uncertainty produced by this situation is evident in some texts of the 1950s which attempted to posit a more complex moral universe than that depicted by the simple binary labeling of "goed" and "fout". One reflection of it may be found in a number of Dutch fictional texts, such as several novels by W.F. Hermans. One paradigmatic example of this theme is *The Dark Room of Damocles* (1958), in which the main character thinks he has run errands for a hero of the Resistance only to find himself accused of collaboration after the war. The only evidence he thinks he may be able to produce that he was indeed working for the Resistance is on a photographic film which, when finally located, turns out to have been destroyed. The text progressively denies the main character and the reader any sense of confidence that he or she understands what is going on, so that at the end the protagonist knows only that he meant to be working for the Resistance but does not actually know who benefited from the secret errands he had run.

There is evidence for such anxiety in history; the Dutch Resistance was not centrally organized, so that members of various groups took serious risks when seeking to contact other organizations. Even the distribution of underground papers was difficult. The ambivalence and ambiguity reflected in Hermans' novel toward historical clarity is also found in other literature, such as several Vestdijk novels of the immediate postwar era, but is at odds with commonly held assumptions among the Dutch populace. The common and unheroic past of the Dutch is a sad secret which, as A.P. Dierick shows, often becomes visible in literary texts.[22]

THE MEANING(S) OF COLLABORATION

Collaborators – and in some cases those only thought to have been collaborators – were reviled as traitors to the national cause and as opportunists who benefited from the suffering of others, or of course simply as weaklings. The issue of treason is complicated for a variety of reasons. Practically speaking, the Dutch Nazi organization (N.S.B.) was not illegal in the Netherlands before the German invasion, except that government employees were forbidden to join. Nevertheless, membership was frowned upon by those who were not in sympathy, presumably most of the population.[23] Naturally the Dutch were concerned that members of the N.S.B. would aid and abet the enemy before, during, or after the invasion.[24] By the end of the occupation, popular opinion had it that members of the N.S.B., those who had voluntarily joined the German war effort as members of the Waffen-SS or work detail in Germany, those who had – perhaps willingly – taken up (or failed to quit) positions in the occupation government of the Netherlands (which was loyal to Germany), any who had done business with the occupation forces, and any who had betrayed members of the Resistance, counted as clear traitors to the Dutch nation. Those who betrayed Dutch citizens who were in hiding (such as Jews, or men refusing to join forced labor details in Germany), and those who engaged in petty business with the occupation forces were viewed as selfish people who benefited from the suffering of others; their actions might not fit the stricter definition of treason, but they were resented during the war, and, since they were considered "fout," were in some cases also "punished" after the war.

The prominent Dutch historian E.H. Kossmann[25] argues that the concept of treason inhabits a unique position in the ethical world of the modern nation-state. In his history of the Netherlands, after tracing the genesis of the Dutch state, Kossmann argues cogently that there is something about the concept of treason that strikes us as so dangerous that a traitor must be excluded from the national identity. He reminds us that lies are against the rules, but we refer to some as little white lies; politicians commit peccadilloes; there is a category of homicide which may be said to be justifiable – or justified – , but the Dutch have no word for "justifiable treason". If the act in question was justifiable, then by definition it wasn't treason, and one who commits an act of treason will likely not only lose his or her Dutch citizenship, but also any sense of acceptance by or belonging to the community.

Human nature being what it is, those who viewed themselves as suffering or sacrificing for good causes during the occupation, those who considered themselves "goed", loyal Dutch citizens, anticipated that they would be rewarded after the war and that there would be appropriate retribution for those of their compatriots who had chosen to cooperate with the enemy in various ways. This view was not discouraged by the government-in-exile in London. A famous radio address beamed over to the occupied Dutch people promised that their sacrifices were being recognized by the free Dutch government and that the legal judgment of collaborators would – in a phrase which would become famous – be "Snel, streng en rechtvaardig": "Rapid, stern and just".[26] This expectation, the execution of which was doomed to leave room for disappointment, combined with the power vacuum and chaos which pertained as a matter of course as the occupation was broken, created a space in which some citizens took matters into their own hands and persecuted individuals they viewed as collaborators, people who had been "fout." Some justification from this attitude may have been found in a speech by Queen Wilhelmina during the war, in which she spoke of "traitors for whom there would be no room in post-war society".[27]

Thinking of the possible function of practices of inclusion/exclusion as a component of community-building sheds light on the possible motivations for not only spontaneously persecuting (former) collaborators[28] right after the war (an act which many outsiders can understand if not justify), but also for refusing to recognize their children as innocent and even for continuing this persecution for many decades –

13. Dutch children during the liberation. (RIOD)

long after outsiders would think it time to forgive and forget. One of the functions of of such practices, sometimes taking the form of public sacrifice, is to create social cohesion or a sense of solidarity among the individual members of a society. One can argue convincingly that Dutch society in the immediate post-war period, which was very much in need of healing after the occupation's effective regime of divide-and-conquer, used the very public and sometimes indiscriminate "sacrifice" – by humiliation, by economic ruin, or by incarceration – of people who had (purportedly) collaborated with the Nazi regime as a method to restabilize itself and to cement a sense of community. Whereas during the occupation, closeness in the community was reinforced by the loss of members of that community who were sacrificed by the (German) Nazi authorities and their Dutch collaborators, after the war, the people explicitly built a new community, one cemented by the sacrifice of collaborators.

According to Dutch views of the time, collaborators richly deserved whatever punishment was meted out to them, no matter how unbalanced the scale of justice. This view was often based on rather simplistic formulations of retribution – the notion that the "Germans", the collaborators' allies, had been no less unjust in their dealings during the occupation. The loyal Dutch had suffered during the occupation, and came to see their allegiance in the face of hardship as central to their self-image as a nation after the war. Thus the simple fact of the collaborators' not having suffered (hunger, loss of life, loss of family members and loved ones) during the war in itself became a sign and symptom of collaboration, an indication that one "deserved" to be punished.

The notion of retribution seemed an adequate basis on which any legal – and some illegal – sanctions seemed justified. But in the rebuilders' zeal, and partially inevitably – how could it have been otherwise? – the children of the collaborators were included in this ousting from society, and were punished or persecuted in a variety of ways. At the very least – as the inevitable result of their parents' punishment – these children were usually denied the "normal" experience of growing up as part of a family because one or both parents were imprisoned and/or the children were put into foster care. Separation from parents is a stressful experience for children. In addition, lacking the protection of a normal family, the children were often subject to discrimination and various kinds of persecution by both their peers and by adults.

Issues of identity versus cultural diversity are a particularly powerful theme in contemporary Dutch literature, a fact which reflects their social importance and political relevance. Several causes for the prevalence of these concerns may be readily identified. The meaning of national/ethnic identity has become a significant issue in Dutch society in the late '80s and the '90s as a response to the reunification of Germany, the pressure created by a flood of asylum-seekers from Eastern Europe, and the (anticipated ongoing) unification of Europe, which in itself raises important and pressing concerns about identity and belonging. In the Netherlands, German reunification also raised the specter of the Nazi occupation during World War II and of the Holocaust, engendering a debate about the political intentions of Germany and about the question whether or not "Germany" had changed in the last five or six decades.

This study investigates and accounts for the continuum of ways of posing and answering these questions of identity and diversity in works which constitute two poles, and the continuum between them, of the anxiety about identity and diversity which meet and clash in the middle.

One reason the Nazi occupiers were so successful at deporting and exterminating a large number of Dutch Jews was that they succeeded early on in removing the Jewish population from the mental landscape of Dutch society in general; they isolated the Jews by deftly driving a wedge of fear between them and their neighbors. A similar approach was taken (though less systematically) after the end of the war to attempt to "separate" good Dutch citizens from those presumed to have been collaborators and sympathizers with the Nazi regime. Citizens such as the families of collaborators, or young women who had had relationships with German men, were isolated from society, making their children vulnerable not only to public abuse by members of society (presumably "good" patriots), who stigmatized and "punished" them for their parents' collaboration, but also to simple cruelty – child abuse in its various guises – at home, perpetrated (in many cases, including that of the protagonist of Rinnes Rijke's *Niet de schuld, wel de straf*) by a stepparent. Thus, we are faced with the curious cultural phenomenon that the children of (presumed) "collaborators" are "punished" for the crimes of their parents' generation by child abuse at home.

THE SINS OF THE FATHERS

It is only in recent decades, particularly since approximately 1980, that the children of Dutch collaborators have found themselves capable of complaining about and rejecting the abuses perpetrated on them from their childhood and into adulthood. In this same time period, Dutch psychotherapists have also recognized and come to treat the damage done by the way these children were treated in the immediate postwar era, and in some cases up to the present.

One of the types of new texts mentioned in the Anbeek van der Meijden lecture, as mentioned earlier, is the emergence of "getuigenisboeken", or testimony books. Van der Meijden's example of this nonfictional genre is Rinnes Rijke's *Niet de schuld, wel de straf. Herinneringen van een NSB-kind* (1983). But although Rijke's book is presented as non-fiction, I do not think that any critical reader can view it as anything but a fictionalized memoir inhabiting approximately the same epistemological status as an historical novel – except that the author and publisher explicitly expressed the desire that the book be read as a memoir. "Not Guilty" purports to "be" the memories of Piet van Weelden – Rinnes Rijke is a pseudonym – the son of a collaborator who, the text on the back cover of the book asserts, describes his experience of the end of the German occupation and the period immediately following. Nevertheless, for reasons which I explain below, I propose that we consider this book to be at least partially fictional, an otherwise historical narrative which is substantially fictionalized by the inclusion of confabulations by its narrator/author. The reader in any case is likely to question the accuracy of narrative detail such as descriptions of the interior of a building which Rijke visited only once. A few paragraphs on the back cover of the book sum up its agenda:

> After his wanderings through the German Reich and the front lines, little Rinnes proved to be an outcast and marked for life upon his return to liberated Rotterdam in 1945. Not only because of his father's membership in the N.S.B., but also because Rinnes had been a member of a Dutch division of the Hitler Jugend during his stay in Germany.

> ...Rinnes Rijke informs the reader of the terrors of a child-refugee of war in a very direct style and with an incredibly clear memory.

> The misunderstanding and disappointments, the loneliness, hardships and humiliations which the child had to endure prove repeatedly that reality is stranger than fiction.

Thus prepared to be outraged at a society which makes a child culpable for the political mistakes his father made, the reader becomes increasingly frustrated as he or she proceeds through the book. As the tale progresses, it becomes clear that although the memories being narrated are lively and colorful and the text is lent an air of verisimilitude by the editorial decision (explicitly stated in a postscript to the book) not to standardize the obviously "rustic" working-class accents in the author's Dutch, most of the unpleasant memories of experiences outside the home in Rijke's text are simply the quotidian dilemmas of any person attempting to survive in the climate of hardship which characterized postwar economies.

Additionally, there are only one or two occasions in which the narrator is forced explicitly to face the fact that his father's political commitments were the subject of intense disapproval. Finally, the level of detail being presented suggests that the author uses his imagination (not just recollections or contemporary notes to himself) to flesh out details in the story. And yet, this text is intended to be read as a memoir; as will be discussed in the next chapter, it is amazing that Rijke is spared the critical pillorying which accompanied the publication of Jeroen Brouwers' *Sunken Red* – an explicitly fictional text. But what makes this text problematic is neither the narrator's undercutting of his "testimony" by embellished recall nor the unconvincing litany of unique, personal hardship. Rather, the real problem is that what appears to be the most cruel treatment of the narrator occurs in the context of the home – usually at the hands of his stepmother or other foster parents whose presence is necessitated by his mother's untimely death during the war. If Rijke intended his memoir to causally link his abuse to his characters' political commitments, he fails to make this either clear or convincing.

In addition, Rijke further undercuts the testimony of his mistreatment by repeatedly showing himself eating well and enjoying at least some of his adventures during his sojourn in Germany, long after his non-collaborating peers in The Netherlands have been deprived of regular meals.

After we rode the train for about an hour, it began to get dark. We had stopped
a few times along the way to let people on or off the train. During the trip I
let my mind wander. I wished my friends could see me here! It would certainly make them envious.[29] (69)

The narrative begins on "Dolle Dinsdag", Crazy Tuesday, the fifth of September
1944, when a mistaken report in a Radio Orange broadcast which announced that the
English had liberated Breda sent many collaborators fleeing the country in panic and
in fear for their lives (fearing the arrival of "bijltjesdag", alternately translated as "Day
of Reckoning", "Lynching-Justice Day" or "Hatchet Day"). Little Rinnes is roused
early in the morning by his father, who presents him with the news that they will be
taking an unexpected journey. Although I am not claiming Rijke did any conscious
borrowing from other texts, there are parallels to the journeys taken by protagonists
of other novels examined in this study, such as the travels of Marga Minco's character Stella, and Jeroen in *For a Lost Soldier*, and Anton in *The Assault*.

The reader is stunned to discover that Rinnes' and his father's hejira seems marked
everywhere along the way not so much by peril, but by helpful women and young
people (members of the Hitler Youth organization) who help Rinnes and his father
by caring for his younger siblings and by providing food for all of them. The fleeing
collaborators and their families seem threatened mostly by late and overcrowded
trains offering them transportation to presumable safety in Germany, and by occasional bombing raids. Any Dutch reader with a head full of stories about the fate of
the children of average Dutch families at this time – where starvation diets and lack
of heating fuel were standard facts of life – would find it difficult to feel much sympathy for such a tale of terror and woe. Rather than being confronted with the notion
of the culpability of children with respect to the deeds of those in power over them
as one expected to be upon opening this book, the Dutch reader is offered the testimony of the child Rinnes, who is forced to take a long trip into a foreign country
where he is well-fed, fairly warm, and relatively safe. Such a tale hardly seems pitiful
in comparison with the tales of privation, starvation, life in hiding and forced conscription by the Nazis which have defined the reality of that time for the Dutch of
recent generations.

Rijke's book continues with the story of his education and indoctrination as a
pupil in a Hitler Youth training facility. His suffering here consists of his having been
separated from his family at age nine and forced to adhere to military school rules,
admittedly a difficult experience for someone ill prepared. This material is certainly
of interest as a (semi)historical document which provides some colorful details from
times and places which are relatively unknown. Again, the reader, in light of his or
her knowledge of the starvation of children of similar ages refused the barest mini-
mum of food by the German occupiers because their parents were not collaborators
is likely to be skeptical of the exemplary magnitude of Rijke's suffering. Perhaps the
real meat of Rijke's testimony lies in his experiences after the war.

Little Rinnes' real suffering only begins upon his return to Rotterdam after expe-
riencing many adventures along the way. Since his father has been sentenced to a

work camp, Rinnes is initially placed into the custody of the woman whom his father married during Rinnes' sojourn in Germany. It is soon made evident that his father's new wife has a lover besides her husband, and that her children are treated fairly well, while Rinnes becomes the stereotypical "fairytale stepchild". The couple abuses him by withholding proper nourishment, keeping him out of school, forcing him to work instead. Rinnes sneaks into his father's work camp in hopes that his father will protect him from his stepmother's cruel treatment, but is not offered any support. The father – certainly not able to alter conditions outside the camp – in fact sides with the evil stepmother, claiming that "If she punishes you, you must have deserved it". (199) Life is clearly unfair. While this segment of the book does indeed entail the abuse of young Rinnes, it fails to demonstrate to the reader either that this poor treatment is causally related to his father's history of collaboration, or what the connection is. It thus fails to fulfill the stated objective of the book to provide an incisive critique of a society willing to hold children responsible for the political sins of their parents.

14. "Sure, why not?" – Dutch newspaper announcement for boys' camps in Germany. Boys aged 16 to 18 can spend a month engaged in sports, fieldwork, small-caliber weaponry and – if it snows – skiing. (RIOD)

At the book's conclusion, the sad tale of punishment for collaboration which had been promised to the reader by the book's cover is withheld, and indeed seems to have been undercut repeatedly along the way. If Rinnes' stepmother abused him and his father was unable or unwilling to protect him, how is his tale political? Why wasn't the book advertised as a book about child abuse in a Dutch family?

The fact is that both Rijke's testimony and his book were well received in the Netherlands. Rijke wrote a sequel published in 1985; as the foreword and back cover suggest, Rijke wrote this volume after receiving hundreds of letters from readers who wished to know how the story continued. The relative success of a book which seems widely accepted as an example of a testimonial while appearing to fail in making its moral and historical argument in nearly every respect seems to me to raise an uncomfortable question: to what extent might the apparently uncritical acceptance of this book imply the existence of a reading public which has failed to confront its own communal experience and critique of collaboration?

A FAIRY TALE

In attempting to understand the reasons for Rijke's success with his readership, one must view this work as reflecting a particular construction of the past and the present. Taking into account the lack of any political or historical analysis – the fact that the book does not differentiate between the hardships which accrue from the narrator's father's politics, from Rinnes' mother's death, those due to the exigencies of life in wartime and the immediate postwar period shared by the populace as a whole, and those troubles arising from any period and to which all human beings are subject – the "common speech" of the text and the obvious references to Rijke's working-class background, and the testimony's odd narrative voice (which alternately speaks a childish language and suddenly switches without warning to the perspective of the adult Rijke), the best analog or model I have been able to conceive for the social function of this tale and as an explanation of its success is that of the fairy tale – one which replaces the difficult analyses and complex moral questions of dominance and the moral stage of World War II which Rijke's book purports to share with its fictional counterparts of evil stepmothers and journeys into darkness with the aid of kind strangers. Viewed in this way, one might consider Rijke's text and its reception in light of Bruno Bettelheim's analysis of the function of such fairy tales as he describes it in *The Uses of Enchantment;* that of allowing children at various stages of cognitive development to come to terms with their subconscious fears at whatever level they are able to. As Bettelheim states in his "Introduction":

> As with all great art, the fairy tale's deepest meaning will be different for each person, and different for the same person at various moments in his life. The child will extract different meanings from the fairy tale, depending on his interests and needs of the moment. When given the chance, he will return to

the same tale when he is ready to enlarge on old meanings, or replace them with new ones.[30]

The fairy tale does not analyze, describe motives or consider sociohistorical factors, but describes occurrences and perhaps the protagonist's feelings. This seems an entirely adequate description of Rijke's text, and of some of its recent uses. To borrow an image from a fairy tale, we have taken an ax to the wicked wolf and split him open, only to liberate the hapless victims who were the wolf's last meal, none the worse for wear. Alternately, Bettelheim's notion of returning repeatedly to a tale to replace old meanings with new ones, very much echoes contemporary views of the function and character of autobiography. As Jerome Bruner puts it:

> On this view, a life is created or constructed by the act of autobiography. It is a way of construing experience – and of reconstruing and reconstruing it until our breath or our pen fails us. Construal and reconstrual are interpretive.[31]

If Bruner is right, then just as – according to Bettelheim – human beings can find new meaning in a single fairy tale at various points in their lives, so each individual can – perhaps must – retell, reinterpret his or her own story in light of recent experiences and the world view one holds at a certain time.

One argument for interpreting "Not Guilty" as a fairy tale is the figure of the mother, or rather the evil stepmother.

> So the typical fairy tale splitting of the mother into a good (usually dead) mother and an evil stepmother serves the child well. It is not only a means of preserving an internal all-good mother when the real mother is not all-good, but it also permits anger at this bad "stepmother" without endangering the goodwill of the true mother, who is viewed as a different person.[32]

This analysis of the role of the mother adds an interesting dimension to Rinnes Rijke's postwar difficulties, with the caveat that Bettelheim's description of the evil stepmother/dead good mother dichotomy is the description of a fantasy, whereas in Rijke's case his biological mother, who is of course favorably compared to his stepmother, is in fact deceased. The pathos of the image of a dead mother, who is perfect except that she has abandoned her hapless, victimized son, is calibrated for a popular audience:

> I relived it all again. If only mama were still alive. I looked up at heaven. That's where she is now.[33]

Such an analysis might suggest an important question: Does the positive reception of a book such as Rijke's suggest that significant segments of the Dutch reading public might be sufficiently troubled by fears or feelings of guilt related to the post-war treatment of the children of collaborators to wish to "atone" for their collective history by sympathizing with this child? Rijke's approach not only plays heavily on the widespread view of the "innocence" of children, but it simultaneously provides permission to discuss the equally touchy subject of child abuse by depicting it in connection with the universally vilified collaborator rather than locating the abuse's causation elsewhere, such as in the patriarchy or by locating the causation of the abuse in a particular society or sub-culture at a certain historical point in time. Also, since fairy tales exist outside of and entirely apart from our chronology and geography, one avoids the uncomfortable questions implied by the existence of child abuse in that context: if social conditions in the Netherlands in the 1940s were such that child abuse was encouraged, have these conditions been sufficiently altered to relieve the problem of child abuse? What are the causes of child abuse in the first place?

One must not overlook the fact that Rijke's text provides a superficial, non-analytical approach to the problem. To stretch the metaphor: are – or were – the readers still at a relatively "childlike" stage, so to speak, in coping with their wartime experiences, making it easier to simply express an indubitably appropriate sympathy for the victims without engaging in the historical analysis necessary for preventing crimes against humanity from occurring again?

Perhaps it is all simply a matter of timing. Perhaps Rijke's story merely served the function of preparing an audience for the more reflective, more analytical, in some cases more academic studies of the children of World War II collaborators in the Netherlands which have been published since then (such as Inge Spruit's *Onder de vleugels van de partij. Kind van de Führer* (1983) ["Under the Wings of the Party, The Führer's Child"], Hanna Visser's *Het verleden voorbij* (1989) ["Beyond Past"], and Duke Blaauwendraad-Doorduijn's *Niemandsland* (1989) ["No Man's Land"].

One must, however, note the fact that most of Rijke's worst sufferings were brought upon him by his stepmother with the blessing of an emasculated father whose sole authority seems ironically to reside in his ability to bluster about the appropriateness of punishment. It seems unlikely that Rijke himself was attempting to make the subtle point (but is it really so subtle?) that collaborators of the Nazi regime (or those who married collaborators) were likely to be authoritarian personalities who were at risk for abusing their children, thus showing Nazism to be an inhumane system. Little evidence for such an interpretation is provided in the text. It is true that the narrator's stepmother's lover refers to the father's political alliance in the midst of an altercation, but it is clear that he is simply taking advantage of the opportunity to threaten the child; nowhere does he exhibit any political scruples himself.

> He got involved too, and said: "I'm warning you, filthy N.S.B.-member, or else I'll pin you to the wall with a knife."

> He punched me in the chest. I had a hard time breathing. They walked off, laughing. I whispered to myself: "Jerks!"(188)

136   I submit that the phenomenon of Rijke's book and its popularity may be explained in light of the prevailing construction of social reality at the time of its publication. Rijke would be more likely to gain an audience for a narrative about child abuse if it were couched in the mythology of the child of the collaborator abused by a vengeful society than if he had attempted to advertise his book as an exposé (however subjective) of the causation and consequences of child abuse. It is appropriate in this context to consider the sentences which continue the Bruner quote given above:

> Like all forms of interpretation, how we construe our lives is subject to our intentions, to the interpretive conventions available to us, and to the meanings imposed upon us by the usages of our culture and language.[34]

Both the history of the postwar treatment of collaborators and their children and the problem of child abuse must be faced by Dutch society; however, the likelihood that each will be dealt with adequately would increase if each complex of problems could be considered on its own merits and in its own sociohistorical context(s). Where the two complexes of problems intersect, as they indubitably do, the dynamics involved should be carefully articulated.

THE RIGHT PLACE AT THE RIGHT TIME

It is apparent that at the time of the publication of "Not Guilty," the Dutch public was generally ready to read about the mistreatment of the children of collaborators; perhaps they were more eager to discuss that topic than to entertain questions about the poor treatment of children presented simply as child abuse. As is clear from Kossmann's writing on treason, which I have discussed above, collaboration has traditionally been assumed to be far beyond the pale by most Dutch citizens who fancy themselves "average" – therefore "goed" or loyal during the occupation – so that child abuse due to collaboration, even child abuse by a collaborator, could easily be set aside as a consequence of the inferior moral character of the parent, the lack of backbone having already been proven by his or her (serious or not-so fundamentally treasonous) behavior.

In his lecture for the 1985 conference which commemorated the fortieth anniversary of the end of the Second World War in The Netherlands, Willem Frederik Hermans points out that a time once existed when wars were strictly a matter for professionals, i.e. those in power who declared them, and those soldiers hired to fight them, and that a concern for loyalty and political rectitude among the population in general, and among writers in particular – such as has occurred in the Netherlands with respect to World War II – was not necessarily an improvement. He refers to this phenomenon as the "increasing tendency to involve everyone in everything". (88)

Ian Hacking, in "The Making and Molding of Child Abuse", argues that the current concept of the meaning of child abuse is a recent phenomenon: "...it comes as a surprise that the very idea of child abuse has been in constant flux for the past thirty

years. Previously our present conception of abusing a child did not even exist." (253)
He shows that this historical development has important implications:

> ... as we evolve an idea about a kind of person or of human behavior, people
> change, behaviors change. Children experience their hurt differently. ... Like-
> wise the abusers' own sense of what they are doing, how they do it, and even
> what they do is just not the same now as it was thirty years ago. New kinds of
> people come into being that don't fit the wisdom just acquired, less because
> the recent knowledge was wrong than because of a feedback effect. There is not
> strictly a truth of the matter that, once discovered, will remain the truth, for
> once it is counted as true and becomes common knowledge, it will change the
> very individuals – abusers and children – about whom it was supposed to be
> the truth.[35]

The popularity of Rijke's book suggests that an opportunity exists to engage some
serious concerns in Dutch society. The publication of books such as "Not Guilty",
and their success, is an indication that the issues surrounding the post-war treatment
of collaborators and their children have recently been of concern to a significant segment of the Dutch population. However, if, as Hacking shows, additional "information" and discussion of concepts such as child abuse, or collaboration, modify the
descriptions and classifications of the social problems being discussed, then a book
such as "Not Guilty", and the dialogues surrounding it, are not merely interesting.
The stakes may well be high, in terms of both literary and their social implications.
If the discourse of literature is to provide any valuable contributions to the debate, be
it about political issues or familial piety, the reading public must demand books of
integrity and receive them critically.

AN ALTERNATIVE APPROACH TO A PARENT'S COLLABORATION

On the other hand, Hanna Visser's *Het verleden voorbij* ["Beyond the Past"] is a
record of another work of memory – the author's attempts to come to terms with the
poor treatment to which she was subjected as a child because her father had been a
member of the N.S.B. and – more importantly – her own feelings of guilt at what
her father had done. Her history shares a number of similarities with that of Rijke: a
fear of rejection outside the home as well as verbal abuse within the family, feelings
of insecurity lasting well into adulthood, and a strong sense of alienation from the
Dutch people. One apparent difference from Rijke's experience is that there was a
time in the postwar era when Hanna's parents believed that nobody else was aware of
their past, and the child was told in brusque tones not to sing certain songs she had
previously heard around the house; only later did she learn that the reason was that
they would have identified her with her father's N.S.B. past. The significant difference between Rijke's and Visser's book, however, is that his is an indictment of the
Dutch people, and – I would argue – of his parents and stepparents for the poor treat-

ment he received as a child, but her book is *as well* an attempt at reconciliation – insofar as possible – with her father and with her past. With encouragement from Dan Bar-On, she meets with Jewish survivors in an attempt to forge such new relationships as might be possible. Unlike Rijke, who found no solution to his problem – think of his need to write a second book at the reading audience's request – "Hanna Visser" achieves and reports a moment of peaceful resolution at the end of the book: she and Dan Bar-On agree to stay in touch and support each other as each of them faces a future filled with promise.

"Beyond the Past" combines a number of different kinds of texts: historical/narrative, theological, psychological. It contains prose, poems, diary fragments, and letters. It alternates between first- and third-person narrative; interestingly, the "frame story" of her journey to Israel to meet the Israeli psychologist Dan Bar-On is in the present tense and third person, whereas memories of her childhood and her self-analysis are in the first person. She details her sense of guilt; she was born in the middle of the war, literally in the shadow of the Nazi regime, while her father, wearing his N.S.B. uniform, was sitting at the foot of the bed. Visser writes:

> *Born guilty,* the title of Peter Sichrovsky's book, means to me the very concrete image of my very first moments on this earth: born under the curse of the swastika, the symbol of death and destruction. How then is it possible to find the way to life?[36]

This image of being born into evil, of having participated in it from childhood on, of the possibility that she may somehow have benefited from it – though she is convinced from a moral point of view that she would have been much better off without any such "advantage" – shakes her sense of herself as a person, and precipitates her search for forgiveness and reconciliation.

As I suggested above, although this book relates some very similar experiences to those Rijke tells, the tone is entirely different. Her treatment of "Dolle Dinsdag" will illustrate this point. Her family, like Rijke's, fled to Germany after "Dolle Dinsdag".[37] Visser worries about how her mother managed to take care of her, a baby in diapers, during the trip. She reports having interviewed other, older people who had made the trip in an effort to reconstruct her own history. She relates that the accommodations on the train had not been luxurious, but immediately adds that they provided "considerably more space and luxury than the trains with which the Jews had been transported".[38] The stay was uncomfortable, the locals were unfriendly, and the mood in the camps was depressing, but she comments that they were not abused. She does note that the situation was difficult for the many wives, including her mother, who were there because of political choices their husbands had made without consulting them, and regret that the women often expressed their irritation toward each other instead of standing by each other. On the way back to the Netherlands, they travel in freight cars and are delayed for several hours because their locomotive is bombed, but she does not complain. The neutral tone of her report – a clear contrast with Rijke's text – does not let up even when she reports that she, her siblings and mother, while being led to an internment camp, were ridiculed, cursed, and spit on by people who had gathered to watch: "At that moment we were driven out of the community of the Dutch people. Today I say that my own people spit me out. That was the first time it happened, and it has been repeated many times since."[39]

Like Rijke, Visser calmly reports a rough home life with an authoritarian father and a weak mother. She speculates briefly that there might be a connection between his authoritarian behavior and his earlier commitment to the National Socialist party, but relinquishes that hypothesis when she cites a Dutch study on the topic in which no correlation was proven. She concludes that her father's unhappiness – which she hopes derives in part from secret remorse over his political past – in combination with the stresses of postwar life in a society hostile to him and his lack of knowledge about how to interact with young children were the cause of her unhappiness within the family.

I will return to the possible similarities between the experience of child abuse and a child growing up in a family where the parents were collaborators later on in this chapter after discussing the significance of collaboration in Dutch society.

RAISING THE STAKES: HISTORY AND FICTION

The enormous weight of what is at stake when a Dutch person is discovered to have collaborated gives rise to a great deal of discussion in Dutch society, and the author Adriaan Venema was often at the center of such debates. As mentioned above, his novel *Het dagboek* ["The Diary"] raises intriguing questions about the relationship between historical veracity and truth in texts which take on a collaborator's past. The publication date – 1990 – situates this text at the very end of the period this study is concerned with. I will not discuss the novel in detail – I do not find that it succeeds as a novel – but only mention it for the interesting space it carves out for itself between fiction and non-fiction, as yet another hybrid form (a variety of historical novel, perhaps) between the poles of what used to be called "fiction" and "history".

As the text on the back cover explains, the story is based on historical figures, Dutch authors, who are not named in the book; others have identified the two closest models as Voeten and Hoornik. On the copyright page, Venema writes: "This novel quotes from the work of: ..." and then follows a list of Dutch authors.[40] The citations are there for verisimilitude. However, the entire exercise raises the question, why write a novel about this material? At the time this book appeared, Venema was in the midst of publishing his four-volume set of historical works. Why did he feel the need to "duplicate" his efforts in a different genre? The text on the back cover presumes to answer the question: his multi-volume history of collaboration in Dutch publishing circles raised questions about the historical figures' motivations – "the psychological dimension" – which he did not attempt to answer unless the historical sources provided evidence. "Yet while he was doing the research, this question occurred to him many times." The text specifically states that "The Diary" is Venema's answer.

Venema the novelist has used his liberty (as a novelist) to weld facts and imagination into a whole in order to (as it were) *add* [my emphasis] to his material the normal "human, all too human" reality which determined life during the war.[41]

The last sentences of this text on the back cover attempt to make absolutely clear to the reader what the truth status of this text is:

The dialogues in this book are those of a novel. They were different in reality. The characters were imagined by Adriaan Venema, but their fates were not.

As I will show in more detail in the next chapter, the Dutch reading public is particularly interested in separating "fact" from "fiction" or "untruth" when tales of the war are concerned. Venema wisely anticipates its questions. It is highly significant, though, that he finds in fiction a more adequate medium to communicate the crucial information about human choice – thus ethics – which he found unavailable within the strictures of history, or rather: within the strictures of history writing as he understood its rules. What he does not mention is that his view oddly parallels that of Sem Dresden[42] who argues that the horror of the Holocaust was such that its reality or truth could never be adequately represented by historical narrative, that only the superior evocative power of literature (i.e. fiction) is adequate to the task. The reason why literature is considered best is different in these two cases – in one, it is because of the (qualitatively and quantitatively) overwhelming aspects of the truth, in the other, because private emotions and motives are hidden – and Venema would have been subject to terrible criticism had he himself made this parallel. However, it is interesting to note that the privileges which Venema and Dresden attribute to literature are also ascribed to autobiography in more recent literary, psychological and cultural theory; they would be much helped by Bruner's notion that even autobiography is a form of interpretation which is subject to reinterpretation, and that each act of writing such a life is "subject to our intentions, to the interpretive conventions available to us, and to the meanings imposed upon us by the usages of our culture and language."[43] When writers and readers in the 1980s look back at the history and memory of collaboration and what was done to collaborators and their children after the occupation, it is useful to remember that they are – *and properly should be* – engaging in an act of reinterpretation in light of the cultural values which pertain in the time in which they do so. Thus it is probable that recent texts about collaboration and its aftermath depend for their production and reception on attitudes which were prepared by the entire move in the 1980s toward attending to the needs of the children of the war.

The writings and research of the psychologist Dan Bar-On provide another piece of the puzzle – the ways that views of the children of the war changed in the 1980s. He has studied the psychological dynamics which occur in the families of persons associated with the Nazi regime during World War II. Bar-On is an Israeli psychologist, the child of German-Jewish parents who had left Germany in time. He studied the children of German war criminals and other (less famous) perpetrators (such as soldiers, death camp guards, and so on) from the German Reich. Bar-On embarked on this research program because he found that the spate of data on the children of Holocaust survivors[44] was not matched by an equal body of information concerning the children who found themselves on the other side of the perpetrator-victim divide after the war.

In essence, he found that children of perpetrators shared many psychological symptoms with the children of survivors, despite the fact that they frequently were unaware of their parents' past activities while growing up. Bar-On's explanation is that the second generation is damaged by the trauma hidden in parents' past; although – rather, since – the parents carefully avoid discussing their war past, the children sense that there is a dark secret there, a topic which may not be discussed within or outside the family.

This knowledge sets up a damaging "double-wall" dynamic within the family which Bar-On has described as being visually representable by a psychological model of a system of relationships in which the family's history is kept inside a set of two opaque cylinders, one of which rotates inside the other. Each cylinder – one representing the parent, the other the child – has a small opening in its side, representing a "window of opportunity", a time when the individual is receptive to a discussion of the past. Thus the past is only (if ever) discussed on those rare occasions when the windows in the two cylinders are coincidentally lined up with each other, that is, when both parties are ready to talk; a constellation which will be very rare. The parents will naturally be loath to discuss their history during the occupation because of society's disapprobation of their political positions and behaviors, and therefore parents will in most cases attempt to keep such shameful information from their children. Possible motivations for evasive behavior may include a desire to save the children grief by shielding them from unpleasant facts concerning (and assumed to be *in*) the past, or saving themselves embarrassment or worse, such as the loss of a job, business associates, friends – reasons which are more self-interested, but easy to understand. As various examples have proven repeatedly, even decades after the end of the war a previously undisclosed wartime association with any Nazi organization, or even with any Germans, could prove disastrous to one's career and standing within the community.

In order to comprehend the meaning attributed to collaboration in the Netherlands during and following World War II, it is imperative that one understand the central constitutive function which the experience of the war fulfills in Dutch self-understanding of its identity as a nation in the post-war period, and exactly what meaning the experience of the war is thought to have (had). Dutch historian J.C.H. Blom states this point quite clearly:

> In other words, "the war", as we usually call it in the Netherlands, constituted an important element of the national consciousness, with a strong signifying function and thus an ethical charge; back then we had discovered who was goed/good and who was fout/bad.[45]

Blom states that in the construction of a national identity after the war, the point of departure is commonly the suffering experienced by the population and its perseverance in the face of overwhelming odds during the occupation. As he explains, although the Netherlands was on what ended up as the winning side, triumphalism is very uncommon, and military events are not accorded a central role. The Dutch are more likely to recall the humiliation they experienced in May of 1940, when the Germans overran the country and forced the Dutch to surrender within a matter of days, than they are to remember feats of the Resistance. One might argue that these foci of memory reflect the reality of the lives of most Dutch survivors of the war: most were neither members of the Resistance nor collaborators in any strict sense, but bystanders. If, as a whole, the populace did what it could to avoid cooperating with the occupation government, yet without losing its survival instinct, that would mean that individuals resisted only passively and in little ways. Even if the cumulative effect of the minor acts of resistance frustrated the Nazis at times, the people would not have felt themselves to be heroes, but would be all the more acutely aware of their own suffering.

In her sensitive and deft introduction to a volume entitled *Rescuers* which tells the stories of perhaps otherwise unremarkable individuals throughout Europe who had risked their lives in order to shelter Jews from deportation, Cynthia Ozick carefully distinguishes between collective guilt and individual responsibility, between the normalcy which caused most individuals to be bystanders and the peculiar events or impulses which made some into heroes. She identifies heroic behavior as exceptional by definition.

> When a whole population takes on the status of the bystanders, the victims are without allies; the criminals, unchecked, are strengthened; and only then do we need to speak of heroes. When a field is filled from end to end with sheep, a stag stands out. When a continent is filled from end to end with the compliant, we learn what heroism is....

> Taken collectively, as I dared to do a moment ago, the bystanders are culpable. But taking human beings "collectively" is precisely what we are obliged not to do. Then consider the bystanders not as a group, not as a stereotype, but one by one. If the bystander is the ordinary human article, as we have agreed, what can there be to puzzle us?[46]

Bar-On too, recognizes that it is difficult to know what motivates human individuals to choose the right course of action when suddenly asked to make a portentous decision, and that thus it is important not to be overly critical of those who fail their own or another's highest ideals:

> Newer approaches have suggested a psychology of "ordinary people" ...

> Being able to identify potential perpetrators and rescuers only in exceptional cases means that there is no simple way humanity can defend itself, psychologically, from similar future calamities. Coupled with this is the problem of disbelief.[47]

Both the fact that one cannot predict on the basis of some psychological test who will behave either well or poorly and the fact that evil is often ignored, kept secret, or only reluctantly recognized for what it is, are true of child abuse. It is easy to point to cases of both child abuse and of collaboration – even the kind of cooperation with the Nazi regime in which the individual perpetrates violence against other human beings – in which acquaintances and family members suffer from disbelief. As Bar-On states: "Obviously, these disquieting facts require a new definition of "normalcy.""[48]

Blom, too, has connected the notion of collaboration and the Dutch view of themselves; his work shows that what is eventually important to "the" Dutch world view about the "ordinary human article" is not exceptional heroics but rather the refusal to cooperate with the occupying forces and the consciousness of having suffered. In this calculus, the suffering of the bystander counts, even though any suffering due to heroics is of course better. It is possible that the bystanders share collectively in the heroics of the resistance and in the extraordinary suffering which occurred as corollary to paramilitary actions; given the penchant of the occupation forces for taking hostages and killing them in retribution for acts of resistance or sabotage, all families, even those of pure bystanders, were in danger of being touched by death, and thus lived with the emotional trauma of this possibility.

The Assault[49] illustrates the perception – embodied in a story typical of the 1980s – that no families were immune from retribution, that all Dutch citizens, even those not heroic enough to perpetrate acts of resistance themselves, might lose family members or be forced to give up their lives. According to Blom, these patterns – of viewing resistance during the occupation and the "suffering" endured as the constitutive element of the new society – remained important not just after the war, but almost to the present, though with a shift in emphasis.

> The extent to which the constitutive elements of the memory of the war and the meaning which was assigned to it have remained largely the same in the half-century since 1945 is certainly remarkable.[50]

Blom's analysis is particularly interesting because of the manner in which it sets this construction of the memory of the war within the context of the Dutch view of national identity which has, he argues, applied for centuries. If he is right, the Dutch may have been conditioned by their self-image not just to think of themselves as people who suffer, but this view of themselves may predispose them to remember their suffering with particular clarity, and to find in it the meaning of their experience. It would then follow that this meaning becomes the basis for the construction of society after the war.

In Blom's analysis, there are three basic tenets of Dutch society, or of the self-image of the Dutch, based on the experience of World War II in light of other signifying moments in Dutch history. Blom's first characteristic of the Dutch people's self-image is one of a "small, but brave" country. Collaboration was beyond the pale, since it was often defined from the start as an act of cowardice. Secondly, according to Blom, the Dutch have prided themselves on being able to form a nation in which a variety of oppositions are united. This principle causes dissonance in the case of collaborators, as the Dutch are unwilling to include collaborators under the umbrella of nationhood. The reason for this exclusion may be explained in the terms used by Kossmann, or as corollaries of items one and three in Blom's article on "Dutchness". Blom's third element of Dutch self-fashioning is that the Dutch embody high moral standards. This assumption complicates the thought of forgiving collaborators, as they are seen as having besmirched the national honor. Thus, despite – actually, because of – the stock the Dutch have put in their ability to assemble under the umbrella of the Dutch state various camps which disagree with each other and to inculcate values of tolerance, collaboration offends against the very values which have allowed diversity to coexist in some semblance of harmony, and thus must be repudiated with a firm hand by anyone "really Dutch" enough to live by proper principles.

One strategy cultures and nations have used over the centuries to iron out inconstancies and disunity has been sacrifice; it (re)creates a sense of community or solidarity. One might speculate that one reason the Dutch seemed amidst all their suffering to enjoy a sense of togetherness during the occupation was a sense of unity in opposing the occupation forces. Such positive attitudes in the face of hardship are reflected in various cultural products, such as the evocative title of a recent article by Renaat Ramon named "Alleen in de brand waren wij gelukkig: schrijvers en tijdschriften in een prachtige, getraliede tijd," which translates as: "We were happy only in the midst of the fire; writers and journals during a wonderful time behind bars."[51]

Sacrifice also sets up an us-against-them dynamic, and can thus be used to create (the illusion of) unity. In the years immediately after the end of the war, collaborators' children and wives fit the sacrificial type: they were socially powerless and easily identified and marked. However, three, four, five decades later they no longer conform to this image: although they feel marginalized, they are no longer identifiable by others as a fringe group. They do not look different: they look and speak like loyal Dutch citizens; in fact, they would argue, for they have learned to recognize this fact: they are, and perhaps always have been, loyal Dutch citizens. Their only offense was that they had been born into families in which one or more of the adult members – often the father – had made an "incorrect" political choice; as they matured and began to see themselves as (somewhat autonomous) individuals, they began to realize that their persecution could not be justified on the basis of the rules to which the Dutch people claimed to adhere: individuals are punished justly for their own deeds. Discriminatory sacrifice maintains its power particularly when it is not explicitly acknowledged as such. Therefore, it is understandable and predictable that these family members of former collaborators would call the Dutch nation to account.

Perhaps one may identify some influence here of the newly multicultural aspects of Dutch culture: as the more recent immigrants arrive, and the majority and minority cultures redefine their spaces relative to each other, such hidden/invisible minorities as the family members of former collaborators would consider joining the fray; if a multicultural society is being negotiated in which there is room for people of other races (certainly a novel experience for the Dutch people), then certainly the Dutch ought to be ready to recognize these loyal but ill-treated white citizens who have been living within the culture all along – those whose families have provided the "lambs" who were sacrificed for the sake of postwar Dutch society.

As the discussion of treason above suggests, those branded collaborators and their families were eager to avoid the public eye when possible. This need to avoid attracting attention from outside the family, and a need for the family to forget the past, set up the dynamic of family secrets which lead to problems later in life as described by Dan Bar-On. Because of this silence at the center of the family, and the ethos of secrecy, these symptoms are similar to those thought to be common to victims of child abuse. It is possible that a similar psychological process occurs in both cases. It is also true in both cases that a child will hesitate to call attention to the family's problems because doing so would involve exposing the adults' transgression and also bring shame and possible persecution upon the child. Thus, Hanna Visser wrote her book under a pseudonym because her mother was still alive at the time of publication, and Visser did not wish to see her tranquil life in an old people's home disturbed. A subtitle of an interview in *Het Parool*, "The intuitive silence of an N.S.B. child",[52] identifies the core of her difficulties. An article in *Het Vrije Volk* ends on a positive note: Visser has resolved her concerns to such a degree that she has recently felt free to participate in the national celebrations of the liberation.[53] This is an important step forward for someone who previously feared being identified as a collaborator when she enrolled in a Jewish Studies class at university.

PROBLEMS OF ABUSE AND MEMORY

Readers might expect a cross-cultural comparison of studies concerning the memory of World War II, specifically the occupation of the Netherlands, with research into the issues surrounding memories in the USA of wars such as the Vietnam or Korean war. It is in fact true that psychological research is being done and that counseling is being offered to some American veterans of the Second World War. It has recently become more common knowledge that there are American World War II veterans who are just now recognizing that they have partially "repressed" their memories of wartime experiences and need to deal with them. One explanation for this delayed reaction is that these soldiers (and members of their support staff) were too busy upon their return to the USA participating in the baby boom, building careers, raising their children, and buying their famous tract houses, to emotionally deal with their experiences, and only now in retirement are they at leisure to remember and to grieve.

However, it is also relevant that from an American perspective, those war experiences were events occurring to and perpetrated by soldiers, "professional" or designated – if in many cases temporary – warriors, not families with small children, not persons whose country or community, whose homes (and often bodies) were literally and figuratively occupied by the enemy. The better American parallel to the Dutch situation lies in issues surrounding child abuse (recently known as physical, sexual, emotional or "satanic ritual" abuse) and the research field and topic of discussion in the popular press now emergent in the USA centering around terrorism and hate groups.

In recent years, however, the problems of child abuse (be it physical, emotional or sexual – or what has come to be known under the term "satanic ritual abuse") and problems of memory (first "recovered memories", now expanded to "falsely recovered memories") have been in the forefront of public discussion in the United States. Several psychologists have recently published studies on memory issues intended for a general audience. Lawrence Wright's *Remembering Satan. A case of recovered memory and the shattering of an American family,*[54] describes the destructive capacity of incorrect uses of a method of recovery of memories, in which a well-meaning father – the alleged perpetrator – apparently "induced" false memories in himself, in which he "remembered" that he and other adults had sexually abused his daughters. Michael D. Yapko's *Suggestions of Abuse. True and False Memories of Childhood Sexual Trauma,*[55] and Lenore Terr's *Unchained Memories. True Stories of Traumatic Memories, Lost and Found,*[56] describe various aspects of lost and "recovered" memories, and attempt to show how to distinguish between accurate recovered memories and false ones. Judith Lewis Herman, writing in *Trauma and Recovery,*[57] draws a connection between three forms of psychological trauma which have "surfaced into public consciousness"[58] in the last century; firstly, hysteria, secondly, shell shock or combat neurosis, and thirdly, sexual and domestic violence. It would be tempting to "diagnose" Anton, the protagonist of *The Assault,* with the second kind and Rijke with the third, compare their symptoms, and declare them comparable. Offering a psychological diagnosis of fictional characters does not make much sense, however, and it rather misses the point. I am not pretending to be a "therapist of culture", whatever that would be, but rather am interested in noting convergences between discourses which make available new ways of discussing old problems. What matters for the story of the children of the war developing in the Netherlands is that an approach exists which opens up the possibility of discussing trauma from the effects of war in the same breath with trauma from the effects of child abuse. The notion of psychological similarities among children of the war was recognized and is documented as early as 1987 by a volume containing the texts of a series of lectures (held between January and April of 1986) entitled simply *Kinderen van de oorlog* ["Children of the War"][59] which consists of a collection of essays about "trans-generational" transference, about the "second generation" of Jewish victims, about those interned in Indonesia and their offspring, and about the children of members of the N.S.B.

On a more theoretical level, the connection between trauma and trauma is not difficult to describe. Kai Erikson points to the fact that the term "trauma" is more and more often used to mean the effect of an injury and not just its cause, as the term was taken to mean in classic medical usage, where it refers "not to the injury inflicted but to the blow that inflicted it."[60] Erikson argues that this naming of a disorder "for the stimulus that brought it into being" does not confuse, but rather reflects reality better:

> The historian who wants to know where a story starts, like the therapist who needs to identify a precipitating cause in order to deal with the injury it does, will naturally be interested in beginnings. But those are no more than details to everyone else (and not even very important ones at that), because it is how people react to them rather than what they are that give events whatever traumatic quality they can be said to have. The most violent wrenchings in the world, that is to say, have no clinical standing unless they harm the workings of a mind or body, so it is the damage done that defines and gives shape to the initial event, the damage done that gives it its name. It scarcely makes sense to locate the term anywhere else.[61]

Thus we need not argue about whose past was worse; one person's experience of the war and the postwar era, or the other. We need not even decide exactly whether Rinnes Rijke's past was more pitiful than that of Hanna Visser; what matters most is that they were both wounded by their past and that the one – apparently – came to terms with it and found at least partial healing, and the other either did not, or did not report on it. The debate about whether Rijke's past is better described as one of child abuse (related to his father's politics) or as a strongly political one, is more a matter of interest because the reader recognizes that he fashioned his own story in ways he found more easily discussible at that time in history, than because the actual details of the history should matter to most readers.

In *Rewriting the Soul: Multiple Personality and the Sciences of Memory*,[62] Ian Hacking argues that the vigorous debates about memory (including the discussion involving repressed and recovered memory and multiple personality disorder) in the United States and Europe are part of an ongoing process by which Western medicine has attempted to remove the soul from the province of religion. Hacking argues that this is to be achieved by developing a scientific analog to the soul, to wit, memory. The details of this proposal are beyond the scope of my study of Dutch literature about the children of the war in the 1980s, but it does raise the enticing possibility – which would fit quite well with my conclusions in this study – that the Dutch project of arguing about memory and history is in fact a variety of what Hacking – referring to the construction of "selves" – has called "making up people."

Taking Hacking and Blom together with the notion that we are talking about memory because we want to get at something else, the texts about the children of the war may then be said to engage in a dialogue about "making up Dutch people." When one considers these representative examples of the literature of the 1980s about collaborators in context with the explicitly fictional texts we have considered earlier, the common element in all these narratives is a childhood trauma, its causes in society, the consequences for the children involved as they become adults, and the consequences for society as these traumatized individuals attempt to find their place in the community. In including the largely nonfictional texts discussed in this chapter, I am seeking to synthesize the insights from the stories we invent explicitly and the stories about "what actually happened". I work from the assumption that the debates about the place in society for those with memories of childhood trauma who feel isolated or marginalized because of their pasts take place in literary texts as they do in the writings of social scientists. As contributions to a larger discussion, they engage in the dialogue which constitutes us.

6. *Distant Cousins*

Throughout this text, I have identified a number of works in Dutch literature which show a marked interest in the history and memory of children of the war, and I have discussed a number of fictional and non-fictional texts published in the Netherlands in the 1980s which use the memory of World War II as their thematic material. Evoking the memory of World War II allows the Dutch authors I have considered to take on any of a number of issues; their reasons for doing so range from predominantly formal concerns to the engagement of notions centrally important to the culture. First, the war as a thematic element can provide challenges to the writer's craft by providing a means to inject excitement and upheaval in a (fictional) society which otherwise sees itself as a stable and placid land populated by persons whose everyday lives

15. Children from Tjideng prison camp, Batavia, Java. Photograph taken after the liberation. (RIOD)

are calm and safe. On a more significant level, the use of the war as a subject engages a larger fund of cultural assumptions which may also allow the writer to address various social issues and ethical concerns such as victimization, the question of what exactly constitutes a victim, the definition and consequences of guilt (and the question whether anyone can be wholly free thereof), memory and forgetting, the abuse of the powerless (children and the Jewish victims of the Nazi regime), and the meaning of national identity in a small European country which has always had a lively international orientation toward the end of the Twentieth Century.

But my purpose is not to impose some simple taxonomy for a body of texts which appear within a temporal boundary (i.e., the decade of the 1980s), but rather to tease out the ways in which I believe these texts participate in the formation of taxonomies of their own within the community of Dutch readers, writers, and thinkers. In particular, I have tried to suggest that, taken as a whole, these texts participate in the creation of a kind of "calculus of suffering" and demonstrate some remarkably similar approaches to the notion of what separates the traumas of a "lived present" from a "remembered past". They interrogate the traditional Dutch cultural notions of "goed" and "fout" and provide a more nuanced account of the events of – and following – World War II. In turn, this more nuanced account in itself becomes a way in which other cultural practices (the development of sexual identity, the work of grief, the discussion of social taboos) may be introduced into the ongoing discussion.

It will, I hope, come as no surprise that I believe that this ongoing discussion cuts across the traditional boundaries some readers impose when regarding fictional texts and nonfictional ones as qualitatively different. While the conventional wisdom is that we expect fiction to tell us "good stories" and history or (auto)biography or clinical studies to tell us "what really happened", I find that the texts I have analyzed here suggest a more complex reality. My purpose is neither to argue that good fiction about suffering is necessarily a clinically precise account of trauma and recovery, nor that the terrible histories and heinous crimes of the Nazi era are mere stories we have chosen to somehow "agree upon" – to do so would be to dishonor the memory of the dead and to marginalize the work of telling stories by reducing the art of writing to mere mimesis. Rather, I have been interested in the ways that these two kinds of writing act and interact, and the ways that one might productively view them as a part of an ongoing dialogue about memory, history, and meaning in Dutch society.

In that light, I have chosen to end this study by discussing another story – that of a fictional text whose appearance generated the kind of fierce debate and squabbling from various perspectives that any member of a large family cannot help but think of as a kind of "family argument". While, as we will see, the original fictional text itself shares many of the thematic concerns which have been discussed throughout this study and is certainly worthy of inclusion on its own terms, the most interesting part of the story is "outside" the narrative itself. Jeroen Brouwers' *Sunken Red*[1] constitutes an unusual case of the fiction of the 1980s in that it tells the story of wartime trauma from a position outside of the texts considered thus far – it concerns the Dutch experience of World War II in Indonesia. Its narrative strategies, while similar to those found in other texts discussed earlier, attempt to mediate the stories of an unusual sort of outsider – the repatriated Dutch expatriate. The traumas at the heart of the narrative also involve the ambivalent attitude of contemporary Dutch society toward a colonial past whose memory it may wish, like Anton Steenwijk did with his memories in *The Assault*, to "narcotize". The final transgression at the heart of *Sunken Red* can be read as a question of representation or a debate on the validity of the "history" embedded in a fictional text. This chapter will thus set in relief a unique combination of certain aspects of the debate about literature, history and memory.

My discussion in this chapter concerns the postwar history of Dutch colonials in Indonesia and their families as reflected in Jeroen Brouwers' *Sunken Red* and the debate following its appearance in 1983. I do not offer a comprehensive historical treatment of the realities of life in the "East Indies" in the 1940s or of their existence after the return of these people to the Netherlands. Rather, the experiences of the Dutch "colonials" provide another set of lessons concerning the meaning attributed to the war and its aftermath within Dutch postwar history. A brief examination of the Dutch response to the returned colonials themselves will illustrate and more precisely define the issues of identity which are central to this study as a whole. *Sunken Red* is only one of a number of texts and only one of a number of different kinds of writing about Indonesia, concentration camp life, and the Japanese occupation which one could choose to discuss. I have selected it not only for the representative value of the work itself, but particularly because the debate surrounding the book provides opportunities to engage concepts which shed new light on the other works I have discussed, and on many of the various issues already engaged.

Throughout this study, I have heretofore concentrated on the aftermath of the experiences of Dutch citizens who survived World War II – i.e., the German occupation of the Netherlands. While this is more or less in accordance with the predominant image of the war in the Netherlands, it is inaccurate. For the Dutch, World War II was fought on two fronts. A large group of Dutch civilians were not in the Netherlands; they resided in the Indonesian colony at the outbreak of the war and therefore became subject to the occupation of Indonesia by the Japanese. Their experience and attitudes toward memory are interesting both for the remarkable similarities they share with those of the Dutch in the Netherlands, and for several significant and telling differences in the patterns by which they have processed and dealt with the past and the memory thereof decades later. Like the other groups I have discussed in previous chapters, survivors who were repatriated from Indonesia also found their history and trauma to be more "discussible" in the 1980s than ever before.[2] In both fictional and nonfictional texts, they participated in the debates about identity, responsibility and memory in which the Dutch "family" engaged in that decade. Because this group has its own peculiar blend of traits which does not fit the standard "*goed-fout*" dichotomy of "good Dutch" or traitors, their experiences provide a different sort of way to test and fine-tune hypotheses concerning postwar Dutch memory and identity discussed earlier.

For those readers unfamiliar with the history of Dutch citizens living in Indonesia during World War II, a brief summary may be in order. After the Japanese attack on Pearl Harbor in December of 1941, the Dutch government in London declared war on Japan, and all "European" adult males in Indonesia were mobilized. After a series of losses, Dutch-Indonesia surrendered to the Japanese on March 8, 1942. At that point, 60,000 members of the colonial army (KNIL) were taken captive by the Japanese on Java alone; of these, non-European and mixed-race military personnel were soon released. In the end, perhaps 37,000 to 41,000 Dutch men were held as long-term prisoners of war.[3] Approximately 20% of these did not survive their internment.[4]

After Japanese citizens in areas under Allied control had been interned, the Japanese decided to intern all "pureblooded" European citizens in Dutch Indonesia in order to prevent or end all Western influence on the local populations. This process of gathering and moving people proceeded by stages. It is important to bear in mind that there were variations of type and degree in "locations, times of internment and camp regime".[5] Toward the end of 1943, the Japanese occupiers began to concentrate all the interned in areas where they did not expect any Allied troops to land. This concentration of many people in relatively small areas only exacerbated already miserable camp conditions, with the result that the loss of life was worse in some of civilian camps than among those interned in POW camps. Almost half of all Europeans in Indonesia – a much greater proportion of civilians directly affected by the war than in the Netherlands – were imprisoned or interned in concentration camps for some period of time. Beyond the already difficult internment, an additional factor which distinguishes the Dutch as an interned rather than an occupied population was the fact that women and children (including boys up to age ten) were separated from the adult males, who were usually assigned to work details under dangerous conditions instead of merely being interned.

The central theme of Jeroen Brouwers' *Sunken Red* is "Nothing exists that does not touch something else".[6] Although I will be considering this single novel here, Brouwers' aphorism extends beyond its meaning in the narrative. First, *Sunken Red* "touches" other fictional texts in Brouwers' oeuvre. As Jos Paardekooper asserts in his monograph about Brouwers' work, the novel is not only recognizably a part of his oeuvre as a whole, it is also the center of a trilogy[7] whose other volumes were published in the 1970s. As a text in the context of this study, *Sunken Red* also touches on themes discussed previously; it provides yet another piece of the puzzle of the relationship between memory and history in the Dutch fiction of the 1980s dealing with the experiences during and after the war of the so-called children of the war. Finally, the reader cannot help but notice the thematic similarity between Brouwers' statement and the one about the child of the war which opened this study – Anton Steenwijk, protagonist of *The Assault*[8] – whose narrator states:

Boundaries have to be continuously sealed off, but it's a hopeless job, for everything touches everything else in this world. A beginning never disappears, not
even with the ending. (79)

This similarity suggests that what is at stake in *Sunken Red* is, again, the centrality of
memory/history for the experience of the present in and among children of the war.
In some sense, this theme of interconnectedness which militates against the possibility of closure (and the possibility of a kind of "final answer" to the argument between
the present self and the past selves of memory or history) suggests the presence of the
same quarrels which came to occupy those Dutch "families" who survived the war –
whether in the West or the East. But I have chosen to discuss Brouwers' novel in a
separate chapter, rather than together with novels about the other child victims such
as Minco's *Glass Bridge*, Van Dantzig's *For A Lost Soldier*, and Mulisch' *Assault*, in part
to underscore the notion of the separateness of Dutch residents of Indonesia during
World War II as a group; Dutch citizens repatriated from Indonesia after the war were
not generally recognized as war victims by the Dutch populace at first. The Indonesian past with which Brouwers' narrator wrestles is worthy of separate consideration
since it concerns a war history which most of the Dutch population who survived the
war on native soil did (and often do) not necessarily recognize as similar to their own.
One may argue that it is in part the search for ways to represent that similarity which
is at the heart of the debates which followed the publication of *Sunken Red*.

The main character of *Sunken Red* is thus to a certain degree an outsider in Dutch
culture, who – though a Dutch citizen – at the end of the war is a migrant from a
different part of the world. As an outsider, he must learn to assimilate, even in superficial ways. By contrast, the child protagonists of *The Assault*, *The Glass Bridge* and
For a Lost Soldier begin the occupation fully integrated into domestic Dutch culture
or their particular subculture; they are still able to pass for "normal" on the surface
when they return at the end of the war, although they have changed internally. They
may feel themselves to be completely different people, and most readers will grant
that they are fundamentally changed. However, their otherness is internal – they are
still able to speak Dutch without an accent. They eat potatoes, not rice. Insofar as
their suffering has changed them, it is recognized as such and respected – even
admired – by other civilians. This contrasts with those repatriated from Indonesia
after the war. All their experiences, including their own wartime suffering, constituted a barrier between them and the Dutch civilians who had resided in Europe the
whole time, and functioned as signs of their difference, and so they ceased to speak
about their pasts to outsiders (i.e., those thought of as "normal" Dutch citizens). The
term "outsiders" itself raises the issue at the center of this group's dilemma: those considered insiders in their group were outsiders to the culture at large, and vice versa.
They were seen as separate by virtue of the historical circumstance of having left their
homes and moved to a country on the other side of the world which was officially
thought to be their "homeland," but which was, practically speaking, foreign to
them, and in which they had not been welcome.

Those Dutch citizens repatriated from Indonesia at the end of the war or at the time of Indonesian independence in 1949 did not leave their painful experiences behind when they left the country to move across the world. It is obvious that the necessity of abandoning what was in many cases the only country these people had ever known and coming to a nation with a cold climate and with a populace which often treated the repatriates with indifference, only intensified the trauma. And, due to the magnitude of the pain and anxiety, these events were more likely to induce them to push far away those memories of war in order to be able to concentrate their emotional energy on assimilating into a "new" culture, which – though familiar in some respects – presented a parade of subtle differences. It is clear that it was exceptionally difficult to be confronted with a "homeland" which was supposed to seem welcoming and familiar, but did not feel like home at all.

This difficulty is again reminiscent of Freud's formulation of the "narcissism of minor difference".[9] Most of the repatriates who returned to the Netherlands spoke Dutch, though not exactly like the "natives". They were culturally Dutch, but with a difference; they were more skilled at cooking rice than potatoes. They considered themselves Dutch, but were not-really-Dutch to the survivors of the German occupation who were concentrating their efforts on the physical, economic and cultural reconstruction of the country in the late 1940s and 1950s. It was not a time when Dutch citizens were eager to confront novelty or felt particularly appreciative of cultural differences. This focus – as a collateral effect of national reconstruction – on what society considered quintessentially Dutch traits complicated the process by which those being repatriated could integrate into the culture. As the narrator of *Sunken Red* presents his situation:

> After the war, having been repatriated to the Netherlands, I disappear almost at once, for the rest of my childhood, into monastically run boarding schools, because my camp experience and other events in post-war Indonesia have made me "wild". I have "no moral sense", I have no "feeling" for what is "right" and what "isn't right", and I recognize no authority.

> (Indeed, in those days I was immensely happy: never afraid, never a prey to doubt, never sad...).[10]

Those returnees who did not feel welcome or particularly understood as a group adopted a strategy of expediency of their own. In many cases they chose to avoid any emphasis on the differences between themselves and those who had survived the war in the Netherlands.[11] They were often silent, and often – as Jeroen Brouwers reports – laughed about their memories and recalled having laughed in the camps:

> "Well, we did laugh a lot there, you know."

> I noticed little or nothing of that, but perhaps grownups laughed at times when I was asleep or when I was somewhere else.

I remember that at home, long after the war, there would be *screams* of laughter when my parents, my brothers, other relatives or friends, raked up memories from their camp years. The history of those camps has been washed away on waves of hilarity.[12]

The other members of the group of repatriated colonials laughed as they retold stories of their terrible experiences in the camp; the narrator also reports having heard people say that the camps had been filled with laughter. But Brouwers' narrator rejects that notion based on his own experience. This response to the horrors remembered only by insiders in the group – of gathering and telling stories – is easily recognized in retrospect as an attempt at building solidarity among the community of survivors, and functions as a source of comfort within the group. It provides a shield against the lack of understanding, sympathy and acceptance expressed by the culture at large. As Kai Erikson describes the dynamic:

> ...trauma can create community. In some ways, that is a very odd thing to claim. To describe people as traumatized is to say that they have withdrawn into a kind of protective envelope, a place of mute, aching loneliness, in which the traumatic experience is treated as a solitary burden that needs to be expunged by acts of denial and resistance. What could be less "social" than that?
>
> ...
>
> Still, trauma shared can serve as a source of communality in the same way that common languages and common backgrounds can.
>
> So trauma has both centripetal and centrifugal tendencies. The human chemistry at work here is an odd one, but it has been noted many times before: estrangement becomes the basis of communality, ...[13]

In many cases, as texts such as that by Brouwers show, laughter – more specifically, the memory of laughter – shared with those who remembered a similar past ironically became the way out of the "protective envelope" into which survivors from Indonesia had retreated as individuals, while simultaneously reinforcing their separateness from the larger culture. Their laughter was misunderstood by the "average" Dutch – who were not listening carefully – as a sign of happiness and thus an absence of any reason for complaint. A predictable result of the "silence" (or uncommunicative and misunderstood laughter) of the Indonesian expatriates and a reluctance to hear on the part of the Dutch was that the returnees' suffering was neither known nor understood by most Dutch citizens. Ian Buruma echoes the ignorance described here as follows: "The Dutch East Indies meant nothing to me, even though some of my friends had been born there."[14]

Jeroen (Godfried Maria) Brouwers had, however, been "born there" – in Batavia (now Djakarta), Indonesia, on April 30, 1940. He was interned in the Tjideng camp – a camp for women and small children on the outskirts of Batavia – from early 1943 until the end of 1945. After migrating to the Netherlands at the age of ten, he attended several Roman Catholic boarding schools, and became a writer as an adult. His mother, Henriette Maria Elisabeth van Maaren, died in the night of Monday, January 26, 1981.

The chronology recounted above, as the biographies of many of the other writers discussed thus far, also has its "touch" extend beyond the facts of verifiable history. In the case of *Sunken Red*, the death of a woman who is the protagonist's mother figures centrally, or rather her death as the end of the protagonist's relationship (more or less) with her. His relationship with her is seen as being of essential importance to his relationship with other women, and in a broader sense of his entire attitude toward life. And at the center of the relationship with his mother, there are the events of their imprisonment in the Japanese camp during the protagonist's boyhood.

Sunken Red thus presents the same basic constellation of motifs which I have claimed in Chapters 1 and 2 of this study to be typical for novels about the memory of children of the war: they are in some sense stories about trauma, represented as coming of age at a too-tender age, and of a character's being forced to grow up too soon and too fast in the fictional constellation of wartime experiences. As such, these motifs incorporate formative experiences of sex as well as early knowledge of death, the two being as intricately related as would delight any Freudian. Memory, with forgetfulness as its double, is also central. Like Anton, Stella and Jeroen,[15] the first-person narrator of *Sunken Red* has memories of experiences which have changed his life forever, because they have fundamentally shaped or deformed his personality.

The narrative structure of *Sunken Red* presents us with a slightly different view of memory and history, however. The story of the protagonist's experiences and history emerge from a set of smaller narrative fragments which are chronologically disconnected. Often, it is the reader's task to determine the location and time frame of a given fragment. It is as if we are given a set of unlabeled and unordered memory traces and evidence of childhood experience, with the novel's narrator understood as their repository. Moreover, it remains unclear even at the end of the novel what sort of closure has occurred in the main character's existence; we are shown the image of a man in a room – isolated from his wife and child as he considers the fragments which form the narrative core of the novel – whose ostensibly calm narrative voice is at odds with the shaking hand which holds his favorite anodyne – tranquilizers and a drink.

> Later the wind rose and raindrops appeared on the outside of the window, slowly sliding across the pane so that between me and my other self a web-like lattice formed and I saw my face dissolve into liquid in the mist.[16]

In the absence of narrative closure, the reader's attention is thus focused on the way that the component parts of the narrator's damaged personality appear and reappear, or "touch" each other as the reader assembles the novel's fragmentary bits and pieces. In some respects, Brouwers seems to imply that what closure is made possible by this narrative strategy may only reside with the reader; as Brouwers' narrator puts it: "What I have written I need no longer remember. It may now move into the conscious and subconscious thoughts of others."[17] The narrative proposes that as the reader re-assembles the fragments presented by the text, this exercise will function as a species of memory-work.

One consequence of Brouwers' narrative style is that the reader is allowed to glimpse recurrent patterns as he or she assembles the chronological "history" embedded in the novel; this strategy explicitly focuses on a feature of trauma only briefly discussed in some of the other works discussed in this study – the notion that the effects of trauma are often thought to appear and reappear as patterns of repetitive behavior. Assembling the narrator's life as a series of fragments out of time allows this pattern to emerge more clearly and more strongly, and in the absence of anything we might recognize as closure, the reader is left to wonder how these patterns may be repeated again. In describing this approach to representing the pattern of his protagonist's life, Brouwers borrows the word *octaviteit* ["octavity", the quality of behaving like musical octaves], commonly associated with Harry Mulisch's work; Jaap Goedegebuure confirms this borrowing in his essay about *Sunken Red* and the discussions it called forth.[18] *Octaviteit* refers to the recurrence of similar themes or issues at different levels in a text. In the case of these novels about the memory of the war, I would argue that it is not just a literary device, but also a reflection of the reality of the way memory – particularly unresolved memory – works to connect all the subsequent events in life to earlier traumatic experiences. Thus, the narrator of *Sunken Red* has a "misconnected" relationship with his mother caused by their experiences of the camp[19] which is subsequently repeated – at another level – when she delivers him to boarding school: "The same story, in a different key."[20] This same notion also finds expression in similarly "broken" relationships with the women who become his lovers.

This skillful repetition on numerous narrative levels accounts for much of the novel's clarity and power. Rather than attempting to detail them all and thus rob the new reader of the pleasures of performing his or her own assembly of Brouwers' novel, I will briefly touch upon and describe a single one of these narrative strands. One of the motifs at the heart of *Sunken Red* is the protagonist's complex relationship with his mother – a relationship which the reader will probably view as defined by a pathology which expresses itself as love-hate. But it is understood that the situation which precipitated this aspect of the relationship is a direct consequence of the war experience of the family's internment in Indonesia. During the war, the narrator is interned in a Japanese camp with his mother, his grandmother (who was to die there), his sister, and a childhood female friend (who also did not survive the camp), while his father is thousands of miles away on an internee work detail. In the close quarters and otherwise uncertain circumstances in which the interned families lived in the camps, it is to be expected that one method of maintaining some semblance of family life would involve the maintenance of small family rituals as a way of providing some sense of a "normal" existence. Similarly, it would not be surprising that any mother in such circumstances would be protective of her children. Yet the sense in *Sunken Red* is that these two understandable aspects of family dynamics emerge as features of what the boy may have perceived as an unnatural intimacy with his mother. One example of this is reflected when he describes the "secret greeting" they shared.

> A look of astonishment crossed my mother's face when she heard me shout those words at her – they were far too solemn, far too pert, from the mouth of a small boy. But then she laughed, so that I knew for the rest of my life that if I said "ketemu lagi" my mother would laugh.

> The words mean more than "farewell". They mean, may you prosper and be happy wherever you go.

> They became sacred, incantatory code words between my mother and me, who said goodbye to each other hundreds of times until a few years before her death, because we were both like the wind that seldom stays, being always on the way from and to somewhere else. And until the last few times, when we said these words to each other we laughed, although in the end we did so only with our eyes and it would have been more fitting if, just for once, we had wept. (32-33)

Even here, in a discussion of farewells, the theme of laughter presents itself, a laughter which masks sadness. Another sign that something is wrong is harder to overlook; the complicated relationships with women which the narrator reports – at least in his imagination. He recounts at length his violent fantasies throughout the novel. He suffers from a classic, almost simplistic virgin/whore complex; he describes images habitually, silently repeating language such as a list of names of the Virgin Mary during his sexual experiences while imagining violence against his lover or rehearsing violent memories from his camp days. Again, his relationship with his mother is presented at the center of those events; the reader is given the fragments to assemble some view of the narrator's sex life only after being told of his mother's death and after having been exposed to the narrator's memories of her. In a variation on the cliché that one sees one's life flash before one's eyes at the moment of death, the narrator/protagonist of *Sunken Red* reviews not only his mother's life (insofar as he is familiar with it) but his own as well upon being told of his mother's passing; this narration constitutes the novel. The novel asserts that for the narrator "everything is connected to everything else", but in another sense, the unusually close relationship between the son and his mother has been severed, or rather, reconnected incorrectly. They are "misconnected":

(Very infrequently in recent years my mother would phone me, but as soon as I spoke my name she would say, "I'm sorry, wrong number."[21] I knew her voice by the tone and by her Indonesian accent. There are millions of mothers in the world, but only one of them is mine. Before I could answer she would hang up, and I left it at that. I had heard the voice of a mother who was misconnected with her son).[22]

The reason for the faulty connection between the two will turn out to be directly related to their past internment in the Japanese camp in Indonesia. The next lines summarize the narrator's development, the psychological trauma he sustained as a small boy, perfectly:

("Croak croak!")

I received the news of her death by telephone...

I stood naked and shivering by the large living-room window, the receiver at my ear and my hand on my member. (The beloved was called Liza.)...

I thought, what was on television last night that my mother might just have had time to enjoy?[23]

The croaking is a symbol both of the torture of the camp interns by the Japanese (the narrator reports that the internees were forced to hop around on their haunches and make croaking sounds) and also of the unhealthy relationship between the narrator and his mother (and, by extension – by way of *octaviteit* – between the narrator and the women who become his lovers). Both the telephone and croaking are associated with the broken relationship between mother and child, and between the former child and his lovers. The news of the mother's death arrives by telephone, with the narrator's body neatly arranged between two primal forces in his life: his mother and sex, connected in his person – or rather, his mother's death and sex.

The text continues by recounting the narrator's life as a young boy in the camps, who lives in close proximity to a large number of women; the only adult males present were Japanese camp guards who maltreated and tortured some of the women while others (including the children) were forced to watch. The regime not only included arbitrary cruelty, but also punishment when the women were caught with a little extra food (which they had found or stolen) beyond their normal rations. At one point, the protagonist's mother is punished and humiliated for attempting to provide extra rice for her children. Naturally, watching his mother get hurt for her attempts to help him is confusing for the little boy. In addition to the damage done to a child's sense of justice in a setting in which decisions by authority figures appear to be arbitrary, and retribution is meted out unfairly, the boy is particularly hurt by some specific kinds of punishment intended to humiliate the inmates as women. In watching the goings-on in the camp, sex becomes associated in the little boy's mind with violence and punishment.

MATERNAL ROLES

In spite of her suffering and powerlessness in the war, the mother depicted in *Sunken Red* does not appear to be a bad mother. The narrator fondly recalls the days before their relationship was fundamentally altered and damaged in the camps, a time when her role in his life was entirely positive:

> Let me not pretend to be more cynical than I am, and certainly no more sentimental either – but at least I knew my mother then, in those war years in the Japanese camp where she taught me to read.[24]

His mother taught him to read, and during their internment bartered assiduously in order to be able to give him a birthday gift: Leonard Roggeveen's "Danny goes on a trip" [*Daantje gaat op reis*], a children's book. Danny becomes one of the alter egos the narrator uses as he describes, remembers, and deals with his childhood, a habit which began in the camp but persists into adulthood. The Danny persona appears when the character is "pursuing" Liza, the woman who will become his lover: "look-tinkle who-tinkle goes-tinkle there-tinkle, Danny on the chase",[25] illustrating the profound influence and persistence of memory; patterns of thought and self-image developed in the camp stay with him for the rest of his life. The memory pattern, the recurrence of the (delayed) effects of trauma, is reinforced by the literary device referred to as *octaviteit*. Goedegebuure, who does not explicitly connect this story to the theme of trauma in the psychological sense, nevertheless writes:

> The story/history of a child and his mother, confined in a Japanese internment camp, is repeated in the relationship between the older self and Liza, that is: he is the one who – almost compulsively – performs[26] this repetition in his imagination.[27]

The book his mother gave him is an important early influence on the boy's life, both as a book – story and object – and as a symbol of his mother's love, and also because of its instrumentality since it was with this book that he learned to read; phrases from the book form one of the refrains in his memory of the camp. If seeing his mother's powerlessness in the face of the camp guards' cruelty has contributed to his being "misconnected" with his mother, to the thought that she is "broken", and that he now needs a new mother,[28] the other side of the coin is that she valued books and taught him to read, thus preparing him to become a writer. In fact, the narrator views his having learned to read as literally a lifesaver:

In order to stay alive: / Every day I repeated the letters and the words my
mother had taught me by writing them with her finger or a stick in the sand
and at the same time in my brain –

"the", "then", "and", "hand", "on", "oen", "roen", "je-roen"...[29]

The narrator states that her gift of a book for his fifth birthday and her teaching him
to read – a pocket of culture in the midst of the deprivations of the camp – is what
presents itself as the most important memory at the time of her death. In the fictional
realm, reading would be the narrator's memory-work if only he could find the book,
just as the book Brouwers has written embodies a work of memory for survivors of
the camps.

I wanted to remember my mother by the best thing she ever gave me: from
that now-lost little pre-war book, stained, smudged, crumpled, torn, my
mother taught me to read. In the East Indies, in the Japanese camp, in the
early forties. I was given that book on my fifth birthday.

Seated at my desk, at the moment when two hundred kilometers away my
mother vanished into the fiery furnace, I would have wished to read aloud
from that book, in her honor, to pay her homage in the way I thought right.[30]

However ardently the reader may wish that the narrator could have connected with
his mother while she was alive, it is an appropriate tribute that he honor her with a
book at her death. As far as the mother and son are concerned, internment and its
vicissitudes ruined what had probably been a normal, loving relationship. The fact
that this broken relationship with his mother is a sign of events which have had a profound impact on the rest of his life is reinforced by the memories he revisits at the
time of her death. The text refers to the beginning of Dante's *Inferno*:

When I was six or seven years younger than I am now, "I found myself in a
dark wood, for I had lost the right road." My life consisted of drifting about,
always half-drunk, out of disgust with life and a desire not to live.[31]

The decision to quote Dante poses some interesting questions. Since this quotation
does not occupy the same position in the novel as the opening stanzas do in Dante's
Inferno, the reader is left with a set of connections – places where (to recall Brouwers' refrain from *Sunken Red*) the text is "connected" to something else – which
remain unresolved. It is unclear that the narrator, unlike the narrator of Dante's opening stanzas, has emerged from his dark wood and details the circumstances of his life
as a way to describe his emergence. Immediately following this quotation, the reader
of *Sunken Red* is introduced to the narrator's lover Liza. While it is intriguing to consider the possibility that introducing her at this point in the text is intended to evoke
the figure of Beatrice (an idealized female figure who may be inserted into the con-

tinuum of the narrator's images of women), the text remains ambiguous on this point as well – her introduction is merely contiguous to the Dante quote. Finally, the reader will surely know that it is Virgil and not Beatrice who guides Dante from the dark wood – the image is, itself, a kind of faulty connection which more generally may be seen to symbolize the narrator's predicament. It is, in fact, unclear who (if anyone) is present to help guide the narrator out of the dark wood. Finally, despite many similarities with war novels set in the Netherlands, it is also true that – in addition to the issues of how memory and the traumas of youth deform the adult lives of survivors encountered previously in this study – Brouwers' dark wood is also one whose contours may remain relatively unknown to some members of his Dutch audience.

Brouwers' audience's relative unfamiliarity with the experience of the Japanese occupation is further compounded by the expedient silence of those Dutch citizens repatriated in the period following the war, a historical fact which presents some interesting problems to the writers whose texts take Indonesia as their setting. In some measure, telling such a story may involve breaking a silence, an act which works against the desire to culturally assimilate. In this light, the choice of a child protagonist and the story of wartime trauma may be seen as another example of telling a different story (that is, the experience of World War II in Indonesia) by adopting narrative conventions already well accepted among a Dutch reading public.[32] Those already-familiar narrative conventions extend well beyond descriptions of childhood, and – as we have seen – beyond the simple notions of "goed" and "fout". They also participate in a variety of conventions of representation. And those representations themselves extend well beyond the conventions of fictional narrative. In some sense, they may be said to be at the heart of what constitutes "truth" and "falsehood" in Dutch cultural practice.

REPRESENTATION AND VERISIMILITUDE

It is this question of representation and verisimilitude which provides another reason for setting *Sunken Red* apart from other novels concerning children of the war. The appearance of the novel in 1983 "touched" something else again; the remarkable history of critical responses to this text became the occasion for a lively debate in the Dutch press which is noteworthy for its vehemence, a debate which circled around questions about the "veracity" of Brouwers' representation of the experiences he gives his narrator in the Japanese internment camp. This debate seems to suggest that many Dutch readers do not always make a careful distinction between fictional and non-fictional genres. An examination of the debate thus allows us to rehearse the reasons why the combatants did or did not view historical truth as an essential requirement for such a text.

My discussion of the debate is not intended to be a blow-by-blow history or analysis, as there is little to be gained from a detailed summary in the context of this study. I believe it will suffice to consider several signal moments from this "family squabble". As I hope my analysis will communicate, the discussion which followed the appearance of Brouwers' Sunken Red does, indeed, fit the term "family argument" in more than one sense: first, as with members of a family, similarities seem clear to the outside world while their differences are most obvious within the confines of the group. What I present here is a debate among members of a group with a clear identity, or rather, several different branches of such a group. Second, (as is the case with all good arguments within families), the subtext of the discussion is about the exercise of power and inclusion – to ask who will be permitted to be or remain a family member in good standing.

At this juncture I proceed by pointing to and engaging some of the issues which the combatants raise in the course of their argument. Rudy Kousbroek is one of Brouwers' most persistent critics; in fact the notion of "sibling rivalry" as a set of bitter arguments over a commitment to similar issues closely held seems profoundly relevant to their debates. Kousbroek accuses Brouwers of having assembled *Sunken Red* as if "uit een Neurembergse bouwdoos" (using a child's building set), and applies his famous coinage, "East Indies Camp Syndrome" *(Oost-Indisch Kamp Syndroom)*, to Brouwers' views. The Dutch expression "to pretend to be deaf in the way of the East Indies", (zich Oost-Indies doof houden), which dates to colonial times and a lack of

16. Rudy Kousbroek as a young boy, with his cat. (September, 1938) (Letterkundig Museum)

sensitivity to cultural difference, means "none so deaf as those that will not hear."[33] In this case, Kousbroek defines this "East Indies Camp Syndrome" as an unwillingness to recognize that one's "memories" are either false or exaggerations, an attempt to gain sympathy, an appeal to a victimhood which is as serious as that of survivors of German camps, and a tendency to accuse of heartlessness anyone who does look for the "objective" truth (or "an unwillingness to figure out how things really were and to prefer to hold on to an unrealistic image, a myth.")[34] Or, as related by de Vos, "the tendency on the part of former victims to exaggerate the horror ("badness") of the Japanese camps. They put those camps on a par with the German camps."[35]

Another line of argument attacks individual details in Brouwers' book and complains that they are not historically accurate. These arguments, in turn, invited counter-arguments from others who rushed to Brouwers' defense. This confusion about the accuracy of historical facts concerning the camps is understandable in light of the fact that there was a good deal of individual variation among the Japanese camps, both in physical design and in the manner in which they were run, which depended to a large extent on the camp leadership. This variation stands in stark contrast to the treatment prisoners received in the German camps, which were centrally planned and much more uniform in their administration and layout. It is thus likely that aspects of camp life as presented in *Sunken Red* which some reviewers criticized might have been correct with reference to some camps, but not to others. As Goedegebuure mentions, some of Brouwers' facts are confirmed in an article by D.M.G. Koch entitled "De Japanse bezetting van Indonesië" ("The Japanese Occupation of Indonesia"); Brouwers in fact cites this source in his novel.[36] The following examples of such criticisms of the factuality of Brouwers' text may help to illustrate this point.[37]

What is striking to me as I look at this debate is the way certain themes emerge within this argument about historical veracity. Several strains of types of information stand out as particularly important to these critics. For instance, Fred Lanzing[38] in a scathing review in *Maatstaf*, argues that the watch towers, machine guns and search lights which are mentioned in *Sunken Red* are entirely fictional. But there are witnesses such as Van Velden, who claim the Japanese had built hideaways for machine-gunners which surrounded the camps.[39] Lanzing complains about the "razzias" in which the children are taken out of the camp on work detail while the mothers wonder whether they will ever see them again, but H.E. Keizer-Henzeveldt[40] reports situations in which children are taken away and returned the same evening which mirror the events described in *Sunken Red*. Hans Vervoort and H.L. Zwitser also respond to accusations leveled against Brouwers, and claim on the basis of their own experiences and of written history that machine guns, rape, beatings, and water torture were indeed historically accurate details.

In short, there is a chorus of complaints which state that Brouwers has gotten his details wrong, often based on an appeal to the authority of the critics' own experiences: "I was in a camp, and that never happened to me." And then there are those who confirm a detail or two, and also those such as Jos Paardekooper, who states: "One gets the impression that of the descriptions of circumstances and occurrences in *Sunken Red* against which many critics... have protested, altogether there are few which cannot be supported by one source or another," in other words, that independent testimony is available in the form of "yes, but at some other point in time", or "not in Tjideng". At least some kind of confirmation is possible that such things did happen in some place at some time, and that poetic license should cover any minor discrepancies. *Sunken Red* is a novel after all.[41] Paardekooper even argues that Brouwers had been actually quite restrained in his descriptions of the rats, lice, and flies, and that he is by no means exaggerating since he fails to mention other legitimate facts, such as the backbreaking work of being forced to sit in the burning sun and pick grass from among the bricks in the street, the unpleasant early morning roll call in the cold tropical nights, and so on.

Kousbroek, for one, is not willing to grant poetic license in this case, because in his view there is too much at stake. He underscores that several facts mentioned by Brouwers about contemporary Dutch life are incorrect, facts which Brouwers could have confirmed relatively easily. For instance, Brouwers' narrator mentions watching *Kumonosuyo*, "The castle in the forest of spider webs", a Japanese version of the Macbeth story, a film directed by Akira Kurasowa and broadcast by a German TV station. The point of his telling this is that the film is dubbed in German:[42]

> I stared absentmindedly at the screen, not trying to follow the plot, but when I did pay attention, I felt irritated: those barbarous Krauts had dubbed the Japanese dialogue in German.[43]

There are other instances in *Sunken Red* where the narrator uses elements of the experience of Japanese camps to refer to German Nazi behavior, a pattern of signs and symbols which angers his critics. He does not equate the two experiences, but questions and ridicules the notion of comparison. The passage continues:

(Who were "worse" in the war, the Germans or the Japanese? And which camps were more gruesome, the Germans or the Japanese?

No surviving victim has ever spoken of the German camps with affection and nostalgia. Those who survived the German camps did not laugh at them in the way that ex-prisoners of the Japanese laughed at the Japanese camps, supposedly to make a relative matter of what cannot be made relative.

The servants of death spoke German and they spoke Japanese too. Sometimes I hear on television how the servant language of one civilized nation is replaced by the servant language of the other, and I observe: the Jap speaks German – just as it can be imagined that in Japan the language of the Kraut is dubbed in Japanese.

Death doesn't care what language his servants speak.)[44]

DISTANT COUSINS

This implied claim that those interned in the Japanese camps also suffered and died in large numbers under the improper treatment of an occupying Japanese army (and who thus might be accorded some position of importance along the continuum of the sufferings of the Dutch people in World War II) in combination with the use of symbolism reminiscent to the Dutch of the Nazi extermination camps has brought down upon Brouwers the wrath of his opponents.

DISTINCTIONS WITH A DIFFERENCE

It makes sense to distinguish clearly between the evil intentionality of the orderly executions which took place in Nazi extermination camps on one hand and the more random cruelty of the Japanese camps on the other; the historical circumstances and the stated intentions which created each of the two situations were clearly different. Likewise, the horrifyingly efficient mobilization of the machinery of the German Reich in the service of the annihilation of the Jews and entire groups of people whose only crime was their ethnic or religious identity, should never be downplayed or discounted. Nevertheless, from the perspective of the victims – and in particular the children of the war(s) – there may be some correspondences between some of the experiences of the camps themselves. Brouwers' usage of symbols of Nazi cruelty and oppression in his text need not necessarily be read as a claim that the evils of the German and Japanese camps are equal. Rather, Brouwers' use of them is an acknowledgment of the ready recognition, symbolic value, and emotional weight of the signs of Nazi power and evil for Dutch readers. The use of such symbols does not necessarily constitute a claim of moral equivalency, but rather an attempt to appropriate (with some license) some images from the common fund of the Dutch experience of World War II into a narrative that tries to bridge the experiential gulf which separates those in Europe during the war from those in Indonesia. The evocation of the sound of jackboots marching down a fictional street will instantly make Dutch readers cringe; the fact that there is no comparable emotional response associated with symbols of the Japanese camps for most Dutch citizens is both a constitutive factor in the difficulties the repatriated experienced after their "return" to the Netherlands and a sign of their continued alienation.

Kousbroek's uncompromising formulating of the issues may work against his point by polarizing the argument – a polarization which extends to any number of quibbles. Kousbroek has noted (as have others) that the broadcast of the Kurasowa film dubbed in German was not on the evening the narrator's/author's mother died, and uses what seems a straightforward bit of poetic license as a pretext to accuse Brouwers of sloppiness (since it would have been a relatively simple matter to check this fact). Besides the Kurasowa broadcast mentioned above, Kousbroek argues with a variety of other details which are as easily matters of poetic license (e.g., the dates of Sone's tenure as camp commander in Tjideng mentioned in *Sunken Red* are also not "accurate"). Kousbroek's uncompromising stance forces one to choose between

Brouwers' indulging in a "private truth" or a lie – an oversimplification I believe to be offered in the spirit of a larger polemic.

Unfortunately for those who consider clarity important, Brouwers himself does little to help matters in some regards. In an interview in the *Haagsche Post*,[45] Brouwers perversely, or perhaps just carelessly, suggested that people who do not like to read novels could read his book as history. This kind of language plays right into the hands of fact-mongers and is thus a stumbling-block for those who would wish to excuse Brouwers' inaccurate details by a simple and appropriate appeal to the text's status as fiction. Nevertheless, it is of paramount importance to remember Brouwers' concern, stated in the novel itself, that "The history of those camps is in danger of being lost",[46] because of the silence which surrounds them. Brouwers' concept of history may have more to do with communication about the past to those living in the present in terms to which they are likely to connect, with an understanding and with a sense of his subjective experience, than with a correct listing of numbers and dates. His is certainly a legitimate concern.

But this is not the only relevant aspect to the discussion; some survivors of the Japanese camps who comment on *Sunken Red* are angry out of a pragmatic concern that they are now receiving "too much" sympathy; such critics feel that the attention will turn to disdain once readers discover Brouwers' "mistakes". Mischa de Vreede,[47] a well-known Dutch author, declares that she no longer has calluses on her feet (thus denying the literal truth of one of Brouwers' more banal but effective images). She is angry because she fears that he has contributed to an atmosphere in which the legitimate claims for acceptance of the people repatriated from Indonesia in the Netherlands will be discredited, because others will certainly disbelieve the reports of suffering in the Indonesian camps if the book becomes known as "inaccurate". Such critics expect readers to reason that if Brouwers felt a need to "embellish" the facts as he wrote his novel, then such exaggeration must count as a sign that the historical reality could not have been so bad. Thus, Brouwers is accused of ruining the returnees' chances at appropriate sympathy and a normal sense of solidarity from other Dutch citizens. Brouwers responds that the camp experience had been actually much worse than he had presented it in *Sunken Red*.[48]

A species of moral argument already alluded to above is also raised, as put forth by Kousbroek. He states that it is inappropriate to claim to have "symptoms" similar to those of survivors of German death camps because the camp situations differed fundamentally. Echoing some of the standard views about the uniqueness of the Holocaust, he argues that those who returned from the Shoah had lived with the knowledge that the goal of their internment was their extinction, and had thus had essentially different experiences. They had suffered both more and qualitatively differently than had those in Japanese camps, where internees who did not return perished as a "collateral" effect of camp life rather than as the result of a well-executed plan of mass extermination.

It is important to note that many of Brouwers' combatants are themselves survivors of camps similar to "his" Tjideng. Their motivations in arguing with Brouwers about the verisimilitude of his text and its function in society range from expressions of piety toward survivors of the Holocaust to concern that complaints about their own past will hamper their acceptance within Dutch society, a strategy which Brouwers dubs "mildness".

> The history of these Japanese camps threatens to be forgotten, because those who were there have kept silent about them and those who have broken the silence have done so too late, after their indignation and their hate had softened or faded, and they had already died the death that is called mildness.[49]

The silence or "mildness" Brouwers refers to failed as a strategy of integration because it not only did not help the survivors gain the place they desired in Dutch society, but also prevented them from coming to terms with their past. The "symptoms" of the trauma sustained during the internment and the motifs related to the narrator's memory of camp life might at first blush seem extreme. They are, however, consistent with the expectations of certain current psychological and therapeutic models. If the symptoms seem extreme, it is interesting to know that this fact need not be interpreted as exaggeration on the part of Brouwers the author. It should rather be noted that the phenomena mentioned fall within the realm considered normal or expected by psychological practitioners who deal with delayed traumatic symptoms, and in particular resemble patterns of behavior of men who were interned in Japanese camps as young boys. Whether this fact means that Brouwers' characters' experiences are generally "true" in some sense, or whether one concludes that this demonstrates only

17. Children and adults in a former Japanese prison camp. (RIOD)

that knowledge is culturally mediated, and emerges from dialogue with other participants in our culture, is a matter of debate.

SOCIAL AND POLITICAL REPERCUSSIONS

ICODO ["Informatie- en Coördinatie Orgaan Dienstverlening Oorlogsgetroffenen"] is a Dutch foundation of psychologists and counselors who specialize in delayed response to trauma sustained during the war. ICODO has identified the former inmates from Japanese camps, including children of the war, as having war-related trauma symptoms, a fact which could be a significant factor in the process of their recognition as "legitimate" war victims. Such symptoms are said to include a sense of alienation, difficulty in forming connections with others, a sense of disengagement from loved ones, consistent mistrust of other human beings, depression and a tendency to make the past (the camp experience and subsequent losses, in this case) into a central constitutive event in one's life, which one identifies as being of prime importance. From these complex combinations of behavioral or psychological traits, it follows that the traumatized person is likely to remain isolated from the culture at large, because others "do not understand", and to retreat into the self, or perhaps into a group of individuals who have had similar traumatic experiences, and who are thus thought to be able to fathom the other's feelings.[50] It is in this sense that Kai Erikson states that "...trauma can create community..."[51]

The symptoms traditionally associated with trauma can be identified in the child protagonists Anton, Stella, and Jeroen,[52] as well as in the protagonist of *Sunken Red*. In addition to being similar fictional constructs, I would suggest that they gain their power as narrators to some extent from the fact that they are fictionalized instantiations of the real-world symptoms of trauma sustained during or after – in any case, as a result of – the war.

I have already mentioned the relationship of "misconnectedness" between the protagonist of *Sunken Red* and his mother. Alienated personal relationships with others are typical of the other children of the war whom I have discussed in earlier chapters, with this difference: the protagonist of *Sunken Red*, sometimes in the guise of his child alter-ego Daantje, feels alienated not only from members of Dutch society at large who did not share the experience of the camps, but even from his mother who was with him throughout the war and the entire time in the camps. Critics have accused Brouwers of exaggeration, since his camp experience was – within the "calculus of suffering" often subconsciously adopted – certainly less horrific than that of the 25% of Dutch Jews who survived the Holocaust. I submit, however, that what is at stake here is not a calculus – qualitative or quantitative – but a text which (in addition to the obvious aesthetic reasons for reading it) may function as an argument in support of legitimate claims to recognition. The novel thus participates in the Dutch "family discussion" about memory and identity: who belongs, who does not, and why.

In addition, the protagonist's "misconnected" relationship with his mother is also represented as related to his violent fantasies about his (female) lovers, an effect which may on the surface seem extreme. Aesthetically speaking, this repetition is another instance of "*octaviteit.*" On the other hand, an ICODO study on the experiences of young boys interned in Japanese camps offers evidence of possible developmental reasons for such reactions from the psychological point of view. If this is correct, the feelings and responses represented in *Sunken Red* are not nearly as extreme or exaggerated as some readers have claimed, but rather very much in concert with what would be predicted on the basis of psychoanalytic theory applied to the situations of the camp. Once again, the appropriate conclusion would be not that Brouwers lied, or exaggerated – thus losing credibility with the general public – but rather, that his presentation of the past falls within the realm of responses considered appropriate, "normal", by his culture. Whether one considers his symptoms in line with what psychological theory has indicated to be appropriate, or whether one prefers merely to note that his responses are in concert with what would be expected of those in that specific cultural situation, there is no doubt that the feelings and behaviors he attribut-

18. A mother and two children at Tjideng camp, Batavia, Java. (RIOD)

es to his protagonist exist in the context of his cultural expectations and are expressed within that particular culture. As such, they form a contribution to the dialogue about what the Dutch think of the function of memory within their culture.

In addition, Ellemers and Vaillant identify three general causes of suffering or emotional stress in former colonials. First, they note the difficulty of working through the psychological pain caused by the war, the internment, and the ensuing difficult period ["Bersiap-periode"]. Secondly, they point to a pattern of social and cultural isolation, particularly among the older Indonesian-Dutch, and thirdly, they speak of some issues related to integration, such as difficulties caused by clashes in value systems which are to some extent inconsistent.[53]

Kousbroek raises the issue of ulterior motives, that being able to show that one has sustained psychological damage during the war has not just psychological advantages, but financial ones as well. He takes this as a suggestion that certain individuals may claim damage for the sake of financial benefit. Then, in a move which rivals those of the debunkers of notions of "recovered memory" in the US movement,[54] he accuses some therapists of displaying "a certain enthusiasm, a kind of conversion fever, which would itself justify psychological research, implying that ulterior motives might play an inappropriate role."[55]

Writing in *ICODO INFO*, J.N. Schreuder[56] suggests a psychological profile of men who as little boys lived in Japanese camps for women and children which sounds remarkably consonant with the representation offered in *Sunken Red*. Schreuder states, first, that the absence of the father influenced the cognitive development of the boy children. In his view, fathers traditionally represent the world beyond the family to the children, particularly to little boys. While women and girls tend to use their linguistic skills to solve problems, men employ abstract reasoning and an intolerance of ambiguity. Schreuder quotes Harris[57] to support the view that boys raised without a father in their latency period tend to favor linguistic problem-solving over the more "masculine" type of problem-solving one would otherwise expect.

Secondly, according to Schreuder, the absence of the father would also affect the development of the child's conscience. As the conscience develops, its self-regulating mechanisms are new and unreliable, and it tends to be strict. Schreuder notes that such strictness coincides well with the role of the Japanese in the camps, and states that the Japanese camp guard, in his powerful position and wearing a uniform, would have been an attractive substitute representative of the outside world to the little boy in need of an alternate male role model. In turn, the Japanese man loved male children.

Even if no sexual abuse occurs – Schreuder does discuss the occurrence of sexual abuse – the child would experience internal conflict at this constellation of relationships. He desperately needs a male role model, and the only one available is the enemy who victimizes his parents. As the narrator of *Sunken Red* reports: "...I also seem to remember sitting on the knee of a Japanese soldier and being allowed to take a drag at his cigarette."[58] Schreuder notes that shame at emotionally ambivalent responses must have played an important role in such conflicts.[59] In places, Brouwers' narrator uses the word "remorse", which implies guilt, but the cause is the same.

172 The negative emotion is caused by the little boy's lack of clarity: was he to identify with the powerful, but cruel and abusive male role model, or the victimized, loving mother?

> What am I to do with my "camp syndrome", the remorse that I try to drive away by slapping myself in the face whenever, unexpectedly, film scenes from my life in that camp appear before my eyes?[60]

Schreuder also emphasizes how difficult it would be for a young boy to work out his Oedipal conflicts in the camp. As he explains, the absence of the father and the seeming omnipresence of the mother – or many "mothers" – would tend to confuse the process. "It seems unavoidable that the mother contributed to this [impression]."[61]

He acknowledges the possibility that mothers or other women might have behaved seductively or had a sexual relationship with the boys,[62] but confusion seems likely even in situations where this was not the case. Such confusing dynamics – seeing his mother without a husband in "his rightful place" – complicated the child's developmental need to give up incestuous ties to the mother.

Although *Sunken Red* makes no suggestion of incest, the "misconnection" between mother and son does present a child who is confused about the relationship between authority and sexuality in the relationship; his use of "*ketemu lagi*" as a greeting: "[those words] were far too solemn, far too pert, from the mouth of a small boy...They became sacred, incantatory code words between my mother and me...,"[63] his dismay at his mother's powerlessness toward the camp guards, and his association of sex with guilt and violence all point in that direction. Thus, instead of suggesting that Brouwers has exaggerated the suffering, and made the negative effects of camp life seem worse than they actually were, Schreuder's report on ICODO's experiences with and research on their clients only confirms that Brouwers' representation is well within the "normal" range.

FICTION AND HISTORY

Where the representation of suffering is concerned, it is important that the reader be assured that the author has not been irresponsible, that the text represents the suffering of human beings with an appropriate sense of proportion. When, on the other hand, one is considering inaccuracies of fairly arbitrary facts such as dates in history, it is more acceptable simply to conclude that *Sunken Red* is a novel, and is to be read as fiction. Once this premise is granted, one is free to consider the ways in which Brouwers tweaks his readers' assumptions about fiction and reality in his work, and what exactly he gains by calling attention to the clashes between fictionality and historical "truth".

Admittedly, Brouwers made the comment to an interviewer which I have already quoted above, that people who do not like to read novels could read his book as history. However, he also planted red herrings for the "truth versus fiction" crowd in the novel itself. Consider the following example: On page 23 of *Sunken Red*, the narrator reports that he is working on a piece on Jacob Hiegentlich, a Dutch writer who took his own life. If the reader perchance wonders whether this reference is to a historical fact about the author, or a fictional "fact" about the narrator, and proceeds to track this down, he or she finds *De laatste deur*, (" *The Last Door*") a book-length study by Jeroen Brouwers on Dutch writers who committed suicide.[64] On page 295, one finds a chapter entitled: "Jacob Hiegentlich 1907-1940 – "Men liet den Jood niet binnen", ["They did not admit the Jew."]" According to Brouwers' text, Jacob Hiegentlich swallowed poison during the night of 14-15 May, 1940. Hiegentlich finally died on the 18th, without regaining consciousness.

Thus the careful reader who may have expected to find that the reference to a piece written about a certain Hiegentlich was a simple fictional element of the novel, finds not only that matters are more complex, but also finds her- or himself standing face to face with the reality of the Holocaust, in a book about the experience of civilian prisoners of war in Japanese camps.

The reality which the reader uncovers is uncomfortable to confront. Brouwers quotes Abel Herzberg, who writes in *Kroniek der Jodenvervolging*.[65]

> It must have been busy in the hospitals during those days, not just with war casualties, but also with people who did not wish to go along with the new era, but preferred to follow (in the footsteps of) the old one, which had died. They were not exclusively Jews, but most of them were. He who does not believe it should visit the Jewish cemeteries and count the tombstones which read May 15 and 16 and the following days. He will see famous names. He will also find wide graves with names of a man and his wife and their children... If people had had a better grasp on techniques of voluntary departure, then those rows of tombstones displaying the first days of the occupation would have been a good deal longer.

And Brouwers quotes Louis de Jong, the famous historian of the Netherlands in World War II: "In Amsterdam the deaths of one hundred twenty-eight Jews were reported, whose suicide attempts had succeeded", and "In The Hague there were 'more than thirty' successful suicide attempts in Jewish circles".[66]

In Brouwers' novel (or rather just outside it, at the point where a reader follows up on the reference embedded in *Sunken Red*), the historical fact of Hiegentlich's death, a reference to "real" suffering of a Jewish civilian at the occupation of the Netherlands by Nazi Germany, a "real", quintessential victim, not one about whom a fractious debate is possible, connects to the story of those who suffered at the other end of the world. It anchors the story in history twice: first, the narrator of *Sunken Red* describes an event which turns out to be historically true for Brouwers, the author of *Sunken Red,* and secondly, the historical fact being mentioned is related to suffering which is not contested in the way Brouwers' suffering, or that of his novel's main character, is challenged.

174 Of course Brouwers "should" have known that his readers would expect his text to be "historically accurate". I have offered evidence in this chapter that Brouwers was aware of issues of historical accuracy and the autobiographical aspects of his text, and playfully addressed them in various passages in his book, for example in his narrator's reference to "his" writing a study of Dutch authors who had committed suicide while, as it turned out, Brouwers was writing exactly such a book.

Brouwers certainly muddied the waters with his comment in the *Haagsche Post* in which he stated that his work could be read as history if the reader wished to do so. Although there are good reasons for checking one's facts, when one looks at this debate from a somewhat more detached and perhaps calmer point of view, it is clear that the "It isn't" – "It is!" argument about the accuracy of the historical facts he mentioned misses an important aspect of what we do when we write and read.

Brouwers responded to his critics by stating that he had written a novel. In the discussion of Dutch texts concerning the children of the war in the 1980s, one recurrent theme among Dutch readers and critics is an apparent failure to distinguish clearly between fiction and non-fiction, with the category of "ego-documenten"[67] (letters, diaries) serving to bridge and soften the contrast; in reality, these genres of texts exist together on a continuum. Rinnes Rijke's two volumes of autobiography or "ego-document", for instance, show clear signs of not being entirely based on personal memory or factual notes taken contemporaneously by the author. One can only assume that the text was at least embellished, that passages were fleshed out with details or descriptions supplied by imagination or historical research at the time the book was written. This process shows some similarity to what historical novelists would do. Nevertheless, this work was marketed, sold and read as "autobiographical" writing. *Sunken Red*, on the other hand, is labeled a novel, but frequently read – as the selected examples I have given in this chapter have shown – with an expectation that individual details mentioned would be accurate. Armando's "Street and Foliage" – a highly stylized novel which uses some of the author's experiences of the occupation, as chapter 4 has shown – is reissued in the inexpensive paperback series by De Bezige Bij[68] with a banner printed on the front cover which identifies the work as "autobiographical".

Margarethe Ferguson[69] attempts to defend Brouwers by arguing from a position which essentially confirms poetic license. First, she states that emotions cloud the memory in the transformation of experience into literature. Second, she argues that the inaccuracies are the effect of Brouwers' superior concern with his artistic considerations for a "carefully composed novel in which various narrative elements are ultimately combined to produce a grand climax".[70] Emotions called up by experiences which the author has kept repressed for many years have a great influence, and on more than one occasion contribute to a demonstrable deformation of what "one normally believes to be able to call the truth, or rather reality". She finds such "deformations" somewhat defensible, but scolds Brouwers for using dates without confirming their accuracy.

The model Ferguson uses for the process by which a narrative is constructed is not the only one available. She identifies "experience" with something like objective truth, or – as she corrects herself – "reality". If, however, one recognizes that experience itself occurs within a specific cultural context in light of which it is experienced and given meaning, then it is inherently a construct, something immediately interpreted within certain conventions. In that case the model is not: experience (or truth) plus emotion (or rules of literary composition) equals literature (with or without (in)advertent inaccuracy as part of the package), but rather: any autobiographical narrative is – as Jerome Bruner phrases it – a "renegotiated life", a life (re)interpreted within the horizons of expectation. Thus it is not Kousbroek's "private truth" (which seems remarkably like a euphemism for "lie"). It is rather a truth which belongs to a certain community, such as that of children of the war, or the community of Dutch-Indonesians interned in Japanese camps who were traumatized by that experience, and who now seek a connection with those children of the war whose traumas were sustained in the Netherlands, or who seek at least a more explicit connection with other members of their own immediate "group".

In sorting out this debate, it is important to keep in mind what a narrative text – even one as "historical" as an autobiography – does and is. It is not a listing of "true facts" which have been independently verified. It is a retelling of certain facts and details from a personal point of view at a specific time in history. It is not unthinkable that one person would rewrite his or her own life several times; each version would have different emphases, and would interpret certain early events or facts about the subject in the new light shed by recent experience or new insight. The experiences and insights which change one's view of one's past may be personal or communal. As Jerome Bruner puts it:

> ... I want to assert that an autobiography is not and cannot be a way of simply signifying or referring to a "life as lived." I take the view that there is no such thing as a "life as lived" to be referred to. On this view, a life is created or constructed by the act of autobiography. It is a way of construing experience – and of reconstruing and reconstruing it until our breath or our pen fails us. Construal and reconstrual are interpretive. Like all forms of interpretation, how we construe our lives is subject to our intentions, to the interpretive conventions available to us, and to the meanings imposed upon us by the usages of our culture and language.[71]

I have suggested in each of the chapters in this book that the Dutch texts by and about children of the war present their experiences and memory within the interpretive conventions which come into their own in the 1980s. Moreover, they are conventions to whose development these texts also collectively contribute. This recognition is as relevant to fiction as it is to non-fictional texts. Each is a part of the dialogue I have called "a family occupation", the process of sorting out what Dutch identity means, what the role of memory is in the present, and how one – or the community – is going to develop in the future. It is clear that constructing a Dutch identity in the postwar era requires that one include the history of the occupation and the suffering considered central to this past. This view is confirmed by C.M. Jacobs-Stam, who in describing the experience of the returnees first notes that the country to which the "colonials" were being repatriated was poverty-stricken, and next that many citizens feared economic disaster and were concerned that Dutch international influence would be lessened because of the loss of the colony. She notes that these negative concerns were expressed in a tendency toward unfriendliness to the returnees. Then Jacobs-Stam states: "One certainly was not interested in hearing the stories of this group, 'our' war had after all been much worse."[72] Such statements count as evidence that the population did have a "calculus of suffering" in mind, and that they did privilege the experience under the Nazi occupation – not necessarily in the camps – over that in the Japanese camps in Indonesia.

If all this is so, then the interesting and more telling question becomes not whether each detail mentioned in *Sunken Red* is accurate, but rather why these novels are marketed as autobiographies and why the Dutch reading public is so insistent on correct detail. If the author of an autobiographical novel or a novel with autobiographical "content" is held to extremely high standards of historical accuracy, it is because something significant is being negotiated in the culture. One can only surmise that something important must be at stake, and I posit that it is the heart of the debate about memory, history, and identity.

WHY SUCH HIGH STAKES?

It is important to ask why a fictional text was received with such extremely critical and intensely combative responses. Several important factors pertain here. The historical context in which the failed colonials returned to the Netherlands after the end of the war is central to understanding their behavior at the time, the responses of Dutch citizens to them, and – by extension – the writing and reception of such works as *Sunken Red* roughly three decades later.

Following the analysis by the historian J. C. H. Blom,[73] it is clear that World War II suffering is such a central, explosive issue in Dutch society, and thus such a rich source of material for writers (of fiction *and* of non-fictional texts, such as "ego-documenten"), because the meaning given to suffering during the war, *that which is at stake*, is ultimately in some sense "Dutchness" itself,[74] and that therefore those who have not suffered in the same way as others have cannot claim to be fully Dutch, members of the "family". It is for this reason that the group of those entitled to say that they have suffered must be carefully controlled. As is the case with cultural systems, all would-be citizens know the rules, and often self-edit what they say in public. Thus it is possible to explain the emphasis among the former residents of Indonesia on remembering the laughter experienced in the camps and their indignant response at the thought that Brouwers' text might have exaggerated their suffering. As not-quite-insiders, it is never to their advantage to risk offending those who are at the center: victims of the war (particularly survivors of the Holocaust proper) and Resistance fighters. It is for this reason that I take note of the validation of the symptoms represented in *Sunken Red* offered by psychologists such as Schreuder. Accusations of "inaccuracies" in such details as dates and times may be shrugged off as either – possibly pardonable – carelessness on Brouwers' part, or a playful refusal by the author to fall into line. Accusations of exaggeration of suffering, on the other hand, should be countered, as they would perpetuate the silence and isolation of a legitimate branch of the "family".

An examination of former Indonesian colonials as a group provides good material for my study because in response to *Sunken Red* these individuals engaged in explicit discussions about suffering and victimization and about the usefulness of discussing their suffering in public.

There are at least three separate but related issues vying for pre-eminence within the debate from the point of view of those repatriated from Indonesia. The first is related to issues of integration, the second and third concern recognition by other members of Dutch society. First, the issue of integration is centrally important. If you keep quiet and don't call attention to your history, you may be accepted as Dutch and may be able to integrate. If, on the other hand, you keep speaking of the past, you repeatedly remind the others of your difference, and you will accomplish little. Second, Brouwers and others consider it important that the pain of those repatriated from Indonesia be recognized. Delayed effects are considered significant in the case of legitimate trauma. Third, such official recognition opens up avenues for treatment.

Note that "recognition" has emotional ramifications as well as financial benefits. In a country such as the Netherlands, where the official recognition of certain illnesses and syndromes has a direct bearing on whether medical procedures will be paid for or permitted under the Dutch health care system, or whether a special pension or allowance will be paid, it is important that an official institution recognize a group's trauma as real. From their perspective, Dutch citizens who did not have an Indonesian past had emotional and political reasons to exclude colonialists from their inner circles. First, those repatriated from Indonesia were a reminder of the loss of the colony, a loss viewed with enormous trepidation by Dutch citizens; as Kossmann[75] states, the Dutch were terrified of not being able to succeed without Indonesia as a colony. These concerns militated against allowing colonials to consider themselves fully Dutch; they would contaminate the pool, and since the Dutch were investing "Dutchness" with such enormous significance, they could not afford to have the meaning of loyalty to nation and political principle diluted. The returnees were outsiders, and although they were not guilty in the way collaborators were, they suffered from guilt by association. Ironically, they were associated with a colonial past considered shameful because of the loss of the colonies, which in turn seemed to presage financial hardship. Their presence in the Netherlands was a constant reminder of an event many found painful, and the resentment of the "local" Dutch did not enhance their chances of integration. Secondly, some Dutch citizens who had survived the occupation in the Netherlands viewed the repatriates with suspicion because they were presumed to have participated in the dirty colonial past. Neither group welcomed them.

In the previous chapter, I have referred to Blom's views on the central importance of patient suffering to the Dutch self-image, and to Ian Buruma's views on how identity and otherness are related: If knowing that the Germans are evil "makes" us, the Dutch, the "good guys" and if this conviction of being a good – though small – nation is somehow at the center of our self-image, then this equation constitutes an explanation for why the community – or some members thereof – would wish to exclude certain would-be members. Some members of the community would have a stake in preventing someone who had not suffered at the hands of the Germans from claiming to inhabit the same position, not only the position of "having suffered" but the same apparently significant condition of having suffered at the hands of the Nazis, whose evil is epitomized by the brutal intentionality and efficient instrumentality of the Holocaust.

What I have shown to be the case about *Sunken Red* confirms my findings in earlier chapters – that when we as readers think about the memories of the children of the war, we are interested in issues much more basic than those related to World War II and its aftermath only. The vehemence with which critics have attacked the "untruths" and "inaccuracies" in *Sunken Red* suggests that some seemingly more important cultural value is at stake. The crux of the issue in the debate about *Sunken Red* is not just the verisimilitude of a novel or autobiographical text by Jeroen Brouwers; the vehemence of the debate is proof that something close to the heart of Dutch culture is at issue in the questions we ask about the memories of the children of the war. At issue is the question of what it means to be a member of Dutch society.

The title of this study, "A Family Occupation" is meant to represent all those issues which occupy a family, and to place in the foreground the fact that the arguments, although heated at times, are ones that are part of the life of a family. They are arguments among people who – for better or worse – belong together. And yet it is also possible for a family to argue about who does and who does not belong to the family, who is or is not loyal, who does or does not do the family proud, whose features or behavior do or do not seem typical for the family. Where an outsider would not question an individual's membership in the family unit, the insiders are more likely to notice and be offended by minor differences.

In previous chapters, we have seen that this debate on the relationship of the past to the present has often emphasized issues of memory: what one remembers, whether one remembers correctly, who has a right to remember, what influence (damage or enhancement) memory has on life 50-odd years later. Such questions are at the center of what a culture is, who people are, how people – members of a community – invent and reinvent themselves and influence the development of others. This same complex of problems is investigated in the novel *Sunken Red*, and also in the debate which followed its publication. Both events created an opportunity for further work to be done in the family occupation of deciding what the memory of the war means for a modestly sized European country consisting mostly of civilians who were once occupied, one way or another.

Notes

CHAPTER I

1. *NRC Handelsblad,* July 23, 1992.
2. *Volkskrant,* July 24, 1992.
3. Dick Schram, "De verwerking van de Tweede Wereldoorlog in de literatuur," in *Overal Sporen: De verwerking van de Tweede Wereldoorlog in literatuur en kunst.* Amsterdam, VU Uitgeverij, 1990, 94.
4. J.C.H. Blom, A.C. 't Hart and I. Schöffer. *De affaire Menten 1945-1976. Eindrapport van de Commissie van onderzoek betreffende het opsporings- en vervolgingsbeleid inzake Menten vanaf de bevrijding tot de zomer van 1976 en de invloeden waaraan dat beleid al dan niet heeft blootgestaan.* The Hague: 1979, 205; cited in A.G.H. Anbeek van der Meijden, "De Tweede Wereldoorlog in de Nederlandse roman," in *1940-145: Onverwerkt verleden? Lezingen van het symposium georganiseerd door het Rijksinstituut voor Oorlogsdocumentatie, 7 en 8 mei 1985.* Utrecht: H&S, 1985, 73-87.
5. A.G.H. Anbeek van der Meijden, "De Tweede Wereldoorlog in de Nederlandse Roman," in *1940-1945: Onverwerkt verleden? Lezingen van het symposium georganiseerd door het Rijksinstituut voor Oorlogsdocumentatie, 7 en 8 mei 1985.* Utrecht: H&S, 1985, 80.
6. Madelon de Keizer cf., ed. *'Een dure verplichting en een kostelijk voorrecht': Dr. L. de Jong en zijn Geschiedwerk.* 's-Gravenhage: SDU Uitgeverij, 1995, particularly the biographical details provided by Madelon de Keizer in the Introduction, 7-20.
7. RIOD in Dutch: Rijksinstituut voor Oorlogsdocumentatie, the research institute for the history of World War II in the Netherlands.
8. L.(Louis) de Jong: *De bezetting. Een weergave in boekvorm van de uitzendingen der Nederlandse Televisie-Stichting over Nederland in de Tweede Wereldoorlog.* Volume 1-5. Amsterdam: Querido, 1963-65.
9. *Het Koninkrijk der Nederlanden in de Tweede Wereldoorlog,* 12 vols. Leiden: Martinus Nijhoff, 1969-1988.
10. Madelon de Keizer cf., ed. *'Een dure verplichting en een kostelijk voorrecht': Dr. L. de Jong en zijn Geschiedwerk.* 's-Gravenhage: SDU Uitgeverij, 1995, 7-20.
11. Original title: *De val.* Amsterdam: Bert Bakker, 1983.
    De glazen brug. Amsterdam: Commissie voor de Collectieve Propaganda van het Nederlandse Boek, 1986.
12. The Hague: BZZTôH, 1987.
13. The Hague: BZZTôH, 1984.
14. The Hague: BZZTôH, 1985.
15. Other titles by Armando published in this decade include *Aantekeningen over de vijand.* Amsterdam: De Bezige Bij, 1981, and *Krijgsgewoel.* Amsterdam: De Bezige Bij, 1989.
16. Sliedrecht: Merweboek, 1989.
17. The Dutch term "ego-documenten" ["ego documents"] is useful as a collective term to describe these non-fictional or not-wholly fictional texts.
18. Bussum: Van Holkema & Warendorf, 1982.
19. Weesp: Van Holkema & Warendorf, 1985.
20. Utrecht: Veen, 1989.

21 Haarlem: In de Knipscheer, 1985.

22 I prefer this term to those, such as "second generation", which suggest the possibility and even desirability of precise delineation of certain numbers of years, and thus require one to argue about the age of consent or the age at which children become aware of the important events which occur in their environment. For my purposes, the primary recognition beginning to emerge is that several generations of Dutch civilians were deeply affected by the occupation. The term "children of the war" includes all those who were touched by the war but were too young to have had any sense of agency, any reasonable opportunity for choice, of allegiance to one side or the other during the war, and therefore to whom no responsibility of personal guilt can be assigned. I am not alone in asserting that there is some commonality among several "generations" of survivors of the occupation; cf. G.F. Bögels, "Vormen van psychische verwonding. Klinische Aspecten van transgenerationele oorlogsgevolgen in historisch perspectief." in: Hans Ester and Wam de Moor, ed., *Een halve eeuw geleden. De verwerking van de Tweede Wereldoorlog in de literatuur.* Kampen, Kok Agora, 1994, 37-46, page 37. The argument for similarity is also made by J.N. Schreuder, "De conspiracy of silence en de kinderen van de oorlog," in: ICODO Info 90-3/4, 7e jaargang, December 1990, 4-13. Schreuder attributes the first use of the term "children of the war" to Mario Montessori.

23 A printed version of this material was published as dr. L. de Jong, *De bezetting. Een weergave in boekvorm van de uitzendingen der Nederlandse Televisie-Stichting over Nederland in de Tweede Wereldoorlog.* Volume 1-5. Amsterdam: Querido, 1963-65.

24 E.H. Kossmann: *De Lage Landen 1780/1980. Twee eeuwen Nederland en België II.* Amsterdam: Agon, 1986, 381ff.

25 One fictional illustration of this phenomenon is found in *The Assault,* where members of a memorial committee for war victims are thought to have debated about whether to include the name of a young boy – shot by the Germans – on a memorial. The argument against including him was that, since he had picked up a revolver in self-defense, he should be excluded from the list of "pure" victims, and included with resistance fighters instead: "they shouldn't just be mixed up together...". (74)

26 The Dutch are notorious "joiners". It would be interesting to know whether the Dutch habit of associating in groups and clubs is a result of having become accustomed to pillarization, or rather whether pillarization developed because the nation was made up of "joiners", who were thus predisposed toward such structures.

27 Bussum: Van Holkema & Warendorf, 1982.

28 Of course, this recognition occurred much earlier in certain less public circles; I here refer to its recognition within the wider culture.

29 J.C.H. Blom: "Lijden als waarschuwing. Oorlogsverleden in Nederland." *Ons Erfdeel,* Vol. 38, September-October 4, 1995, 531-541.

30 Surprising, at least, to those who have uncritically accepted stark dichotomies between "good victims" and "evil perpetrators", a common scheme in the Netherlands during the postwar decades.

31 Though, given the history of Anti-Semitism, Jewish victims constitute the most quintessential example of intentional genocide by the Nazi authorities.

32 The "continuum of survivors" is a chain which exists at a given point in time.

33 This can be seen in the movement from group therapy to self-help books to truths accepted at face value on talk-shows.

Sem Dresden, *Persecution, Extermination, Literature.* Translated by Henry G. Schogt.
Toronto: University of Toronto Press, 1995, 13. Originally published as *Vervolging, ver-nietiging, literatuur.* Amsterdam: Meulenhoff, 1991.

35 cf. chapter 4 in particular.

36 Hunt, Lynn, ed. *The New Cultural History.* Berkeley: U. of California Press, 1989.

CHAPTER 2

1 Another reason for beginning with this text is that it may, in some form, be the best-known story of life in the Netherlands during and after World War II besides *The Diary of Anne Frank.* The novel was made into a film which won an Academy Award for best foreign film in 1987 and has enjoyed wide distribution in Europe and North America. I quote in English from: Harry Mulisch, *The Assault.* Claire Nicholas White, transl. New York: Pantheon, 1985. The Dutch edition is Harry Mulisch, *De aanslag.* Amsterdam: De Bezige Bij, 1987. Mulisch is one of the most prominent Dutch authors of the post-war period; in the earlier post-war period, Mulisch was mentioned with Louis Paul Boon, W.F. Hermans, and G.K. van het Reve as one of a number of authors who "use the war as a decor" which serves as a foil for their protagonists' more general – psychological or philosophical – questions. cf. G.J. van Bork, N. Laan, editors, *Twee eeuwen literatuur-geschiedenis: poëticale opvattingen in de Nederlandse literatuur.* Groningen: Wolters-Noordhoff, 1986. I argue that *The Assault* both conforms and does not conform to this view of the function of the war in fiction; the locus of the discussion shifts in the 1980's.

For studies of Mulisch and his earlier work, cf. Hans Dütting, ed., *Over Harry Mulisch: Kritisch Nabeeld.* Baarn: De Prom, 1982 and Maritha Mathijsen, *Harry Mulisch: Een bibliografie.* The Hague: BZZTôH, 1979. These works precede the publication of *The Assault,* and thus do not discuss it. I have published a brief article which touches on *The Assault:* "The Occupied Mind: Remembering and Forgetting; Some Recent Examples in Dutch Literature," in *The Low Countries: Multidisciplinary Studies,* ed. Margriet Bruijn Lacy, 157-164. *Publications of the American Association for Netherlandic Studies* 3. Lanham: University Press of America, 1990.

2 Bernd Müller cites the success of *The Assault* as evidence of "how important memories of World War II are in Holland." Bernd Müller, "The Second World War in Dutch and German Literature" in *The Berkeley Conference of Dutch Literature, 1991. Europe 1992: Dutch Literature in an International Context.* Edited by Johan P. Snapper and Thomas F. Shannon. *Publications of the American Association for Netherlandic Studies* 6. Lanham: University Press of America, 1993, 123-131.

3 A.G.H. Anbeek van der Meijden is such a reader. In his essay "De Tweede Wereldoorlog in de Nederlandse Roman," *in 1940-1945: Onverwerkt verleden? Lezingen van het symposium georganiseerd door het Rijksinstituut voor Oorlogsdocumentatie, 7 en 8 mei 1985.* Utrecht: H&S, 1985, 84, he argues that a major strength of the novel is the subtlety of the manner in which issues of guilt and responsibility are handled. Dick Schram revisits similar issues and responds to Anbeek van der Meijden in "De verwerking van de Tweede Wereldoorlog in de literatuur", in *Overal Sporen: De verwerking van de Tweede Wereldoorlog in literatuur en kunst.* Amsterdam, VU Uitgeverij, 1990, 93-126.

4 The title translates as "Don't get annoyed"; the game is essentially the same as one known as "Parchisi", a game of chance in which a player's pawns may be knocked off the board by another player who lands on the same space on the roll of the dice. This game was certainly

very popular and thus its appearance in the Steenwijk household requires no special explanation; it may be just a coincidence that it also is a classic image of the theme of occupation.

5   "Steen" is Dutch for "stone".

6   Unfortunately, the English translation somewhat obscures this fact; readers of the English may also miss the hint in the family name, *Steen*wijk. This device has of course been mentioned in other studies of the novel as well, e.g. Jan Heerze, *Harry Mulisch, De aanslag*. Apeldoorn: WalvaBoek, 1983.

7   The notion of recurrence at various levels is known in a coinage by Mulisch as "octaviteit"; see chapter 6 where I discuss this concept and the point of using it to describe the workings of (repressed) memory.

8   Jacques Presser, *Ondergang. De vervolging en verdelging van het Nederlandse jodendom* (1940-1945) (The Hague: Staatsuitgeverij, 1965; this work is Monograph number 10 in the series published under the auspices of the State Institute for War Documentation). Mulisch also quotes from *Ondergang*.

9   Presser, 64.

10 Harry Mulisch: *Mijn getijdenboek*. Amsterdam: De Bezige Bij, 1985.

11 The Dutch term "moffen" for "Germans" is actually a more strongly negative term than some current usages of the term "Krauts" in post-"Hogan's Heroes" American English.

12 cf. Marcel Janssens, "The Prolog in Mulisch' *De Aanslag:* A Novel in a Nutshell." In *The Berkeley Conference of Dutch Literature. 1987: New Perspectives on the Modern Period*. Edited by Johan P. Snapper and Thomas F. Shannon. *Publications of the American Association for Netherlandic Studies* 2. Lanham: University Press of America, 1989, 81-92. The images in the Prologue which attract Anton are also discussed by John Michielsen, "Coming to Terms with the Past and Searching for an Identity: The Treatment of the Occupied Netherlands in the Fiction of Hermans, Mulisch and Vestdijk". in *Canadian Journal of Netherlandic Studies* VII i-ii, 1986, 62-68 (64). The novel is also briefly discussed in Wam de Moor, *Deze kant op: Kritieken en profielen van boeken en schrijvers 1979-1984*. Amsterdam: De Arbeiderspers, 1986, 191-195.

13 The facts surrounding "verduistering", or blackout are described in Evert Werkman, Madelon de Keizer, Gert Jan van Setten, editors: *Dat kan ons niet gebeuren... Het dagelijks leven in de Tweede Wereldoorlog*. Amsterdam, De Bezige Bij, 1980, 33. Starting on May 10, 1940, all streetlights were turned off and houses were not allowed to emit any light whatsoever, so that the country was cloaked in pitch darkness as soon as the sun set. Flashlights were permitted if adjusted so as to allow only a tiny bit of light to shine, and in any case batteries became scarce almost immediately. In this tale, the mysterious worker is also out after curfew, and thus would not have used a flashlight even if she had had one.

14 "He/she didn't live through (experience) the war." See chapter 1, p. 14.

15 Also see the discussion of Dan Bar-On's explanation of this phenomenon in chapter 5.

16 This cruelty is well symbolized by the statue which forms the war memorial for the city. The fact that the Allied forces bombed the harbor and boats toward the end of the war is not as widely known or mentioned.

17 "De oorlog"

18 J.C.H. Blom: "Lijden als waarschuwing. Oorlogsverleden in Nederland." In *Ons Erfdeel*, 38e Jaargang, september-oktober nummer 4, 1995, 531. cf. Chapter 4 for a more detailed discussion of this idea.

19 Umberto Eco. "An Ars Oblivionalis? Forget It!" *PMLA* 103 (1988): 254-261, 254.

20 Eco, 254.

21 Eco, 259.

22 For a description of the structure provided by these historical "benchmarks", cf. Jan Heerze: *Harry Mulisch, De aanslag.* Apeldoorn: WalvaBoek, 1983.

23 Arnold Heumakers, "Harry Mulisch en de politiek", in *Maatstaf* 8/9, 37e jaargang, August/September 1989, 101-111, 104.

24 Gay Block and Malka Drucker, *Rescuers. Portraits of Moral Courage in the Holocaust.* New York: Holmes & Meier, 1992. Prologue by Cynthia Ozick, xii.

25 Jaap Goedegebuure, *Haagsche Post*, October 9, 1982.

26 *The Assault,* 5.

CHAPTER 3

1 I quote from Marga Minco, *The Glass Bridge.* Stacey Knecht, transl. London: Peter Owen, 1988. The translations from van Dantzig's book are mine.

2 I have very briefly suggested the broad outlines of such an inquiry in the article on Marga Minco in *Women Writers of the Netherlands and Flanders, Canadian Journal of Netherlandic Studies* XI, ii, Fall 1990, 51-56. For an additional brief essay which touches on some of this material, cf. "The Occupied Mind: Remembering and Forgetting; Some Recent Examples in Dutch Literature," in *The Low Countries: Multidisciplinary Studies,* ed. Margriet Bruijn Lacy, 157-164. *Publications of the American Association for Netherlandic Studies* 3. Lanham: University Press of America, 1990.

3 It is a truism – one which the author herself has mentioned – in Dutch literary circles that Minco "writes the same book over and over." The negative version of that view would underestimate her talent, skill and commitment. Some critics, such as J. Huisman, recognize the advantages, however. He writes: "She is one of those writers who repeatedly writes the same book, but who can get away with it perfectly because it is new every time." J. Huisman, "Twee juweeltjes. Indrukwekkende geschenken van Minco en van Dis," in *Algemeen Dagblad,* March 8, 1986.

4 A. Van den Hoven *"Het Bittere Kruid* by Marga Minco. Paradise Lost: Paradise Regained," in *The Low Countries: Fin de Siècle;* ed. Robert Siebelhoff, Augustinus P. Dierick. Special issue of *Canadian Journal of Netherlandic Studies* 9 (1988) 2 (Fall), 92-96.

5 For a historical study in English of the families of Holocaust survivors, and in particular the second generation, see Aaron Hass: *In the Shadow of the Holocaust. The Second Generation.* Ithaca: Cornell University Press, 1990.

   Henry Schogt, "Motives and Impediments in Describing War Memories: The Tragedy of the Jews," in *Canadian Journal of Netherlandic Studies* 11 (1990) 1 (Spring), 3-7, offers a discussion of a number of Dutch fictional and non-fictional texts by Jewish writers which describe the experiences of World War II. Schogt cautions against focusing exclusively on stray hopeful statements, such as the famous ones by Anne Frank and Etty Hillesum, and forgetting that "for most people there was no hope." (6)

   Standard histories of the Jewish people during World War Two in the Netherlands include Jacques Presser: *Ondergang. De vervolging en verdelging van het Nederlandse jodendom (1940-1945).* The Hague: Staatsuitgeverij, 1965; this work is Monograph number 10 in the series published under the auspices of the State Institute for War Documentation; an abbreviated English translation by Arnold Pomerans was published under the title *The Destruction of the Dutch Jews.* New York: Dutton, 1969;

Louis de Jong: *De jodenvervolging I and II,* Amsterdam: Rijksinstituut voor Oorlogsdocumentatie, 1978, is a historical study of the persecution of the Jews in the Netherlands during World War Two.

Louis de Jong: *Het Koninkrijk der Nederlanden in de Tweede Wereldoorlog,* 12 vols., Leiden: Martinus Nijhoff, 1969-1988, is a standard history of the Dutch nation under Nazi German rule.

Sem Dresden: *Persecution, Extermination, Literature.* Translated by Henry G. Schogt. Toronto, Buffalo, London: University of Toronto Press, 1995. Original title: S. Dresden: *Vervolging, vernietiging, literatuur.* Amsterdam: Meulenhoff, 1991.

Debórah Dwork: *Children With a Star. Jewish Youth in Nazi Europe.* New Haven: Yale University Press, 1991.

The standard history of the Jews in the Netherlands is Jozeph Michman, Hartog Beem, and Dan Michman: *Pinkas. Geschiedenis van de joodse gemeenschap in Nederland.* Translated from Hebrew by Ruben Verhasselt, with additional research by Victor Brilleman. Joop Sanders, Edward van Voolen, editors. Ede: Kluwer Algemene Boeken and Amsterdam: Nederlands-Israëlitisch Kerkgenootschap, 1992.

Kritzman, Lawrence D., ed. *Auschwitz and After. Race, Culture, and "the Jewish Question" in France.* New York: Routledge, 1995.

6   The death toll among Dutch Jews was the highest in Western Europe, only 35,000 or 25% of the 140,000 Jews present in the Netherlands at the outbreak of the war survived. cf. Miller p. 97.

Cf. Lawrence Langer ed. *Art from the Ashes. A Holocaust Anthology.* New York: Oxford University Press, 1995. The flap text proclaims the book "the most far-reaching collection of art, drama, poetry, and prose about the Holocaust ever presented in a single volume. Through the works of men and women, Jews and non-Jews, figures famous and unknown, those who were there and those separated from the ordeal by time and space, this anthology offers a vision of the human reality of the disaster". Surprisingly and unfortunately, even though the Netherlands lost a greater percentage of the Jewish population of the country to deportation to the Holocaust than any other Western European country, Langer has included no Dutch authors in this collection. This fact serves as an indication that further study is called for, as well as as an illustration of the difficulty Dutch literary texts have had until recently in being read or translated.

7   For a history of the Jewish Council of Amsterdam in an international perspective, comparing it to comparable organizations in Vienna, Germany, Poland, France, and Belgium, see the article by Dan Michman: "De oprichting van de 'Joodsche Raad van Amsterdam' vanuit een vergelijkend perspectief", p. 75-100, in *Oorlogsdocumentatie '40-'45. Derde jaarboek van het Rijksinstituut voor Oorlogsdocumantatie.* Editors: N. D. J. Barnouw, D. van Galen Last, M. de Keizer, R. Kok. P. Romijn (secr.), E. L. M. Somers, C. Touwen-Bouwsma (voorz.) Zutphen: Walburg Pers, 1992. Michman concludes that the model used to rule the Netherlands, in which the SS and the police were much more powerful than in countries such as France and Belgium because the nation was ruled by a civilian government rather than a military regime, meant that the Nazis were able to accomplish the deportation of Jews much more efficiently.

A brief discussion of the role of the Jewish Council of Amsterdam and postwar reactions to it and evaluations of its effects is found in Judith Miller, *One by One by One.* New York: Touchstone/Simon & Schuster, 1991, p. 103-105.

8   At the end of the war, she was the sole survivor in her family, except for an uncle (a brother of her father's) who was never deported because he was married to a gentile.

9 Dresden, 13.

10 Presser II, 505.

11 Minco, 24. Stella will create a persona to go with her new identity card and then hold on to the name Maria for some time after the end of the war; this detail has some grounding in Minco's experience. She was born Sara Menco and called Selma by her mother. During the war, while she was in hiding, she was given several false identities; one of these names was Margaretha, and she has written under the name Marga (Minco) since the end of the war.

12 A. P. Dierick, "War and/as Initiation." In: *Canadian Journal of Netherlandic Studies* 11 (1990) 1 (Spring) 9-16, 10.

13 *Wat was de vrede mooi toen het nog oorlog was. Gesprekken over de wederopbouw.* Hans Olink, ed. The Hague: BZZTôH, 1992.

14 Piet Calis, *Het ondergronds verwachten. Schrijvers en tijdschriften tussen 1941 en 1945.* Amsterdam: Meulenhoff, 1990.

15 Renaat Ramon, "Alleen in de brand waren wij gelukkig: schrijvers en tijdschriften in een prachtige, getraliede tijd." In: *Diogenes.* 7 (1990-1991) 6 (july-aug 1991) 9-18.

16 *Revue,* 24.6.67, interview with Marga Minco by Trix Betlem.

17 Sera Anstadt, *Een eigen plek. Verhalen van een opgejaagde jeugd.* The Hague: BZZTôH, 1984.

18 Bert Jansma, *Amersfoortse Courant,* November 3, 1984.

19 For a study of women's experience of the Holocaust, see Rittner, Carol and Rother, John K, ed. (introductions). *Different voices: women and the Holocaust.* New York: Paragon House, 1993.

   Also, for non-fictional narratives of various aspects of Jewish women's experiences of the Holocaust, in addition to Anne Frank's *Diary,* see Etty Hillesum, Smeelik, Klaas A. D., eds. Tekstverzorging door Gideon Lodders en Rob Tempelaars. *Etty. De nagelaten geschriften van Etty Hillesum 1941-1943.* 3e herziene druk. Amsterdam: Balans, 1986. Also, Etty Hillesum: *Het verstoorde leven: Dagboek van Etty Hillesum, 1941-1943,* Bussum: De Haan/Unieboek, 1981. English edition: *An Interrupted Life: The Diaries of Etty Hillesum, 1941-1943.* New York: Pantheon, 1983.
   Anne Frank: *De Dagboeken van Anne Frank,* The Hague: Staatsuitgeverij, 1986. English edition: *Anne Frank: The Diary of a Young Girl: The Critical Edition,* New York, Doubleday, 1989.

20 Sera Anstadt, *Een eigen plek. Verhalen van een opgejaagde jeugd.* The Hague: BZZTôH, 1984, 152.

21 As I noted in Chapter 1, he would rather solve other people's crossword puzzles.

22 Diny Schouten. "Een wurgende pastorale. Oorlogs- en jeugdherinneringen van Rudi van Dantzig" in *Vrij Nederland,* June 7, 1986.

23 As Diny Schouten notes, the language does not remain consistently in the childlike register of that sentence, cf. Diny Schouten, "Een wurgende pastorale", *Vrij Nederland* June 7, 1986; also in *Een Jaar Boek 1985-86,* edited by Aad Nuis and Robert-Henk Zuidinga, Amsterdam: Aramith, 1986, 53-55.

24 Literally: "locks."

25 From a poster republished as an insert in the *Oorlogskrant* of January 5, 1994. Amsterdam: Florence Uitgeverij, 1994.

26 On children taken in by non-Jewish host families, see Presser II, 513-514 and Michman, Beem and Michman's *Pinkas,* 219-221.

27 Members of his Frisian host family.

28 Jan Brokken, "Rudi van Dantzigs Bittere oorlog", *Haagsche Post,* May 31, 1986.

29 Aad Nuis, in *de Volkskrant* June 6, 1986.

30 Hugo Bousset. "Harry Mulisch als buikspreker" in: *Dietsche Warande en Belfort* 134/2, 194-198.

31 Gary Saul Morson, *Narrative and Freedom.* New Haven: Yale University Press, 1994.

32 March 6, 1987.

33 In the early eighties, a stream of studies and essays begins to be published by psychologists and therapists showing that responses to war trauma among victims and children of victims are in many cases beginning to come to the surface where they have not been recognized before. Miller also refers to a time lag among survivors in revisiting the experiences of the war; cf. pp. 108-111.

CHAPTER 4

1 In the postwar period in the Netherlands, this was what survivors said to their children. Interestingly enough, in the debates about the commemoration of D-Day, a similar argument was used to criticize Bill Clinton, the President of the United States, by critics who felt that his lack of experience in the armed forces during the Vietnam war would reduce his credibility as a representative of the nation in the ceremonies memorializing World War II.

2 This pattern has persisted into the 1990s as well.

3 i.e. war victims, victims of the Holocaust, and their children.

4 The children of the war.

5 cf. Dan Bar-On, *Legacy of Silence. Encounters with Children of the Third Reich.* Cambridge: Harvard University Press, 1989, and a host of psychological studies, such as ICODO's *Psycho-sociale problematiek van de tweede generatie I.* Utrecht: ICODO, 1982 and *Psycho-sociale problematiek van de tweede generatie II,* Utrecht: ICODO, 1985 (3rd edition).

6 *Bzzlletin* 173, vol. 19, february 1990 is dedicated to Armando.

7 The title translates – more or less – as "Street and Foliage." Since no English translation of this novel has been published – an understandable situation, as Armando's text is a challenge to render in English – translations in this text are mine. For the benefit of readers of Dutch, however, I also provide the original in the footnote.

8 Pieter de Nijs: "Ik heb iets vreselijks gezien. De stoere gevoeligheid van Armando", in: *Bzzlletin 173,* vol. 19, february 1990, 8-20.

9 Han Foppe traces the role of violence in Armando's writing from 1951 to 1988 in "Vechten. Was dat het leven? Over het geweld in Armando's literaire werk (1951-1988)." In: *Bzzlletin 173,* vol. 19, february 1990, 31-38.

10 Armando: *Aantekeningen over de vijand.* Amsterdam: De Bezige Bij, 1981.

11 This is almost impossible to translate accurately – meanings for "gedoe" include: carrying-on, business, stuff, what people do.

12 "Waar gaat dat boek over. Dat is moeilijk te zeggen. Volgens mij gaat het over *gedoe.* Men zegt dat gedoe met 'de oorlog' te maken heeft. Ik weet dat zo net nog niet, ik dacht eigenlijk dat het meer met *mensen* te maken heeft, maar ik vergis me wel meer." Armando: *Krijgsgewoel.* Amsterdam: De Bezige Bij, 1986.

13 June 22, 1967. Author identified as R.V.D. (My translation).

14 Ian Buruma: *The Wages of Guilt. Memories of War in Germany and Japan.* New York: Farrar Straus Giroux, 1994, 6. Quoted from the "Introduction: The Enemies", in which Buruma writes about his childhood in the Netherlands during the occupation.

15 Jaap Goedegebuure. "Suspecte bomen. De weerbarstige roman van dubbeltalent Armando: wreedheid als schoonheid, het geweld als hart van het leven", in *Haagsche Post* June 11, 1988.

16 "....I can't escape the anecdote, of course, but I try as hard as I can to abstract and to smear out the conclusion of a story." Also see *De Revisor* 68.

17 Wam de Moor: *Dit is de plek. De betekenis van plaats en emotie in het werk van schrijvers en schilders.* Zutphen: Gaillarde Pers, 1992, 22.

18 Ernst van Alphen: *De toekomst der herinnering. Essays over moderne Nederlandse literatuur.* Amsterdam: Van Gennep, 1993, 100-101.

19 Armando and J. Heymans: "De onvoltooid verleden tijd", in *De Revisor* 1989/4, 62-73.

20 Wam de Moor: *Dit is de plek. De betekenis van plaats en emotie in het werk van schrijvers en schilders.* Zutphen: Gaillarde Pers, 1992, 22.

21 This is suggested, for instance, by the cover of an inexpensive Dutch paperback edition (Amsterdam: De Bezige Bij, 1993) which displays a colored banner on which is printed the word "autobiografisch".

22 This is difficult to translate. Armando here uses three slang terms for "to fall", in addition to the standard expression.

23 "Jonge padvinders heeten 'welpen'. Er waren ook deftige welpen. ...

'Nee', zei de deftige welp, 'ik ben bang dat ik duvel.'

Ik keek verwonderd om me heen, maar niemand verroerde een vin. Wat zou je dan moeten zeggen. Ik ben bang dat ik omflikker. Of: dat ik op de grond pleur. Of gewoon: ik ben bang dat ik val. Maar je zegt niet: ik ben bang dat ik duvel, dat zeg je niet.

Alsof deftige welpen geen aardige jongens kunnen zijn.

Maar wie is er nou bang dat ie valt. Bestaan er mensen die vallen. O ja, genoeg. Maar toen nog niet."

24 cf. 134-135

25 "Je wilde geen handschoenen aan als kind. Je verrekte af en toe van de kou, met sneeuwballen gooien bijvoorbeeld, maar je wilde geen handschoenen aan. Je wilde ook geen muts op je kop. Nooit. Hoe koud het ook was. Je wilde nooit wat." (12)

26 "Op de plek waar de bal steeds terugkwam verrees nog geen jaar later 'het kamp'." (19)

27 or: display of power; "Het wachten was op de overval en de verovering en het machtsvertoon." (31)

28 "Het voorval met de officier, die eigenlijk een christelijke onderwijzer was en tot z'n eigen verbazing een Duitse officier met drie soldaten gevangen genomen had. Hij had het viertal ontwapend, maar de officier op erewoord z'n pistool teruggegeven. De Duitser had z'n pistool aangenomen, de onderwijzer neergeschoten en de rest van het groepje overmeesterd. Een van de overlevenden heeft het beschreven. Het speelde zich af in een bosje.

Had die Duitser nou gelijk of niet. Het was toch oorlog. Nee, erewoord is erewoord." (43)

29 "Overigens, deze soldaten gedroegen zich ter plekke soms wel es wat ruw. Ze hadden een loslopende hond zwart geschilderd en af en toe hakten ze een lange den om en hadden veel plezier als een van hun kameraden 'm bijna op z'n kop kreeg." (54).

30 Certainly the initial occupation of Amsterdam surprised many because of the calm demeanor and discipline of the soldiers as they marched into the city; cf. Evert Werkman, Madelon de Keizer, Gert Jan van Setten, editors: *Dat kan ons niet gebeuren... Het dagelijks leven in the Tweede Wereldoorlog.* Amsterdam, De Bezige Bij, 1980, 31.

31 "Ze hadden gerust kunnen schuilen. Als bezetter mag je best schuilen, lijkt me. Aan het front niet. Daar kun je nauwelijks schuilen." (56)

32 "Vanaf het moment dat er niet meer gevochten werd vertoonde de vijand zich openlijk aan iedereen die kon zien. De vijand was zichtbaar. De vijand was te bezichtigen." (47)

33 "Het bleek dat hij praatte en bewoog: de vijand vertoonde menselijke trekken. Hij liep gewoon door de straat, in een groep of alleen. Hij ging zelfs wel eens een winkel binnen." (47).

34 "Men sprak van 'onze' soldaten, van 'onze jongens'.

Toen de vijand er goed en wel was hielden 'onze soldaten' op te bestaan. Ze moesten hun uniformen uittrekken en als een soldaat z'n uniform uittrekt en verwisselt voor gewone kleren, burgerkleren, dan is ie geen soldaat meer.

Het was eigenlijk je reinste verkleedpartij." (46)

35 "We. Men sprak van 'we'.

Men sprak van 'onze' soldaten, van 'onze jongens'." (46)

36 "Daar waren ze, zo zagen ze eruit: grijs en stoffig. Ze hadden korte laarzen aan. Het waren soldaten. Geen mensen. Geen verklede jongemannen. Nee: soldaten." (46-47)

Ik heb het zelf gezien, ik heb ze goed bekeken." (47)

37 "Mocht dat? Kon je zomaar naar de vijand wuiven? Ik vond van niet. Ik was geschokt." (41)

38 "Hij had natuurlijk gelijk, maar je mag zoiets niet zeggen. Dat wist ie ook wel, anders had ie geen kleur gekregen." (35)

39 "Hij deed het heel voorzichtig, op de tenen van z'n rechterlaars, hij was zeker bang dat ie er doorheen zou zakken. De soldaten moesten lachen. Dat was geoorloofd. Lachen mocht in zo'n geval." (53)

40 "Ik weet nog dat de jongen van tien, die het tafereeltje gadesloeg, stomverbaasd was. Het rijmde niet. Hoe kan dat nou, hoe kan zo'n man nou grapjes maken met een kind, het waren toch moordenaars, ze hadden doodskoppen op hun muts.

Hij wist toen nog niet dat het geen moordenaars waren, maar gehoorzame soldaten, die bevelen kregen en uitvoerden. " (53-54)

41 "Ze roken anders, ze liepen anders, ze droegen andere kleren, ze spraken een andere taal. Dat zegt genoeg.

Toch waren het geen vreemdelingen: het was de vijand, het waren vijandelijke soldaten. Zo was het afgesproken." (48)

42 "Men probeert ons nu wel eens wijs te maken dat het eigenlijk gewone mensen waren, jonge mensen, maar hoe konden wij dat weten. Af en toe hoorde je wel eens iemand zeggen: het zijn ook maar jonge kerels, maar daar sloeg je geen acht op. Ze droegen immers uniformen!

Het was de vijand.

Ik begrijp er niets van." (48)

43 "Kijk, als de man het kind geslagen had of gewoon omgeduwd, dan zou de jongen niet zo verbaasd geweest zijn. Was de jongen verkeerd voorgelicht? Hij moest al iets gehoord hebben. Ja, hij had hier en daar wat opgevangen." (54)

44 "En de vijand zong maar. De soldaten zongen onophoudelijk. Ze zongen en marcheerden. Soms hoorde je ze heel in de verte, bracht de wind even een flard van hun gezang. Maar hoe kort die flard ook was, ik herkende het meteen: het was hun taal, het was hun geluid.

'Afschuwelijk, dat zingen van ze. Zo luid. En dan die afgehakte zinnen. Vreselijk.'

De jongens vonden het wel mooi, ze moesten, met enige tegenzin, toegeven dat ze het mooi vonden, ze kwamen er rond voor uit dat het prachtig was." (50)

45 "Het was nog geen oorlog, het was nog net geen oorlog. Er kon ieder ogenblik iets gebeuren.

Wat is er met die man gebeurd: de oorlog moest nog komen. Dat weet je niet hè." (28)

46 "Het wachten was op de overval en de verovering en het machtsvertoon." (31)

47 "De straten waren geplaveid. Er was een wegdek. Je kon er op lopen. De vijand liep er ook op. Maar wat wil je daar mee zeggen. Nou, dat je elkaar tegenkwam.

Gegroet, beste vijand." (51)

48 The camp and its meaning for Armando is described by Henk Niezink in "Armando en Berlijn", in *Bzzlletin* 173, vol. 19, February 1990, 39-49.

49 Armando, (57)

50 Armando, (58)

51 Armando has also made visual representations of trees; cf. his series entitled *Fichten*.

52 Alternate translation: "Shouldn't that be criticized?"

53 "Er wordt vaak zo laatdunkend (dismissive/ly) gesproken over de mensen die zich in dienst van de vijand stelden. Goed, maar wat dacht je van de denne- en sparre-bomen, die zich volledig onderworpen hebben en zich nog steeds onderwerpen aan welke vijand dan ook. Kijk naar de afbeeldingen waarop de vijand doende is: daar staan ze, de bomen, ze staan op de achtergrond te lachen. En niet alleen de denne- en de sparre-bomen, de andere bomen ook.

Moet daar niet es iets van gezegd worden?

Ik dacht van wel, want ze staan er soms nog, de bomen, de bosrand en het geboomte, op dezelfde plek waar ze destijds ook stonden, je moet niet denken dat ze verderop zijn gaan staan, ze staan er nog steeds als onverschillige getuigen. Ik bekijk ze, ik kijk naar ze, en dan doet zich iets akeligs voor: ze zijn mooi, ik vind ze mooi." (245-246)

54 Ernst van Alphen: *De toekomst der herinnering. Essays over moderne Nederlandse literatuur.* Amsterdam: Van Gennep, 1993. "Armando's oorlog. Isolatie en annexatie als vormen van herinnering", 84-107. One advantage of an indexical relationship between sign and referent mentioned by van Alphen is that it would allow for relationships of meaning without necessarily implying coherence. Thus, Van Alphen argues, one can write literature about the war or even the Holocaust without implying a coherence which is inherently at odds with the Shoah.

55 Consider the example of hair: the State Museum Auschwitz also has a large collection of hair shorn from the heads of victims, which would function as a very effective sign for the victims, since hair is even more private than shoes are. However, hair brings with it certain practical and logistical problems which necessarily engender philosophical discussions. Hair gets dirty: should it be washed, cleaned, combed, or should it be displayed in dirty, matted form? Hair deteriorates. Should serious efforts be made to preserve it, at the expense of making it less accessible in the present? And so on.

56 "De schoonheid moest zich schamen.

En niet te vergeten de schoonheid van de plekken waar de vijand ten onder ging. De schoonheid weet van gekkigheid niet meer wat ze doen moet. De schoonheid is uit het lood geslagen." (247)

57 "De schoonheid van de plekken waar de vijand was, waar de vijand zich bevond, waar de vijand huisde en huishield, waar de vijand z'n schrikbewind uitoefende, waar zich nog de sporen van 's vijands schrikbewind bevinden. Juist daar." (246-247)

58 "Ik heb het al zo vaak gezegd, maar ik kan het niet genoeg herhalen: de schoonheid is geen knip voor de neus waard, de schoonheid trekt zich nergens wat van aan." (247)

59 Er is werkelijk iets aan de hand met de schoonheid, dat is toch niet te ontkennen. Dat de schoonheid niet deugt moet duidelijk zijn. Maar wat wil het geval: juist aan deze schoonheid heb ik mijn leven gewijd. Zij heeft mij in haar macht. Ik dien haar.

Wat moet ik anders. Laat me toch!" (247)

60 Literally: "Where, then."

61 "Waar kan men troost vinden. Niet meer bij de medemens, dat schijn je zelf verknoeid te hebben. Waar dan. Als het niet bij de medemens is, dan wel bij dat wat ie voortgebracht heeft: de kunst. Soms kan men troost vinden in de natuur. De natuur lijkt vredig, maar is het niet. Daarom is de natuur erg mooi.

Maar is troost werkelijk nodig? Kan het niet zonder?" (247)

62 In an interview for the book *Dit is de plek*, Armando repeats the tale as follows:

"They take off with the boy (walking) in front, but he pretends to trip, and in one motion stabs the soldier in the belly. I have called it the beauty of the deed in a besmirched landscape. A place like that is laden. If I myself were guilty of that deed, then I know that there are feelings one could suffer from. I don't think I would suffer from them. In reactions to my work, this story of the boy with the knife has been considered important. I understand. But I will never reveal to what extent it's autobiographical, because that would give just that charge to this story which I wish to prevent. It's also possible that it was another boy. After all, I grew up in circumstances in which an accident like that one was fairly normal."

"De jongen voorop vertrekken ze....aan het verhaal een lading zou geven die ik nu juist wil vermijden. Het kan ook een andere jongen geweest zijn. Ik ben namelijk groot geworden onder omstandigheden waarin zo'n voorval nogal normaal was." (18)

63 "Hoe waren die mensen die in die koetsen zaten gekleed. Waar zouden zulke kleren gebleven zijn. Waar blijft zoiets. [More literally: "Where do such things remain".] Blijft er eigenlijk wel es iets? Weinig, lijkt me. Het verslijt, het vergaat, het lost zich op. [Translator's note: This is a pun: "it dissolves" or "it solves itself."] Daar ben ik het niet altijd mee eens." (25)

64 "Het opschrijfboekje van de vader met de adressen van z'n vrienden van vroeger. Ze hadden ooit gelachen en gepraat, kun je je die en die nog herinneren: dat soort gesprekken.

Maar wat moet je nu met zo'n boekje. Gooi toch weg. Ja en nee." (18)

65 And vice versa.

66 "De vader riep de moeder, z'n vrouw: er is oorlog.

Er stond een man op straat die 'er is oorlog' schreeuwde. Toch was het prachtig weer." (33)

The beautiful weather on May 10, 1940, the day the Germans attacked, is well-established, and a recurrent theme in memoirs of the occupation. See, for example, a memoir by a Dutch person published in the United States by Cornelia Fuykschot, *Hunger in Holland. Life During the Nazi Occupation*. Amherst: Prometheus Books, 1995, which starts with the words: "The sunlight came streaming in through the dormer window, and the sparrows that had built their nest right underneath it were making an enormous racket as they tripped along the eaves, picking up tidbits for their young." (1) "Could they land right near us in the fields[...]? It seemed unimaginable, the weather was so beautiful, the birds were singing, the lilacs fragrant in the garden. (2, my translation)

Dr. L. de Jong's memoirs, *Herinneringen I*, Amsterdam: SDU Uitgeverij, 1993, mentions that the birds were chirping at 4 a.m. (84).

Also Willem Brakman in Wam de Moor (red.): *Duitsers!? Ervaringen en verwachtingen van....*'s-Gravenhage: BZZTôH, 1990, 17. In the context of his discussion of the occupation as something that does not seem real, Brakman not only refers to lovely weather, but describes the parachutes of the occupation force as visually beautiful as they floated down. Brakman confirms the basic thesis of this study, i.e. the central importance of memory in the process of integrating experiences into one's life. "A human being requires three things in order to experience something: He needs to anticipate it, he needs to experience it, and he needs to look back on it. Not until he remembers it, is he able to say: "Now I have experienced something and it's over and done with and it has become my mental property." This is the case with very important experiences. It's an essential aspect of reality that that time needs to become integrated into it." (16, 17) And to prevent the reader from missing the reference here, Brakman continues: "When I think back about the war..." Two factors seem relevant to him when he remembers the war: how unreal the situation seemed, and feelings of shame.

[De mens heeft voor zijn beleving drie dingen nodig: Hij moet ernaar toeleven, hij moet het beleven en hij moet erop terugkijken. Pas als hij het zich herinnert, kan hij zeggen: 'Nou heb ik iets beleefd en dat is afgerond, het is mijn geestelijk eigendom geworden.' Dat gaat op voor heel belangrijke gebeurtenissen. Het is een wezenlijke trek van de werkelijkheid, dat die tijd daarin verwerkt moet worden.

Als ik aan de oorlog terugdenk, vallen mij twee belangrijke aspecten op. Ten eerste vind ik het heel belangrijk dat die tijd zo irreëel was. Als ik mezelf daar in de verte in de oorlog zie lopen, heb ik moeite te bedenken: dat ben ik. Een ander feit dat me opvalt, is een gevoel van schaamte.]

67 Brakman, 17.
68 "Kledingstukken, ledematen, papieren. Rommel. Een dag of wat later werd er opgeruimd en schoongemaakt, er werd gereinigd, de bewoners namen bezit van hun huizen en alles zag er weer uit alsof er niets gebeurd was." (44)
69 "Er is iets gebeurd. Er is iets gebeurd, wat was het ook weer. O ja, de vijand is er. Ik ga vandaag weer naar 'm kijken." (47)
70 "De bezetter was er al. Ik liep op een stille weg, vlak bij wat een maand later *het kamp* zou zijn, het kamp." (49)
71 "– Oorlog, ik vind het zo'n gek woord, oorlog, oorlog, oorlog, oorlog, als je het vaak zegt wordt het woord steeds vreemder, vind je niet?
– Ach, je went er aan." (100)
72 The title chosen for an oral history of the period of reconstruction after the war, which translates loosely as "How beautiful peace seemed to us when we were still at war" serves as an apt illustration of this phenomenon: *Wat was de vrede mooi toen het nog oorlog was. Gesprekken over de wederopbouw,* Hans Olink, ed., The Hague: BZZTôH, 1990. Due to their need to be easily recognizable and to elicit easy identification, titles of such books are a fair index of common sentiment.
73 "Ik moest erg aan de vrede wennen. Al dat geklets over goed en slecht, over zwart en wit." (165)
74 "Juist omdat het mensen zijn waren ze tot zulke dingen in staat." (165)
75 "Is de oorlog eigenlijk wel van jou?" (170)
76 "Weet je dan niet dat de oorlog allang afgelopen is?" (252)
77 169-170
78 See the discussion of these issues in chapter 5.
79 "Nee, ik begreep z'n onbehagen en z'n afkeer niet. Dat kon ik toen nog niet begrijpen." (174)
80 See Chapter 3.

NOTES

81 "Oneindig vele stemmen gehoord gedurende de oorlog. Ook stemmen, die men van de bezetter niet mocht horen, stemmen van overzee.

Later ben ik ter plekke gaan kijken waar die stemmen vandaan kwamen, uit welke kamers, uit welke kamertjes." (238)

82 "Zo. Hier dus. Van hier uit heeft men ons toegesproken.

Maar wat nu? Hoe moet het nu verder? Moet ik eigenlijk nog wel verder? Was dit niet genoeg?

De herinneringen. Herinneringen die zo weining om het lijf hebben en toch het hoofd doen gonzen." (239)

83 "Ik vind dat ze daar niets te maken hebben, maar zij menen dat zij daar wonen.

Er is daar gebouwd. Dat moeten ze niet doen. Ze moeten het laten zoals het was. Ik vind het niet mooi zoals het nu is." (250)

84 "En het nu? Dat is er niet. Dat komt later pas te voorschijn in de gedaante van het verleden. Het nu zal zich vermommen als het verleden. Pas maar op." (250)

85 "Ik ben een overlevende", zei de man, "ik schaam me dood." cf. Brakman quote earlier in this chapter.

86 James E. Young, *The Texture of Memory: Holocaust Memorials and Meaning.* New Haven: Yale University Press, 1993, 5.

87 Translator's note: these terms are difficult to translate into English while maintaining the original sense. Armando uses two nouns (each in the plural), each of which denotes a kind of brick commonly used to pave streets in the Netherlands at that time.

88 Literally: "is lying there." As the child's favorite place to play in the woods was supplanted by the camp, so now the stones which could serve as a monument of the camp and the atrocities for which it (the camp) and they (the stones) stand, have been replaced by others, so that even the indirect connection (stones stand for camp which stands for atrocities which stand for an interrupted childhood) is erased.

89 "Het wordt tijd om de straatstenen en de klinkers te bekijken, elke plek aan een onderzoek te onderwerpen om te kunnen zeggen: kijk, hier liep deze vrouw, hier liep die en die en daar is dat en dat gebeurd.

Een dergelijk onderzoek heeft geen zin.

De straatstenen en de klinkers zijn er niet meer, ze zijn vervangen, ze zijn verdwenen. Er ligt wat anders.

Ze waren nogal ongeduldig, de straatstenen en de klinkers.

Ik hou er van zoals het was en niet zoals het is. Dit is een afwijking." (250-251)

90 "Hoe kun je nou gelukkig zijn als je in het heden leeft. Wat heb je nou aan het heden. Het is te hopen dat het heden gauw voorbij is." (251)

91 "Je kunt beter niet terugkomen.

Je kunt beter niet weten hoe het er hier uitzag, hoe het was. Het ergste is om te weten hoe het was. Als je ergens voor het eerst komt weet je niet beter.

Als je niet weet hoe het was ziet het er hier best aardig uit. Maar als je weet hoe het was vind je het niks. Ik vind het niks, omdat ik weet hoe het was, hoe het er hier uitzag. Dat is het nadeel als je iets ouder wordt. Kun je beter niet worden." (251-252)

92 "Weet je dan niet dat de oorlog allang afgelopen is?" (252)

1   Small segments of this chapter have been published in somewhat different form as "Rinnes Rijke's *Niet de Schuld, Wel de Straf* as a Social Phenomenon: An Attempt to come to terms with a tragic past", *Canadian Journal of Netherlandic Studies* XII, ii, Fall 1991, 28-32.

2   W. T. Mitchell, *Iconology: Image, Text, Ideology.* Chicago: University of Chicago Press, 1986, 38.

3   A.G.H. Anbeek van der Meijden, "De Tweede Wereldoorlog in de Nederlandse Roman", in *1940-145: Onverwerkt verleden? Lezingen van het symposium georganiseerd door het Rijksinstituut voor Oorlogsdocumentatie, 7 en 8 mei 1985.* Utrecht: H&S, 1985, 84.

4   All translations from the original Dutch text are mine.

5   Rolf Wolfswinkel, *Tussen landverraad en vaderlandsliefde: De collaboratie in naoorlogs proza.* Amsterdam: Amsterdam University Press, 1994, is a study of the image of collaboration in Dutch postwar prose. In the preface, Wolfswinkel mentions that he began the work in 1988 (VII).

6   *1945: Consequences and Sequels of the Second World War. Montreal – September 2, 1995 //Bulletin du Comité international d'histoire de la Deuxième Guerre mondiale, No. 27/28 – 1995,* 311. Also Wolfswinkel mentions in the preface to his book (see previous footnote) that some of his interviewees spoke with him while stipulating that they wished to remain anonymous (VII).

7   Inge Spruit. *Onder de vleugels van de partij. Kind van de Führer.* Bussum: Wereldvenster, 1983.

8   Dan Bar-On, *Legacy of Silence. Encounters with Children of the Third Reich.* Cambridge: Harvard University Press, 1989. Also an interview with him in which the "double wall" is explained, by Rinke van den Brink, "Dubbele muur: 'Je kan niet alles verdringen, want dan verlies je al je morele besef.' Psycholoog Dan Bar-On over zijn onderzoek in Duitsland onder kinderen van nazi's en de betekenis voor Israel." *Vrij Nederland,* 49e jaargang, July 9, 1988, 2.

9   Hanna Visser, *Het verleden voorbij.* Sliedrecht: Merweboek, 1989.

10 Adriaan Venema, *Het dagboek.* Amsterdam: De Arbeiderspers, 1990.

11 Adriaan Venema. *Schrijvers, uitgevers en hun collaboratie. Deel 1 Het systeem.* Amsterdam: De Arbeiderspers, 1988; *Deel 2 De harde kern* Amsterdam: De Arbeiderspers, 1989; *Deel 3A De kleine collaboratie.* Amsterdam: De Arbeiderspers, 1990; *Deel 3B S. Vestdijk.* Amsterdam: De Arbeiderspers, 1991.

12 Although an interview by *Elsevier,* a Dutch weekly news journal on April 7, 1990 among the members of *de Tweede Kamer,* the Dutch Lower House of Parliament, netted clear results: World War II is still very much on the lawmakers' minds. cf. *Elsevier,* April 4, 1990, 34-39.

13 Ian Buruma: *The Wages of Guilt. Memories of War in Germany and Japan.* New York: Farrar Straus Giroux, 1994, 3.

14 He further relates the existence of a prejudice against visiting Germany which persists among some until the present day.
    Prof. dr. G. P. Hoefnagels, Criminologist at Erasmus University (Rotterdam): "Mijn ouders gingen in de jaren '20 nog wel eens naar Duitsland op vakantie, maar sinds Hitler aan de macht was, zijn ze er nooit meer geweest. Geen piekeren over dat je als jongen ooit een leuk reisje langs de Rijn zou mogen maken. Het was een zeer ernstige anti-houding. Het anti-Duits-zijn werd mij zo met de paplepel toegediend." Wam de Moor (ed.): Duitsers!? 's-Gravenhage: BZZTôH, 1990, 39.

194   15   Ian Buruma: *The Wages of Guilt. Memories of War in Germany and Japan.* New York: Farrar Straus Giroux, 1994, 4-5.

16   Women who had had Germans as friends or lovers were frequently publically humiliated by having their heads shaved and being dragged through the streets in various stages of undress. Being painted with various dark, sticky substances was common as well. A photograph of punitive barbers at work may be found on the front cover of Rolf Wolfswinkel, *Tussen landverraad en vaderlandsliefde: De collaboratie in Naoorlogs proza.* Amsterdam: Amsterdam University Press, 1994.

17   cf. friendly Germans, or the notion that soldiers out of uniform are just young men.

18   For further evidence of undifferentiated polarization in the assignment of blame for the atrocities of the war and the Holocaust, see for example: John C. Kennis: *De sprinkgerma-nenplaag ... en de stoute dingen die Toontje deed.* Bussum: Van Holkema & Warendorf, 1975. This book, written during the occupation and published well after the war, is a simplistic parody (using child characters with funny names for the public figures, such as the Queen of the Netherlands, Anton Mussert, leader of the Dutch Nazi organization, Hitler, and so on) in comic book form.

19   Michael Ignatieff. *Blood and Belonging. Journeys into the New Nationalism.* New York: Farrar, Straus Giroux, 1993, 21-22.

20   Buruma, 6.

21   Buruma, 6.

22   A.P. Dierick: "War and/as Initiation." In: *Canadian Journal of Netherlandic Studies* 11 (1990) 1 (Spring) 9-16.

23   Jaap van Donselaar, *Fout na de oorlog. Fascisme en racistische organisaties in Nederland 1950-1990,* Amsterdam: Bert Bakker, 1991, 9.

24   See, for instance, John C. Kennis: *De sprinkgermanenplaag ... en de stoute dingen die Toontje deed.* Bussum: Van Holkema & Warendorf, 1975.

25   E.H. Kossmann: *De Lage Landen 1780/1980. Twee eeuwen Nederland en België II.* Amsterdam: Agon, 1986, 381ff.

26   Peter Romijn's study of the postwar legal treatment of collaborators borrows this phrase as part of its title: *Snel, streng en rechtvaardig. Politiek beleid inzake de bestraffing en reclassering van 'foute' Nederlanders 1945-1955.* De Haan, 1989.

27   Jaap van Donselaar, *Fout na de oorlog. Fascisme en racistische organisaties in Nederland 1950-1990,* 11.

28   But the rule: "Once a collaborator, always a collaborator" pertains in many cases.

29   Rinnes Rijke's *Niet de schuld, wel de straf. Herinneringen van een NSB-kind.* Bussum: Van Holkema & Warendorf, 1982.

30   Bruno Bettelheim, *The Uses of Echantment.* New York: Knopf, 1975, 12.

31   Jerome Bruner: "The Autobiographical Process" in *The Culture of Autobiography. Constructions of Self-Representation.* Edited by Robert Folkenflik. Stanford: Stanford University Press, 1993, 38-56, 38.

32   Bettelheim 1975, 69.

33   Rijke, 185.

34   Jerome Bruner: "The Autobiographical Process" in *The Culture of Autobiography. Constructions of Self-Representation.* Edited by Robert Folkenflik. Stanford: Stanford University Press, 1993, 38-56, 38.

35   Ian Hacking, "The Making and Molding of Child Abuse", *Critical Inquiry* 17 (Winter 1991), 253-288, 254.

36   Visser, 15.

Born guilty: children of Nazi families (compiled by) Peter Sichrovsky, Jean Steinberg, transl. Original German title: *Schuldig geboren.* New York : Basic Books, 1988.

37 Visser, 17 ff.
38 Visser, 17.
39 Visser, 18-19.
40 Venema, 4.
41 Venema, back cover.
42 Sem Dresden, *Persecution, Extermination, Literature.* Translated by Henry G. Schogt. Toronto: University of Toronto Press, 1995, 13. Originally published as *Vervolging, Vernietiging, Literatuur.* Amsterdam: Meulenhoff, 1991.
43 Jerome Bruner: "The Autobiographical Process" pp. 38-56, in *The Culture of Autobiography. Constructions of Self-Representation.* Edited by Robert Folkenflik. Stanford: Stanford University Press, 1993, 38.
44 For a clear and readable discussion in English of such research on the families of Holocaust survivors, and in particular the second generation, see Aaron Hass: *In the Shadow of the Holocaust. The Second Generation.* Ithaca: Cornell University Press, 1990.
45 J.C.H. Blom: "Lijden als waarschuwing. Oorlogsverleden in Nederland." *Ons Erfdeel,* 38th Jaargang, September-October 4, 1995, 531-541. "Anders gezegd 'de oorlog' zoals wij in Nederland meestal zeggen, vormde in het nationaal bewustzijn een belangrijk bestanddeel met een sterk zingevende betekenis en dus morele lading: toen was gebleken wat en wie goed was en wat en wie fout." (531)
46 Gay Block and Malka Drucker, *Rescuers. Portraits of Moral Courage in the Holocaust.* New York: Holmes & Meier, 1992, xiii.
47 Bar-On, 7.
48 Bar-On, 7.
49 See chapter 1 of this study.
50 "Wel is opmerkelijk hoezeer de samenstellende elementen van de herinnering aan de oorlog en de betekenis die daaraan werd gegeven gedurende de halve eeuw na 1945 in hoofdlijnen onveranderd zijn gebleven." (532)
51 Renaat Ramon, "Alleen in de brand waren wij gelukkig: schrijvers en tijdschriften in eenprachtige, getraliede tijd." In: *Diogenes* 7 (1990-1991) 6 (July-August 1991), 9-18. The article discusses Piet Calis, *Het ondergronds verwachten: schrijvers en tijdschriften tussen 1941 en 1945.* Amsterdam: Meulenhoff, 1989.
52 Fred Vermeulen, "Ik nam mijn vaders schuld op me", *Het Parool,* September 16, 1989. The title translates as: "I took my father's guilt upon myself."
53 Bert Pol, "Eindelijk verlost van dat schuldgevoel: Dochter van Rotterdams NSB'er legt levensverhaal vast in boek. 'Het blok beton is nu van mij af.'" *Het Vrije Volk,* November 11, 1989.
54 Lawrence Wright, *Remembering Satan. A case of recovered memory and the shattering of an American family.* New York: Knopf, 1994.
55 Michael D. Yapko, *Suggestions of Abuse. True and False Memories of Childhood Sexual Trauma.* New York: Simon & Schuster, 1994.
56 Lenore Terr, *Unchained Memories. True Stories of Traumatic Memories, Lost and Found.* New York: Harper Collins, 1994.
57 Judith Lewis Herman, *Trauma and Recovery.* New York: Basic Books, 1992.
58 Judith Lewis Herman, *Trauma and Recovery.* New York: Basic Books, 1992, 9.
59 R. Beunderman and J. Dane, editors. *Kinderen van de oorlog. Opstellen naar aanleiding van een lezingencyclus, georganiseerd in de periode januari-april 1986 door de RIAGG's Cen-*

195

NOTES

trum/Oud-West Amsterdam en Zuid/Nieuw-West Amsterdam, in samenwerking met de Stichting ICODO te Utrecht. Utrecht/Amsterdam: self-published, 1987.

60 Kai Erikson: "Notes on Trauma and Community", in: *Trauma: Explorations in Memory*. Edited, with introductions, by Cathy Caruth. Baltimore, Johns Hopkins University Press, 1995, 183-199, 184.

61 Erikson, 184-185.

62 Ian Hacking, *Rewriting the Soul: Multiple Personality and the Scienes of Memory*. Princeton: Princeton University Press, 1995.

CHAPTER 6

1 Original title: *Bezonken Rood*, Amsterdam: De Arbeiderspers, 1981. I quote in English from the American edition, in the translation by Adrienne Dixon: *Sunken Red*. Amsterdam: New Amsterdam Books, 1988.

2 In a book entitled "War Traumas after 45 years? Political and Psychiatric Impatience", L. de Jong starts his preface with the words "In 1990, respectively 1992, it will be fifty years since the occupation of the Netherlands by the Germans, and Dutch-Indonesia by the Japanese" (7). Naming both countries and both occupations named together in one sentence, one breath as it were, is a phenomenon characteristic of the 1980's. – A. Engelsman, ed. *Oorlogstrauma's na 45 jaar? Politiek en psychiatrisch ongeduld*. Met een voorwoord van dr. L. de Jong. Amsterdam: Van Gennep, 1988.

3 cf. J.E. Ellemers and R.E.F. Vaillant: *Indische Nederlanders en gerepatrieerden*. Muiderberg: Coutinho, 1985, p. 25ff. They took these figures from E. Van Witsen: *Krijgsgevangenen in de Pacific-oorlog (1940-1945)*. Franeker: Wever, 1971, and N. Beets: *De verre oorlog: Lot en levensloop van krijgsgevangenen onder de Japanners*. Meppel: Boom, 1981.

4 Particularly infamous were several camps which used their prisoners to build railroads through dangerous terrain; best-known of these among the Dutch is the Birma-Siam railroad, but as Ellemers and Vaillant state, the Pakan-Baru railroad on Sumatra is also justly infamous. For a more thorough recent study of these work projects, cf. Harry A. Poeze: "De weg naar de hel. De aanleg van een spoorlijn op West-Java tijdens de Japanse bezetting." p. 9-47, in: *Oorlogsdocumentatie '40-'45. Tweede jaarboek van het Rijksinstituut voor Oorlogsdocumentatie*. Editors: N.D.J. Barnouw (secr.), D. van Galen Last, J.Th.M. Houwink ten Cate, M. de Keizer (voorz.), R. Kok, R. Kruis, P. Romijn , J. Smit, E.L.M. Somers, G.P. van der Stroom, C. Touwen-Bouwsma (secr.), H. de Vries. Zutphen: Walburg Pers, 1990.

5 Vaillant Ellemers, 27.

6 *Sunken Red*, 11.

7 The other titles are *Het verzonkene* ("The Sunken"), Amsterdam: De Arbeiderspers, 1979, and *Zonsopgangen boven zee* ("Sunrises over the Ocean"), Amsterdam: De Arbeiderspers, 1977.

8 "Niets bestaat dat niet iets anders aanraakt."

9 cf. Chapter 1.

10 *Sunken Red*, 34.

11 cf. J.E. Ellemers and R.E.F. Vaillant: *Indische Nederlanders en gerepatrieerden*. Muiderberg: Coutinho, 1985.

12 *Sunken Red*, 52.

13 Kai Erikson: "Notes on Trauma and Community", in: *Trauma: Explorations in Memory.* Edited, with introductions, by Cathy Caruth. Baltimore, Johns Hopkins University Press, 1995, 183-199.

14 Ian Buruma: *The Wages of Guilt. Memories of War in Germany and Japan.* New York: Farrar Straus Giroux, 1994, 6.

15 cf. Chapter 2 and 3.

16 *Sunken Red*, 131.

17 *Sunken Red*, 76.

18 Jaap Goedegebuure, *Tegendraadse Schoonheid. Over het werk van Jeroen Brouwers.* Amsterdam: De Arbeiderspers, 1982, 68ff.

19 It is of note that Brouwers maintains that he respects his mother, that the misconnection is due only to the circumstances in the camp; cf. Johan Diepstraten, *De literaire wereld van Jeroen Brouwers.* The Hague: BZZTôH, 1985, 36.

20 "Hetzelfde verhaal nu, in een ander octaaf:..." *Bezonken rood*, 30.

21 The Dutch term for "wrong number" in a telephone conversation, literally translated, is more or less "misconnected" as the translator suggests a few sentences down.

22 *Sunken Red*, 13-14.

23 *Sunken Red*, 14.

24 *Sunken Red*, 25.

25 *Sunken Red*, 22.

26 Translator's note: Goedegebuure uses the verb "voltrekken", a wonderfully chosen word which can mean to execute (a judgment or decision), to celebrate or perform (a marriage), or to complete (an agreement or deal); each of these translations contributes to the meaning of the concept as a whole. *Van Dale Groot Woordenboek der Nederlandse Taal.* Elfde, herziene druk door prof. dr. Geerst en dr. H. Heestermans met medewerking van dr. C. Kruyskamp. Utrecht: Van Dale Lexicografie, 1984.

27 Jaap Goedegebuure, *Tegendraadse Schoonheid. Over het werk van Jeroen Brouwers.* Amsterdam: De Arbeiderspers, 1982, 61. "De geschiedenis van een kind en zijn moeder, opgesloten in een Japans interneringskamp, herhaalt zich in de relatie tussen de oudere ik en Liza, dat wil zeggen: hij is degene die deze herhaling in zijn fantasie voltrekt, op een haast dwangmatige manier."

28 *Sunken Red*, 22.

29 *Sunken Red*, 50.

30 *Sunken Red*, 16.

31 *Sunken Red*, 20.

32 It is interesting to consider whether one might also read *Sunken Red* as a narrative which is ostensibly "about" World War II, but which actually takes its place as a part of a similar construction of attitudes to the Netherlands' colonial past as a whole.

33 cf. "zich Oost-Indisch doof houden", de schijn aannemen alsof men niet hoort dat men geroepen, aangesproken, of om iets verzocht wordt. *Van Dale Groot Woordenboek der Nederlandse Taal.* Elfde, herziene druk door prof. dr. Geerst en dr. H. Heestermans met medewerking van dr. C. Kruyskamp. Utrecht: Van Dale Lexicografie, 1984.

34 Rudy Kousbroek, "Het tomaten-ketchup-Tjideng van Jeroen Brouwers", *Het Oost-Indisch Kamp Syndroom.* Amsterdam: Meulenhoff, 1992, 445-452, 445. Or, as expressed in *NRC Handelsblad* of January 8, 1982: "Don't contradict me, because I have already suffered deeply."

35 Marjoleine de Vos, "Waar of niet waar. *Bezonken rood* in discussie." In: *Bzzlletin* nr 98, September 1982. Reprinted in: Hans Dütting, ed. *Over Jeroen Brouwers: Kritische Motieven. Beschouwingen over het werk van Jeroen Brouwers.* Baarn, De Prom, 1987, 152-166, 156-157.

36 Jaap Goedegebuure, *Tegendraadse Schoonheid. Over het werk van Jeroen Brouwers.* Amsterdam: De Arbeiderspers, 1982, 76.

37 Critics include reviewers such as Rudy Kousbroek, Fred Lanzing, Etty Mulder, Cyrille Offermans, and Mischa de Vreede.

38 "Wachttorens, mitrailleurs, zoeklichten, m'n neus. De omheining bestond uit een schutting van gevlochten bamboe."

39 H.E. Keizer-Henzeveldt, *En de lach keerde terug.* Franeker, 1982, 331.

40 H.E. Keizer-Henzeveldt, *En de lach keerde terug.* Franeker, 1982.

41 cf. Johan Diepstraten, *De literaire wereld van Jeroen Brouwers.* The Hague: BZZTôH, 1985, 38.

42 *Sunken Red,* 39.

43 *Sunken Red,* 39.

44 *Sunken Red,* 40-41.

45 7-11-81.

46 *Sunken Red,* 22.

47 Mischa de Vreede, "Hoe betrouwbaar is het eelt van Jeroen Brouwers?" In *De Tijd,* January 15, 1982. Cited by Marjoleine de Vos, "Waar of niet waar. *Bezonken rood* in discussie." In: *Bzzlletin* nr 98, September 1982. Reprinted in: Hans Dütting, ed. *Over Jeroen Brouwers: Kritische Motieven.* Beschouwingen over het werk van Jeroen Brouwers samengesteld door Hans Dütting, Baarn, De Prom, 1987, pp. 152-166, 154.

48 cf. Johan Diepstraten, *De literaire wereld van Jeroen Brouwers.* The Hague: BZZTôH, 1985, 39.

49 *Sunken Red,* 26.

50 The insight of this study of Dutch literature concerning the children of the war in the 1980s is that there are *various* groups of "individuals who have had similar traumatic experiences, and who are thus thought to be able to fathom the other's feelings."

51 cf. Kai Erikson: "Notes on Trauma and Community", pp. 183-199, in: *Trauma: Explorations in Memory.* Edited, with introductions, by Cathy Caruth. Baltimore, Johns Hopkins University Press, 1995, 185-186.

52 cf. Chapters 2 and 3.

53 J.E. Ellemers and R.E.F. Vaillant: *Indische Nederlanders en gerepatrieerden.* Muiderberg: Coutinho, 1985, 115.

54 See the discussion of the similarities of structure and content between the debate concerning "recovered memory" in the USA and the discussion about the memory of the "war" in the Netherlands in Chapter 4.

55 *Het Oost-Indisch Kamp Syndroom,* 370.

56 J.N. Schreuder: "Honderd moeders en geen vader, seksuele ervaringen in Jappenkampen." ["A Hundred Mothers and No Father, Sexual Experiences in Japanese Camps"]. In: *ICODO Info* 93-3, 4-12.

57 He refers to Harris, "Variances and Anomalies". In: *Sciences* (1979), 206. 52.

58 *Sunken Red,* 29.

59 *Sunken Red,* 10.

60 *Sunken Red,* 120.

61 *Sunken Red,* 10.

62 Schreuder here refers to A. Stufkens *Een moderne Oedipus.* s.n., s.l., 1993.

63 *Sunken Red*, 32-33.

64 Jeroen Brouwers, *De laatste deur*. Amsterdam: De Arbeiderspers, 1983.

65 Abel J. Herzberg: *Kroniek der Jodenvervolging, 1940-1945*. 5th revised edition. Amsterdam: Querido, 1985. Jeroen Brouwers, *De laatste deur*. Amsterdam: De Arbeiderspers, 1983, 295 (my translation).

66 *Het Koninkrijk der Nederlanden in de tweede wereldoorlog. Deel 3. Mei '40*. The Hague: Staatsuitgeverij, 1970. Jeroen Brouwers, *De laatste deur*. Amsterdam: De Arbeiderspers, 1983, 295 (my translation).

67 cf. H.W. von der Dunk, "Over de betekenis van ego-documenten. Een paar aantekeningen als in- en uitleiding." in: *Cultuur en geschiedenis: negen opstellen*. The Hague: SDU, 1990, 65-82.

68 Armando, *De straat en het struikgewas*, Amsterdam: De Bezige Bij, 1993.

69 Margaerthe Ferguson: "Een schrijver, zijn boek, zijn collega's, zijn lotgenoten, zijn andere lezers. Over de ontvangst van *Bezonken Rood*." Reprinted in: Hans Dütting, ed. *Over Jeroen Brouwers: Kritische Motieven*. Baarn, De Prom, 1987, 177-188.

70 Margarethe Ferguson: "Een schrijver, zijn boek, zijn collega's, zijn lotgenoten, zijn andere lezers. Over de ontvangst van *Bezonken Rood*." Reprinted in: Hans Dütting, ed. *Over Jeroen Brouwers: Kritische Motieven. Beschouwingen over het werk van Jeroen Brouwers*. Baarn, De Prom, 1987, 179.

71 Jerome Bruner: "The Autobiographical Process" in *The Culture of Autobiography. Constructions of Self-Representation*. Edited by Robert Folkenflik. Stanford: Stanford University Press, 1993, 38-56, 38.

72 C.M. Jacobs-Stam, *Oorlog, een breuk in het bestaan*. Deventer: Van Loghum Slaterus, 1981. Series: Leven en welzijn, ed: prof. dr. Kees Trimbos (my translation).

73 Also see the discussion in chapter 4.

74 "In other words, 'the war' as we usually call it in the Netherlands, constituted an important element of the national consciousness, with a strong signifying function and thus an ethical charge; it had been revealed back then who was goed/right and who fout/evil." Blom, J.H.C.: "Lijden als waarschuwing. Oorlogsverleden in Nederland", *Ons Erfdeel*, 38e jaargang, September-October 4, 1995, 531-541, 531.

75 E.H. Kossmann: *De Lage Landen 1780/1980 Twee eeuwen Nederland en België II*. Amsterdam: Agon, 1986.

Bibliography

Aarts, Petra G., H.: "De Indische naoorlogse generatie gezond verklaard! Van kille feiten en verhitte gemoederen", in: *ICODO INFO*, Lies Schneiders, Tom de Ridder, Sytse van der Veen, eds., April 1995, 12e jaargang, nummer 1, 54-64.

Aercke, Kristiaan, ed.: *Women writing in Dutch*. New York [etc.]: Garland, 1994.

Alphen, Ernst van: *De toekomst der herinnering. Essays over moderne Nederlandse literatuur*. Amsterdam: Van Gennep, 1993.

Anbeek van der Meijden, A.G.H.: "De Tweede Wereldoorlog in de Nederlandse Roman", in *1940-1945: Onverwerkt verleden? Lezingen van het symposium georganiseerd door het Rijksinstituut voor Oorlogsdocumentatie, 7 en 8 mei 1985*. Utrecht: H&S, 1985.

Anbeek, Ton: *Geschiedenis van de Nederlandse literatuur tussen 1885 en 1985*. Amsterdam: De Arbeiderspers, 1990.

Anne Frank Stichting: *Anne Frank in the World 1929-1945 / Die Welt der Anne Frank 1929-1945*. Amsterdam: Bert Bakker, 1985.

Anstadt, Sera: *Een eigen plek. Verhalen van een opgejaagde jeugd*. The Hague: BZZTôH, 1984.

Armando (Herman Dirk van Dooideweerd): *Aantekeningen over de vijand*. Amsterdam: De Bezige Bij, 1981.

Dagboek van een dader. Amsterdam: De Bezige Bij, 1990.

Eindhovens Dagblad, June 22, 1967. Interviewer identified as R.V.D.

Krijgsgewoel. Amsterdam: De Bezige Bij, 1989.

De straat en het struikgewas, Amsterdam: De Bezige Bij, 1988.

Armando and J. Heymans: "De onvoltooid verleden tijd", in *Revisor* 1989/4, 62-73.

Armando and Hans Sleutelaar: *De ss'ers*. Amsterdam: De Bezige Bij, 1990. First edition: 1967.

Touwen-Bouwsma, C., N.D.J. Barnouw, D. van Galen Last, M. de Keizer, R. Kok. P. Romijn, E.L.M. Somers, eds. *Oorlogsdocumentatie '40-'45. Derde jaarboek van het Rijksinstituut voor Oorlogsdocumentatie*. Zutphen: Walburg Pers, 1992.

Barnouw, David, Madelon de Keizer, and Gerrold van der Stroom, eds.: *1940-1945: Onverwerkt verleden? Lezingen van het symposium georganiseerd door het Rijksinstituut voor Oorlogsdocumentatie, 7 en 8 mei 1985*. Utrecht: H&S, 1985.

Bar-On, Dan: *Legacy of Silence. Encounters with Children of the Third Reich*. Cambridge: Harvard University Press, 1989.

Beets, N.: *De verre oorlog: lot en levensloop van krijgsgevangenen onder de Japanner*. Meppel: Boom, 1981.

Betlem, Trix: Interview with Marga Minco. *Revue*, 24.6.67.

Bettelheim, Bruno: *The Uses of Echantment*. New York: Knopf, 1975.

Beunderman, R. and J. Dane, eds.: *Kinderen van de oorlog. Opstellen naar aanleiding van een lezingencyclus, georganiseerd in de periode januari-april 1986 door de RIAGG's Centrum/Oud-West Amsterdam en Zuid/Nieuw-West Amsterdam*, in samenwerking met de Stichting ICODO te Utrecht. Utrecht/Amsterdam: self-published, 1987.

Blaauwendraad-Doorduyn, Duke: *Niemandsland*. Amsterdam: Amber, 1989.

Block, Gay and Malka Drucker, *Rescuers. Portraits of Moral Courage in the Holocaust*. Prologue by Cynthia Ozick. New York: Holmes & Meier, 1992.

Blom, J.C.H.: "Lijden als waarschuwing. Oorlogsverleden in Nederland", *Ons Erfdeel*, 38e jaargang, September-October 4, 1995, 531-541.

Blom, J.C.H. and E. Lamberts, eds.: *Geschiedenis van de Nederlanden*. Rijswijk: Nijgh & Van Ditmar Universitair: Infoboek, 1993.

Blom, J.C.H., A.C. 't Hart and I. Schöffer. *De affaire Menten 1945-1976. Eindrapport van de Commissie van onderzoek betreffende het opsporings- en vervolgingsbeleid inzake Menten vanaf de bevrijding tot de zomer van 1976 en de invloeden waaraan dat beleid al dan niet heeft blootgestaan.* Tweede Kamer, zitting 1978-1979, 14252, number 19. The Hague: 1979.

Bögels, Gertie: "Vormen van psychische verwonding. Klinische aspecten van trangenerationele oorlogsgevolgen in historisch perspectief", in: Hans Ester and Wam de Moor, eds., *Een halve eeuw geleden. De verwerking van de Tweede Wereldoorlog in de literatuur.* Kampen, Kok Agora, 1994, 37-46.

Bork, J. van, and N. Laan, eds., *Twee eeuwen literatuur-geschiedenis: poëticale opvattingen in de Nederlandse literatuur.* Groningen: Wolters-Noordhoff, 1986.

Bousset, Hugo. "Harry Mulisch als buikspreker" in: *Dietsche Warande en Belfort* 134/2, 194-198.

Bregstein, Philo: *Gesprekken met Jacques Presser.* Amsterdam: Polak & Van Gennep, 1972.

Bregstein, Philo and Salvador Bloemgarten: *Herinnering aan Joods Amsterdam.* Amsterdam: De Bezige Bij, 1994.

Bril, Martin en Dirk van Weelden. *Terugwerkende kracht. Een leesgeschiedenis van de Tweede Wereldoorlog.* Amsterdam: De Bezige Bij, 1991.

Brink, Rinke van den: "Dubbele muur: 'Je kan niet alles verdringen, want dan verlies je al je morele besef.' Psycholoog Dan Bar-On over zijn onderzoek in Duitsland onder kinderen van nazi's en de betekenis voor Israel." *Vrij Nederland,* 49e jaargang, July 9, 1988, 2.

Broekhuis, Carly, Dirk Jan Broertjes, Simon Franke, Simon Gunn and Bert Janssens, eds.: *Het Collectieve Geheugen: Over Literatuur en Geschiedenis.* Amsterdam: De Balie, 1990.

Brokken, Jan: "Rudi van Dantzigs bittere oorlog", *Haagsche Post,* May 31, 1986.

Brouwers, Jeroen: *Bezonken Rood.* Amsterdam: De Arbeiderspers, 1981.

   De laatste deur. Amsterdam: De Arbeiderspers 1983.

   Adrienne Dixon, transl.: *Sunken Red.* New York: New Amsterdam Books, 1988.

   Het verzonkene. Amsterdam: De Arbeiderspers, 1979.

   Zonsopgangen boven zee. Amsterdam: De Arbeiderspers, 1977.

Bruner, Jerome: "The Autobiographical Process", in Robert Folkenflik, ed.: *The Culture of Autobiography. Constructions of Self-Representation.* Stanford: Stanford University Press, 1993, 38-56.

Büch, Boudewijn: *De rekening.* Amsterdam: De Arbeiderspers, 1989.

Burnier, Andreas (pseud.): *Het jongensuur.* Amsterdam: Querido, 1969.

Buruma, Ian: *The Wages of Guilt. Memories of War in Germany and Japan.* New York: Farrar Straus Giroux, 1994.

Bzzlletin 98: *Jeroen Brouwers.* The Hague: BZZTôH, September 1982.

Bzzlletin 135: *Harry Mulisch.* The Hague: BZZTôH, April 1986.

Bzzlletin 173: *Armando.* The Hague: BZZTôH, February 1990.

Calis, Piet: *Het ondergronds verwachten: schrijvers en tijdschriften tussen 1941 en 1945.* Amsterdam: Meulenhoff, 1989.

Charles, J.B.: *Volg het spoor terug.* 12th ed. Amsterdam : De Bezige Bij, 1994. First edition: 1953.

Corsari, Willy: *Die van ons.* Amsterdam: 1945.

Dane, J., ed.: *Keerzijde van de bevrijding: Opstellen over de maatschappelijke, psycho-sociale en medische aspecten van de problematiek van oorlogsgetroffenen.* Deventer: Van Loghem Slaterus / ICODO, 1984.

Dantzig, Rudi van: *Voor een verloren soldaat.* Amsterdam: De Arbeiderspers, 1986.

David, Kati: *Een klein leven.* The Hague: BZZTôH, 1985.

Derks, Sergio: *Verleden tijd: Nederland tijdens de Tweede Wereldoorlog.* Landsmeer: Robas, 1992.

Diepstraten, Johan: *De literaire wereld van Jeroen Brouwers.* The Hague: BZZTôH, 1985.

202   Dierick, A.P.: "War and/as Initiation." In: *Canadian Journal of Netherlandic Studies* 11 (1990) 1 (Spring) 9-16.

Donselaar, Jaap van: *Fout na de oorlog. Fascistische en racistische organisaties in Nederland 1950-1990.* Amsterdam: Bert Bakker, 1991.

Dresden, Sem: *Persecution, Extermination, Literature.* Translated by Henry G. Schogt. Toronto, Buffalo, London: University of Toronto Press, 1995. Original title: S. Dresden: *Vervolging, vernietiging, literatuur.* Amsterdam: Meulenhoff, 1991.

Dunk, W. von der: "Over de betekenis van ego-documenten. Een paar aantekeningen als in- en uitleiding", in: *Cultuur en geschiedenis: negen opstellen.* The Hague: SDU, 1990, 65-82.

Dütting, Hans (ed.): *Over Harry Mulisch: Kritisch Nabeeld. Beschouwingen over het werk en de persoon van Harry Mulisch.* Baarn: Ambo, 1982.

Dütting, Hans (ed.): *Over Jeroen Brouwers: Kritische Motieven. Beschouwingen over het werk van Jeroen Brouwers.* Baarn: De Prom, 1987.

Dwork, Debórah: *Children With a Star. Jewish Youth in Nazi Europe.* New Haven: Yale University Press, 1991.

Eco, Umberto: "An Ars Oblivionalis? Forget It!" In *PMLA* 103 (1988): 254-261.

Ellemers, J.E. and R.E.F. Vaillant: *Indische Nederlanders en gerepatrieerden.* Muiderberg: Coutinho, 1985.

Engelsman, ed.: *Oorlogstrauma's na 45 jaar? Politiek en psychiatrisch ongeduld.* Met een voorwoord van dr. L. de Jong. Amsterdam: Van Gennep, 1988.

Erikson, Kai: "Notes on Trauma and Community", in: *Trauma: Explorations in Memory.* Edited, with introductions, by Cathy Caruth. Baltimore, Johns Hopkins University Press, 1995, 183-199.

Ester, Hans and Wam de Moor, eds., *Een halve eeuw geleden. De verwerking van de Tweede Wereldoorlog in de literatuur.* Kampen: Kok Agora, 1994.

Ferguson, Margarethe: "Een schrijver, zijn boek, zijn collega's, zijn lotgenoten, zijn andere lezers. Over de ontvangst van *Bezonken Rood.*" Reprinted in: Hans Dütting, ed. *Over Jeroen Brouwers: Kritische Motieven. Beschouwingen over het werk van Jeroen Brouwers.* Baarn, De Prom, 1987, 177-188.

Ferron, Louis: *Hoor mijn lied, Violetta.* Amsterdam: De Bezige Bij, 1982.
    De keisnijder van Fichtenwald. Amsterdam: De Bezige Bij, 1976.
    Over de wateren. Amsterdam: De Bezige Bij, 1986.

Folkenflik, Robert, ed.: *The Culture of Autobiography. Constructions of Self-Representation.* Stanford: Stanford University Press, 1993.

Foppe, Han: "Vechten. Was dat het leven? Over het geweld in Armando's literaire werk (1951-1988)", in: *Bzzlletin 173*, vol. 19, February 1990, 31-38.

Frank, Anne: *De Dagboeken van Anne Frank.* The Hague: Staatsuitgeverij, 1986. English Edition: *Anne Frank: The Diary of a Young Girl: The Critical Edition.* New York: Doubleday, 1989.

Frank, Cobie: *Alsof er niets gebeurd was: Terugblik van een joodse verzetsman.* Haarlem: In de Knipscheer, 1985.

Friedländer, Saul, ed.: *Probing the Limits of Representation: Nazism and the "Final Solution."* Cambridge: Harvard University Press, 1992.

Fuykschot, Cornelia: *Hunger in Holland. Life During the Nazi Occupation.* Amherst: Prometheus Books, 1995.

Goedegebuure, Jaap: *De Nederlandse literatuur 1960-1988.* Amsterdam: Synthese/De Arbeiderspers, 1989.

"Suspecte bomen. De weerbarstige roman van dubbeltalent Armando: wreedheid als schoonheid, het geweld als hart van het leven", in *Haagsche Post*, June 11, 1988.

Tegendraadse Schoonheid: Over het werk van Jeroen Brouwers. Amsterdam: De Arbeiderspers, 1982.

Goodenough, Elizabeth, Mark A. Heberle, and Naomi Sokoloff: *Infant Tongues. The Voice of the Child in Literature.* With a foreword by Robert Coles. Detroit: Wayne State University Press, 1994.

Griffin, Susan: *A Chorus of Stones: The Private Life of War.* New York: Doubleday, 1992.

Hacking, Ian: "The Making and Molding of Child Abuse", *Critical Inquiry* 17 (Winter 1991), 253-288.

Rewriting the Soul: Multiple Personality and the Sciences of Memory. Princeton: Princeton University Press, 1995.

Hanley, Lynn: *Writing War: Fiction, Gender and Memory.* Amherst: University of Massachussetts Press, 1991.

Hass, Aaron: *In the Shadow of the Holocaust: The Second Generation.* Ithaca: Cornell University Press, 1990.

Heerze, Jan: *Harry Mulisch, De aanslag.* Apeldoorn: WalvaBoek, 1983.

Herman, Judith Lewis: *Trauma and Recovery.* New York: Basic Books, 1992.

Hermans, Willem Frederik. "Oorlog en literatuur", in: *1940-1945: Onverwerkt verleden? Lezingen van het symposium georganiseerd door het Rijksinstituut voor Oorlogsdocumentatie, 7 en 8 mei 1985.* David Barnouw, Madelon de Keizer, Gerrold van der Stroom, eds.. Utrecht: Hess Uitgevers, 1985 88-98.

De donkere kamer van Damocles. Amsterdam: Van Oorschot, 1958.

Herzberg, Abel J.: *Verzameld Werk I.* Amsterdam: Querido, 1993.

Heumakers, Arnold: "Harry Mulisch en de politiek", in *Maatstaf* 8/9, 37e jaargang, August/September 1989, 101-111.

Hillesum, Etty: *Het verstoorde leven: Dagboek van Etty Hillesum, 1941-1943,* Bussum: De Haan/Unieboek, 1981. English edition: *An Interrupted Life: The Diaries of Etty Hillesum, 1941-1943.* New York: Pantheon, 1983.

Hillesum, Etty, Klaas A. D. Smeelik, ed. *Etty. De nagelaten geschriften van Etty Hillesum 1941-1943.* 3e herziene druk. Amsterdam: Balans, 1986.

Hooven, A. ten (pseud.): *Lemmingen.* Bussum, Agathon, 1982.

Houten, Boudewijn van: *Fout: Lebensbericht meines Vaters.* Antwerp/Amsterdam: Manteau, 1987.

Hoven, A. van den: *"Het Bittere Kruid* by Marga Minco. Paradise Lost: Paradise Regained", in *The Low Countries: Fin de Siècle;* ed. Robert Siebelhoff, Augustinus P. Dierick. Special issue of *Canadian Journal of Netherlandic Studies* 9 (1988) 2 (Fall), 92-96.

Huisman, "Twee juweeltjes. Indrukwekkende geschenken van Minco en van Dis", in *Algemeen Dagblad,* March 8, 1986.

Hunt, Lynn, ed.: *The New Cultural History.* Berkeley: University of California Press, 1989.

ICODO: *Psycho-sociale problematiek van de tweede generatie I.* Utrecht: ICODO, 1982.

Psycho-sociale problematiek van de tweede generatie II. Utrecht: ICODO, 1985 (3rd edition).

Ignatieff, Michael: *Blood and Belonging. Journeys into the New Nationalism.* New York: Farrar, Straus Giroux, 1993.

Jacobs-Stam, C.M.: *Getekend door de oorlog: feiten en meningen over burger-slachtoffers 1940-1945.* Deventer: Van Loghum Slaterus, 1982.

Oorlog, een breuk in het bestaan: achtergrond en problemen van door de oorlog getroffenen. Deventer: Van Loghum Slaterus, 1981.

204   Jansma, Bert: Interview with Sera Anstadt. *Amersfoortse Courant*, November 3, 1984.

Jansen, Thijs, Frans Ruiter and Jèmeljan Hakemulder: *De lezer als burger: Over literatuur en ethiek*. Kampen: Kok Agora, 1994.

Janssens, Marcel: "The Prolog in Mulisch' *Aanslag:* A Novel in a Nutshell", in *The Berkeley Conference of Dutch Literature. 1987: New Perspectives on the Modern Period*. Johan P. Snapper and Thomas F. Shannon, eds. *Publications of the American Association for Netherlandic Studies* 2. Lanham: University Press of America, 1989.

Jansz, Ernst: *De overkant*. Haarlem: In de Knipscheer, 1985.

Jong, L.(Louis) de: *De bezetting. Een weergave in boekvorm van de uitzendingen der Nederlandse Televisie-Stichting over Nederland in de Tweede Wereldoorlog*. Volume 1-5. Amsterdam: Querido, 1963-65.
    Herinneringen I, Amsterdam: SDU, 1993.
    De jodenvervolging I and II. Amsterdam: Rijksinstituut voor Oorlogsdocumentatie, 1978.
    Het Koninkrijk der Nederlanden in de Tweede Wereldoorlog, 12 vols. Leiden: Martinus Nijhoff, 1969-1988.

Keizer, Madelon de, ed.: *'Een dure verplichting en een kostelijk voorrecht': Dr. L. de Jong en zijn Geschiedwerk*. Rijksinstituut voor Oorlogsdocumentatie / The Hague: SDU Uitgeverij Koninginnegracht, 1995.

Keizer-Heuzeveldt, H.E.: *En de lach keerde terug*. Franeker: Wever, 1982.

Kennis, John C.: *De sprinkgermanenplaag...en de stoute dingen die Toontje deed*. Bussum: Van Holkema & Warendorf, 1975.

Kleinjans, Jos: *Het acces van Meijel: Roman over het verzet in Limburg*. Utrecht: Het Spectrum, 1987.

Kluvers, Elouise and Ingrid: *Jouw oorlog – mij een zorg: Gesprekken over de oorlog met mensen van na de oorlog*. Baarn: Anthos / In den Toren, 1979.

Knoop, Hans: *De zaak Menten*. Amsterdam: H. J. W. Becht, 1977.

Kooiman, Dirk Ayelt: *Montyn*. Amsterdam: De Harmonie, 1982.

Kors, Ton: *Hannie Schaft: Het levensverhaal van een vrouw in verzet tegen de nazi's*. Amsterdam: Van Gennep, 1976.

Kossmann, Alfred: *Familieroman*. Amsterdam: Querido, 1990.
    Een verjaardag: Amsterdam: Querido, 1989.

Kossmann, E. H.: *De Lage Landen 1780/1980. Twee eeuwen Nederland en België II*. Amsterdam: Agon, 1986.

Kousbroek, Rudy: *Het Oost-Indisch Kamp Syndroom*. Amsterdam: Meulenhoff, 1992.

Kouwenaar: Gerrit: *Ik was geen soldaat*. Amsterdam: P.N. van Kampen & Zoon, 1951.

Kritzman, Lawrence D., ed.: *Auschwitz and After. Race, Culture, and "the Jewish Question" in France*. New York: Routledge, 1995.

Kroon, Dirk, ed.: *Over Marga Minco: Beschouwingen en interviews*. The Hague: BZZTôH, 1982.

Langer, Lawrence, ed.: *Art from the Ashes. A Holocaust Anthology*. New York: Oxford University Press, 1995.

Laub, Dori and Nanette C. Auerhahn: "Kennen en niet-kennen van ernstige psychische trauma's: vormen van traumatische herinnering", *ICODO INFO*, Lies Schneiders, Tom de Ridder, Sytse van der Veen, eds., December 1994, 11e jaargang, nummer 3/4, 55-81.

Lindt, Maarten Willem Jan: *Als je wortels taboe zijn. Verwerking van levensproblemen bij kinderen van Nederlandse nationaal-socialisten*. Kampen: Kok, 1993.

Manen, Willem G. van: *Etty: Toneelstuk over Etty Hillesum*. Baarn: De Prom, 1988.

Marxveldt, Cissy van: *Ook zij maakte het mee...* Weert: M & P, 1992.

Mathijsen, Maritha: *Harry Mulisch: Een bibliografie*. The Hague: BZZTôH, 1979.

Meulenhoff: *De bevrijding in de Oost: De bevrijdingsdagen van: Rob Nieuwenhuys, Agnes New-ton Keith, Bep Vuyk, H.L. Leffelaar, Jenny Pisuisse, Oscar de Wit, Margarethe Ferguson, G.F. Jacobs, Eric Lomax, J. Rookmaaker en Paula Gomes*. Amsterdam: Meulenhoff, 1995.

Michielsen, John: "Coming to Terms with the Past and Searching for an Identity: The Treat-ment of the Occupied Netherlands in the Fiction of Hermans, Mulisch and Vestdijk", in *Canadian Journal of Netherlandic Studies* VII i-ii, 1986.

Michman, Dan: "De oprichting van de 'Joodsche Raad van Amsterdam' vanuit een vergelijk-end perspectief", in *Oorlogsdocumentatie '40-'45. Derde jaarboek van het Rijksinstituut voor Oorlogsdocumentatie*. C. Touwen-Bouwsma, N.D.J. Barnouw, D. van Galen Last, M. de Keizer, R. Kok. P.Romijn, E.L.M. Somers, eds. Zutphen: Walburg Pers, 1992, 75-100.

Michman, Jozeph, Hartog Beem, and Dan Michman: *Pinkas: Geschiedenis van de joodse gemeenschap in Nederland*. Translated from Hebrew by Ruben Verhasselt, with additional research by Victor Brilleman. Joop Sanders, Edward van Voolen, eds. Ede: Kluwer Algemene Boeken and Amsterdam: Nederlands-Israëlitisch Kerkgenootschap, 1992.

Middeldorp, A.: *Over het proza van Marga Minco*. Amsterdam: Wetenschappelijke Uitgeverij, 1981.

Miller, Judith: *One by One by One*. New York: Touchstone/ Simon & Schuster, 1991.

Minco, Marga: *Het Bittere Kruid: een kleine kroniek*. Den Haag: Bert Bakker, 1957.

   The Glass Bridge. Stacey Knecht, transl. London: Peter Owen, 1988.

   De glazen brug. Amsterdam: Commissie voor de Collectieve Propaganda van het Neder-landse Boek, 1986.

   Een leeg huis. Den Haag: Bert Bakker, 1966.

   De val. Amsterdam: Bert Bakker, 1983.

Mitchell, T.: *Iconology: Image, Text, Ideology*. Chicago: University of Chicago Press, 1986.

Mitscherlich, Alexander und Margarete: *Die Unfähigkeit zu Trauern. Grundlagen kollektiven Verhaltens*. München: Piper, 1967.

Mitscherlich, Margarete: *Erinnerungsarbeit. Zur Psychoanalyse der Unfähigkeit zu Trauern*. Frankfurt am Main: Fischer, 1987.

Moor, Wam de: *Deze kant op: Kritieken en profielen van boeken en schrijvers 1979-1984*. Amster-dam: De Arbeiderspers, 1986.

   *Duitsers!? Ervaringen en verwachtingen van....*The Hague: BZZTôH, 1990.

   Dit is de plek. De betekenis van plaats en emotie in het werk van schrijvers en schilders. Zut-phen: Gaillarde Pers, 1992.

Morson, Gary Saul: *Narrative and Freedom*. New Haven: Yale University Press, 1994.

Mosse, George: *Toward the Final Solution: A History of European Racism*. Madison: University of Wisconsin Press, 1978.

Mulisch, Harry: *Aan het woord*. Amsterdam: De Bezige Bij, 1986.

   De aanslag. Amsterdam: De Bezige Bij, 1987.

   The Assault. Claire Nicolas White, transl. New York: Pantheon, 1985.

   Mijn getijdenboek. Amsterdam: De Bezige Bij, 1985.

   Op de drempel van de geschiedenis. Amsterdam: De Bezige Bij, 1992.

   Het stenen bruidsbed. Amsterdam: De Bezige Bij, 1959.

   Voer voor psychologen. Amsterdam: De Bezige Bij, 1978.

Müller, Bernd: "The Second World War in Dutch and German Literature", in *The Berkeley Conference of Dutch Literature, 1991: Europe 1992: Dutch Literature in an International Con-text*. Johan P. Snapper and Thomas F. Shannon, eds. Publications of the American Associ-ation for Netherlandic Studies 6. Lanham: University Press of America, 1993, 123-131.

206   Niezink, Henk: "Armando en Berlijn", in *Bzzlletin* 173, 19e jaargang, February 1990, 39-49.

Nijs, Pieter de: "Ik heb iets vreselijks gezien. De stoere gevoeligheid van Armando", in: *Bzzlletin 173*, vol. 19, february 1990, 8-20.

Oberski, Jona: *Kinderjaren*. The Hague: BZZTôH, 1987.

Offermans, Cyrille, ed.: *Oorlog*. Amsterdam: De Bezige Bij, 1994.

Olink, Hans, ed.: *Wat was de vrede mooi toen het nog oorlog was. Gesprekken over de wederopbouw.* The Hague: BZZTôH, 1992.

Paardekooper, Jos: *Jeroen Brouwers: Bezonken Rood.* Tweede, herziene druk. Apeldoorn: Walva-Boek, 1986.

Pam, Max: *De onderzoekers van de oorlog. Het Rijksinstituut voor Oorlogsdocumentatie en het werk van Dr. L. de Jong.* The Hague: SDU, 1989.

Pannekoek, Yvo: *Memoires van Yvo Pannekoek.* Amsterdam: van Oorschot, 1982.

Peene, Bert ed.: *Literatuur in West-Europa na de Tweede Wereldoorlog.* Leiden: Nijhoff, 1992.

Peene, Bert: *Marga Minco, Een leeg huis.* Apeldoorn: Walva-Boek/Van Walraven, 1985.

    Marga Minco: De Val en De glazen Brug. Apeldoorn: Walva-Boek/Van Walraven, 1987.

Poeze, Harry A.: "De weg naar de hel. De aanleg van een spoorlijn op West-Java tijdens de Japanse bezetting." in: *Oorlogsdocumentatie '40-'45. Tweede jaarboek van het Rijksinstituut voor Oorlogsdocumentatie.* M. de Keizer, N.D.J. Barnouw, D. van Galen Last, J.Th.M. Houwink ten Cate, R. Kok, R. Kruis, P. Romijn , J. Smit, E.L.M. Somers, G.P. van der Stroom, C. Touwen-Bouwsma, H. de Vries, eds. Zutphen: Walburg Pers, 1990, 9-47.

Pointl, Frans: *De kip die over de soep vloog.* Amsterdam: Nijgh & Van Ditmar, 1989.

Pol, Bert: "Eindelijk verlost van dat schuldgevoel: Dochter van Rotterdams NSB'er legt levensverhaal vast in boek. 'Het blok beton is nu van mij af.'" *Het Vrije Volk*, November 11, 1989.

Presser, Jacques: *Ondergang. De vervolging en verdelging van het Nederlandse jodendom (1940-1945).* The Hague: Staatsuitgeverij, 1965. Monograph number 10 in the series published under the auspices of the State Institute for War Documentation; an abbreviated English translation by Arnold Pomerans was published under the title *The Destruction of the Dutch Jews.* New York: Dutton, 1969.

    De nacht der Girondijnen: novelle. Amsterdam: Vereeniging ter bevordering van de belangen des boekhandels, 1957.

Ramon, Renaat: "Alleen in de brand waren wij gelukkig: schrijvers en tijdschriften in een prachtige, getraliede tijd", in: *Diogenes.* 7 (1990-1991) 6 (july-aug 1991) 9-18.

Reve, Gerard Kornelis van het: *De ondergang van de familie Boslowits.* Amsterdam: Van Oorschot, 1964.

Ridder, Tom de, Lies Schneiders and Sytse van der Veen: *ICODO INFO. Joodse onderduikkinderen van toen,* (Themanummer). Augustus 1992, 9e jaargang, nummer 2.

Rijke, Rinnes: *Niet de schuld, wel de straf. Herinneringen van een NSB-kind.* Bussum: Van Holkema & Warendorf, 1982.

    Op zoek naar erkenning. Weesp: Van Holkema & Warendorf, 1985.

Rijksinstituut voor Oorlogsdocumentatie: *Het Proces Blokzijl.* Utrecht: Veen, 1989.

    Dagboek fragmenten 1940-1945. The Hague: Martinus Nijhoff, 1954.

Rittner, Carol and John K. Rother, eds.: *Different voices: women and the Holocaust.* New York: Paragon House, 1993.

Ritzerfeld, J.: *De poolse vlecht.* Amsterdam: Querido, 1982.

Romijn, Peter: *Snel, streng en rechtvaardig. Politiek beleid inzake de bestraffing en reclassering van 'foute' Nederlanders 1945-1955.* De Haan, 1989.

Schenkeveld-van der Dussen, M.A., Ton Anbeek et al, eds.: *Nederlandse literatuur, een*
geschiedenis. Groningen: Nijhoff, 1993.

Schneiders, Lies, Tom de Ridder, and Sytse van der Veen, eds.: *Oorlogskinderen toen en nu.*
(Themanummer). *ICODO INFO,* December 1995, 12e jaargang nr. 3/4.

Schogt, Henry: "Motives and Impediments in Describing War Memories: The Tragedy of the
Jews", in *Canadian Journal of Netherlandic Studies* 11 (1990) 1 (Spring), 3-7.

Schouten, Diny: "Een wurgende pastorale. Oorlogs- en jeugdherinneringen van Rudi van
Dantzig", in *Vrij Nederland,* June 7, 1986. Also in *Een Jaar Boek 1985-86,* edited by Aad Nuis
and Robert-Henk Zuidinga, Amsterdam: Aramith, 1986, 53-55.

Schram, Dick: "De verwerking van de Tweede Wereldoorlog in de literatuur", in *Overal Sporen:*
De verwerking van de Tweede Wereldoorlog in literatuur en kunst. D.H. Schram and C.
Geljon, eds. Amsterdam, VU, 1990.

Schreuder, J.N.: "De conspiracy of silence en de kinderen van de oorlog", in: ICODO Info 90-
3/4, 7e jaargang, December 1990, 4-13.
"Honderd moeders en geen vader, seksuele ervaringen in Jappenkampen." ["A Hundred
Mothers and No Father, Sexual Experiences in Japanese Camps"]. In: *ICODO Info* 93-3, 4-
12.

Sichrovsky, Peter, ed.: *Born guilty: children of Nazi families;* Jean Steinberg, transl. Original
German title: *Schuldig geboren.* New York : Basic Books, 1988.

Sokoloff, Naomi: "Childhood Lost: Children's Voices in Holocaust Literature", in: Elizabeth
Goodenough, Mark A. Heberle, Naomi Sokoloff: *Infant Tongues. The Voice of the Child in*
Literature. Foreword by Robert Coles. Detroit: Wayne State University Press, 1994, 259-
274.

Spruit, Inge: *Onder de vleugels van de partij. Kind van de Führer.* Bussum: Wereldvenster, 1983.

Taylor, Jolanda Vanderwal: "Marga Minco," in *Women Writers of the Netherlands and Flanders,*
Canadian Journal of Netherlandic Studies Xi, ii, Fall 1990, 51-56.
"Rinnes Rijke's *Niet de Schuld, Wel de Straf* as a Social Phenomenon: An Attempt to come
to terms with a tragic past", *Canadian Journal of Netherlandic Studies* XII, ii, Fall 1991, 28-
32.

Terr, Lenore: *Unchained Memories. True Stories of Traumatic Memories, Lost and Found.* New
York: Harper Collins, 1994.

Turnhout, Ted van: *Nederland Nederland ik lijd nog steeds: Het onvoorstelbare verhaal van*
verzetsstrijdster Corrie van Ede. Weert: M & P, 1990.

Vanheste, Bert: *'Want uw vijand wie is dat?' Mijn kleine oorlog: Louis Paul Boon als ongelovige*
dromer. Amsterdam: Querido, 1989.

Veen, Adriaan van der: *Het wilde feest.* Amsterdam : Querido, 1952.

Venema, Adriaan: *Aristo revisited.* Baarn: De Prom, 1990.
Het dagboek. Amsterdam: De Arbeiderspers, 1990.
Kleine oorlog. The Hague: SDU, 1990.
Schrijvers, uitgevers en hun collaboratie. Deel 1: Het systeem. Amsterdam: De Arbeiderspers,
1988; *Deel 2: De harde kern.* Amsterdam: De Arbeiderspers, 1989; *Deel 3A: De kleine collab-*
oratie. Amsterdam: De Arbeiderspers, 1990; *Deel 3B: S. Vestdijk.* Amsterdam: De Arbeiderspers, 1991.

Vermeulen, Fred: "Ik nam mijn vaders schuld op me", *Het Parool,* September 16, 1989.

Vestdijk, Simon: *Bevrijdingsfeest.* Amsterdam: De Bezige Bij, 1978. (First edition: Amsterdam:
Salm, 1949).
Pastorale 43: roman uit de tijd van de Duitsche overheersching. Rotterdam, The Hague, 1948.

Visser, Hanna (pseud.): *Het verleden voorbij.* Sliedrecht: Merweboek, 1989.

208   Voeten, Bert: *Doortocht: Een oorlogsdagboek 1940-1945.* Amsterdam: Contact, 1946.

Vos, Marjoleine de: "Waar of niet waar. *Bezonken rood* in discussie." In: *Bzzlletin* nr 98, September 1982. Reprinted in: Hans Dütting, ed. *Over Jeroen Brouwers: Kritische Motieven. Beschouwingen over het werk van Jeroen Brouwers.* Baarn, De Prom, 1987, 152-166.

Vreede, Mischa de: "Hoe betrouwbaar is het eelt van Jeroen Brouwers?" In *De Tijd,* January 15, 1982. Cited by Marjoleine de Vos, "Waar of niet waar. *Bezonken rood* in discussie." In: *Bzzlletin* nr 98, September 1982. Reprinted in: Hans Dütting, ed. *Over Jeroen Brouwers: Kritische Motieven. Beschouwingen over het werk van Jeroen Brouwers.* Baarn, De Prom, 1987, 152-166.

Vries, Theun de: *Het meisje met het rode haar.* Amsterdam: Querido, 1977. (First and second edition 1956).

Beb Vuyk: *Kampdagboeken.* Utrecht: Veen, 1989.

Warren, Hans, and Mario Molengraaf, eds.: *Die dag in mei vergeet ik niet: de mooiste Nederlandse bevrijdingspoëzie.* Amsterdam: Prometheus / Bert Bakker, 1995.

Weinreb, F.: *De gevangenis: Herinneringen 1945-1948.* Amsterdam: Meulenhoff, 1989. Original title: *Die Haft, Geburt in eine neue Welt. 1945 bis 1948.* Thauros Verlag GmbH, Weiler im Allgäu, 1988.

Werkman, Evert, Madelon de Keizer, Gert Jan van Setten, eds.: *Dat kan ons niet gebeuren... Het dagelijks leven in de Tweede Wereldoorlog.* Amsterdam, De Bezige Bij, 1980.

Withuis, Jolande: "De gevoelige erfenis van de jaren '40-'45", in *ICODO INFO,* Toon Nelissen, Tom de Ridder, Lies Schneiders and Sytse van der Veen, eds., April 1991, 8e jaargang, nummer 91-1, 5-18.

Wolfswinkel, Rolf: *Tussen landverraad en vaderlandsliefde: De collaboratie in naoorlogs proza.* Amsterdam: Amsterdam University Press, 1994.

Wright, Lawrence: *Remembering Satan. A case of recovered memory and the shattering of an American family.* New York: Knopf, 1994.

Yapko, Michael D.: *Suggestions of Abuse. True and False Memories of Childhood Sexual Trauma.* New York: Simon & Schuster, 1994.

Young, James E.: *The Texture of Memory: Holocaust Memorials and Meaning.* New Haven: Yale University Press, 1993.

    Writing and Rewriting the Holocaust. Narratives and the Consequences of Interpretation. Bloomington: Indiana University Press, 1988.

Zomeren, Koos van: *Otto's oorlog.* Amsterdam: De Arbeiderspers, 1983.

Index

Note: This index follows the Dutch convention for alphabetization: it ignores "van", "von", and "de". Thus, Rudi van Dantzig will be found under "Dantzig, Rudi van".